In 1947 the theologian and musicologist Friedrich Smend published a study which claimed that J. S. Bach regularly employed the natural-order number alphabet (A = 1 to Z = 24) in his works. Smend provided historical evidence and music examples to support his theory which demonstrated that by this means Bach incorporated significant words into his music, and provided himself with a symbolic compositional scheme.

Since then many people have taken up Smend's theory, interpreting numbers of bars and notes in Bach scores according to the natural-order alphabet.

By presenting a thorough survey of different number alphabets and their uses in seventeenth- and eighteenth-century Germany, Dr Tatlow investigates the plausibility of Smend's claims. Her new evidence fundamentally challenges Smend's conclusions and the book sounds a note of caution to all who continue to use his number-alphabet theory.

Dr Tatlow's painstaking research will fascinate all those with an interest in the music of J. S. Bach and German Baroque culture, and will be of particular importance for music historians and analysts.

Bach and the riddle of the number alphabet

Bach and the Riddle
of the
Number Alphabet

RUTH TATLOW

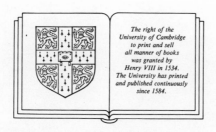

CAMBRIDGE UNIVERSITY PRESS

Cambridge
New York   Port Chester
Melbourne   Sydney

Published by the Press Syndicate of the University of Cambridge
The Pitt Building, Trumpington Street, Cambridge CB2 1RP
40 West 20th Street, New York, NY 10011, USA
10 Stamford Road, Oakleigh, Melbourne 3166, Australia

© Cambridge University Press 1991

First published 1991

Printed in Great Britain at the University Press, Cambridge

British Library cataloguing in publication data
Tatlow, Ruth
Bach and the riddle of the number alphabet.
1. German music. Bach, Johann Sebastian, 1685–1750
I. Title
780.92

Library of Congress cataloguing in publication data
Tatlow, Ruth Mary.
Bach and the riddle of the number alphabet / Ruth Mary Tatlow.
p.   cm.
Includes bibliographical references.
ISBN 0 521 36191 5
1. Bach, Johann Sebastian, 1685–1750 – Criticism and interpretation,
2. Symbolism in music. I. Title.
ML410.B1T18 1990
780′.92 – dc20   90–1550   CIP

ISBN 0 521 36191 5 hardback

LIBRARY
ALMA COLLEGE
ALMA, MICHIGAN

to
Mark
my best friend
my love
my husband
with whom I have walked
talked and laughed
for eleven years

Contents

Illustrations

The illustrations appear by kind permission of the following: Musik-
abteilung, Staatsbibliothek Preußischer Kulturbesitz, Berlin (Illustrations 1 and 2); Kungliga Biblioteket, Stockholm (Illustrations 3, 4, 5, 6,
7, 8, 10 and 11); Stadtbibliothek, Nürnberg (Illustration 9).

Acknowledgements

Bach and the Riddle of the Number Alphabet is a revised version of my doctoral thesis, *Lusus Poëticus vel Musicus: Johann Sebastian Bach, The Baroque Paragram and Friedrich Smend's Number Alphabet Theory*, submitted to the University of London in January 1987. Without the encouragement of Professor Dr Ulrich Siegele (University of Tübingen) my research into this topic would not have begun. I am most grateful to him and to members of the Faculty of Music, King's College London, who listened carefully before commenting wisely upon the evolving ideas.

My thanks are also due to the librarians Dr Stefan Kubów (Wrocław), Dr Günther Thomann (Nürnberg), Dr Günther Klein (West Berlin), Frau Erika Rother (East Berlin) and Dr Wolfgang Goldhan (East Berlin), who made material from their libraries available, and to Dr Walther Dehnhard and Dr Wolf Hobohm for trusting me with the results of their own research.

I am grateful to the British Academy and the Deutscher Akademischer Austauschdienst for financially assisting my research period.

During the course of preparing the thesis for publication many more people have given of their time and experience. Mrs Mary Whittall and Mr Colin D. Monk expertly translated the German and Latin texts; Mr Timothy Wilcox, Miss Terry Barringer, Miss Fiona Divers and members of my family willingly assisted at different stages; but above all it was Mark and Benjamin who made the project possible with their total love, support and co-operation.

Introduction

In 1947 the theologian and musicologist Friedrich Smend (1893–1980) published the first of four studies in which he presented his theory of Johann Sebastian Bach's use of a number alphabet. Smend provided historical evidence and musical examples to support his claim that Bach regularly used the natural-order number alphabet (A = 1 to Z = 24: see Appendix 1) to incorporate significant words into his music as part of a grander scheme of compositional number symbolism.

Bach's use of the number alphabet is a highly controversial topic, kept alive today by a few writers who continue to wrench ideas from their original context in Smend's theory and exaggerate them to the point of academic absurdity. Several bizarre examples appear in a book written in 1985 by Kees van Houten and Marinus Kasbergen:

Johann Sebastian Bach was born on the 21st March 1685 or 21 3 307 in the Rosicrucian calendar. He died on the 28th July which in Rosicrucian terms is 28 7 372. This leads to an improbable but inescapable conclusion: it appears that Bach employed the epitaph of Christian Rosencreuz [ACRC Hoc Universi Compendium Vivus Mihi Sepulchrum Feci = 544] in the *Sinfoniæ*. [The total number of bars in the 15 three-part *Sinfoniæ* is 544.] In the *Magnificat* the epitaph encircles 28 + 7 and in the last three organ sonatas it encircles the number 372.[1] In relation to this inscription we find in one case 28 7 and in the other case 372, the date and year of Bach's death when calculated by the Rosicrucian calendar. The *Magnificat* dates from 1730 and the organ sonatas probably date from 1727. In other words Bach accurately registered the date of his death in relation to the epitaph long before the actual event. The overall structure of many of Bach's most important works is dealt with in the context of the above insights into the esoteric relationship. The connection Bach – Rosicrucian (epitaph) – date of death becomes more and more evident and the numbers involved are very relevant to Bach himself and have a fundamental symbolic meaning. A special chapter is devoted to the number 23,869, the total sum of the days of Bach's life.[2]

---

[1] Discussions of the *Sinfoniæ* and *Magnificat* appear on p. 50 and p. 54 respectively of Kees van Houten and Marinus Kasbergen's *Bach en het getal* (Zutphen, 1985).
[2] Ibid., p. 212.

1

Many other sensational articles and books have been published on Bach's use of the number alphabet. They are all too often written by enthusiasts using Smend's theory uncritically, and do nothing but harm to its reputation among more serious scholars. One indication of this is the absence of an entry under 'Number Symbolism' or 'Number Alphabet' in *The New Grove Dictionary of Music and Musicians* (1980) (although there is an entry under '*Zahlensymbolik*' in the *Supplement* (1979) of its German counterpart *Die Musik in Geschichte und Gegenwart*).

If it were proved sound, Smend's theory could serve as the foundation for the development of an 'authentic' analytical technique, using seventeenth- and eighteenth-century ideas to shed light on eighteenth-century music. Were it to be shown that Bach used a number alphabet as part of his compositional technique, it could increase our knowledge of Bach the man and of his intentions when composing. Furthermore, were it to be discovered that the practice was widespread among Bach's contemporaries, then the implications would be far-reaching. However, the fundamental question of the validity of Smend's theory must be answered first. Some musicologists have looked for fresh evidence to supplement Smend's historical examples. Their material purports to show that Bach was interested in mathematics, cabbalism and number symbolism.

BACH AND MATHEMATICS

The earliest reference to a link between Bach and mathematics can be found in Mattheson's *Ehren-Pforte*. Lorenz Christoph Mizler's autobiographical entry contains a revealing editorial annotation by Mattheson:

The latter [Bach] was certainly and in truth just as little instrumental in teaching him [Mizler] the supposed mathematical bases of composition as the man to be named next [Mattheson himself]. This I can guarantee.[3]

Philipp Spitta uses this quotation to reinforce his point that Bach had no interest in teaching the 'supposed mathematical bases of composition', and adds: 'Even the writers of the Necrology state plainly: "Bach never went into a deep theoretical study of music".'[4] While there is little doubt

---

[3] Johann Mattheson, *Grundlage einer Ehren-Pforte* (Hamburg, 1740), p. 231. Quoted by Hans T. David and Arthur Mendel in *The Bach Reader: A Life of Johann Sebastian Bach in Letters and Documents*, revised edn with a Supplement (New York, London, 1966), p. 440.
[4] Philipp Spitta, *Johann Sebastian Bach: His Work and Influence on the Music of Germany 1685–1750*, 3 vols. transl. Clara Bell and J. A. Fuller-Maitland (London, 1884), reprint edn in 2 vols. (New York, 1951), III, 24.

that the 'supposed mathematical bases of composition' Bach and Mattheson did not teach Mizler refer to well-known aspects of music theory, it is tantalising to imagine that Mattheson was also referring to mathematical devices that included a number alphabet.

The most developed thesis of Bach as a mathematician is that of Herbert Anton Kellner in his articles on the tuning of Bach's keyboard instruments.[5] Many biographers try to show that Bach was something of a mathematician by including general references that link mathematics with music. A frequent example is a verse from the apocryphal book of the Wisdom of Solomon, which was first quoted by Augustine of Hippo in connection with symbolic numbers, and which heads many German mathematical and musical books of the seventeenth and eighteenth centuries: 'But thou hast arranged all things by measure and number and weight.'[6] Another favourite quotation is the definition of music by the philosopher Gottfried Wilhelm Leibniz (1646–1716), which reads: 'Music is the hidden arithmetical exercise of a mind unconscious that it is calculating.' Leibniz' studies on the theory of music may have been stimulated by his correspondence with the mathematician Henfling (1705–9).[7] His definition of music, from one of two letters written to Christoph Goldbach in 1712, is interesting, but almost wholly irrelevant to a study of Bach and the number alphabet, because Bach's use of it would have been *conscious* rather than *unconscious*. The verse from the Apocrypha is perhaps of more value because it helps to build up a picture of how numbers were viewed in Lutheran society.

BACH AND CABBALISM

In the major encyclopædic authority on cabbalism, the *Encyclopædia Judaica*,[8] there is no mention of the natural-order number alphabet. In cabbalistic *gematria* the most common number alphabet used is the Hebrew milesian alphabet (Alep = 1 to Taw = 400: see Appendix 1).[9]

[5] For example, Herbert Anton Kellner, 'Was Bach a Mathematician', *The English Harpsichord Magazine* 2 (1978), 32–6; 'A propos d'une réimpression de la *Musicalische Temperatur* de Werckmeister', *Revue de Musicologie* 71 (1985), 184–7; 'How Bach Quantified His Well-Tempered Tuning within the *Four Duets*', *The English Harpsichord Magazine* 4 (1986), 21–7.

[6] Wisd. 11:20. Quoted by Ulrich Meyer in 'Johann Jacob Schmidts *Biblischer Mathematicus* von 1736', *Die Musikforschung* 32 (1979), 150, and Arthur Hirsch in *Die Zahl im Kantatenwerk Johann Sebastian Bachs* (Stuttgart, 1986), p. 3, among others. See p. 40 below for Augustine's citation of the verse.

[7] *The New Grove Dictionary of Music and Musicians*, s.v. 'Leibniz, Gottfried Wilhelm', by Rudolf Haase.

[8] *Encyclopædia Judaica* (Jerusalem, 1971).

[9] The term 'milesian' is a translation of 'milesisch' from Franz Dornseiff's *Das Alphabet in Mystik und Magie*, Studien zur Geschichte des Antiken Weltbildes und der Griechischen Wissenschaft, vol. VII (Leipzig, 1922; reprint edn Leipzig, 1980), p. 91. The number

Nowhere in cabbalistic literature have I seen *gematria* used for musical purposes: it was always used for interpreting Scripture.

Smend was the first to make a connection between Bach and cabbalism although he neither defined the term cabbalism nor explored the connection.[10] This left the field wide open for all kinds of cabbalistic and pseudo-cabbalistic interpretations of the numbers in Bach's scores. Ulrich Meyer addresses the problem in his article 'Zahlenalphabet bei J. S. Bach? – Zur anti-kabbalistischen Tradition im Luthertum'. Taking a passage from Luther and quotations from several seventeenth- and eighteenth-century sources he shows that Bach did not use the number alphabet cabbalistically. His conclusion reads:

The line I have drawn runs from the sixteenth, through the seventeenth and into the early part of the eighteenth centuries, that is, from the Reformation to the age of Bach. It displays a clear anti-cabbalistic stance throughout. The number, weight and consistency of these sources make it wholly improbable that the Lutheran Bach thought and acted differently in any way from their authors. It is time we bade farewell to the notion that Bach worked with the number alphabet for any musico-theological purpose.

And in the qualifying footnote he writes:

I do not rule out the possibility that Bach occasionally used the process that he had come across in Picander's poems to allude to his own name by means of the number 14 (and only that number), but in a non-theological and non-serious spirit.[11]

Meyer's work is the first major challenge on historical grounds to the validity of Smend's theory, although, unfortunately, he deals only with the interpretation and not with the fundamental premises of the theory.

BACH AND NUMBER SYMBOLISM

Smend's number-symbolism scheme includes the idea that Bach incorporated traditional biblical numbers into his music: numbers such as 3 to symbolise the Trinity, 10 to symbolise the Commandments and 12 to symbolise the Apostles. As Fritz Feldmann's study 'Numerorum mysteria' shows, however, there were frequently five or more possible interpretations of each number in traditional number symbolism.[12]

alphabet with the progression 1, 2, 3 . . . 10, 20, 30 . . . 100, 200, 300, etc. was first used in Miletus as early as the eighth century BC, and I use 'milesian' to describe any number alphabet with this progression. Cabbalistic *gematria* is discussed on pp. 41–2 below.

10 Friedrich Smend, *Johann Sebastian Bach: Kirchen-Kantaten: erläutert*, 6 vols. (Berlin, 1947–9; reprint edns Berlin, 1950 and 1966), III (1947) and IV (1947).

11 Ulrich Meyer, 'Zahlenalphabet bei J. S. Bach? – Zur anti-kabbalistischen Tradition im Luthertum', *Musik und Kirche* 51 (1981), 19.

12 Fritz Feldmann, 'Numerorum mysteria', *Archiv für Musikwissenschaft* 14 (1957), 102–29.

Writing about symbolic numbers in *Musicalische Paradoxal-Discourse* (1707), Andreas Werckmeister gives some musical interpretations of the numbers 1, 2, 3, 4, 5, 6 and 7, but without explaining exactly how the numbers should be incorporated into a musical composition.[13]

It is puzzling that, although many musicians since Smend have been happy to use the natural-order number alphabet in analyses of Bach's music, it was not until 1980 that an eighteenth-century example of the alphabet appeared in a music journal in connection with Bach or his contemporaries.[14] It is similarly perplexing that there is no mention of a symbolic number alphabet in any of the studies I have seen on number symbolism in literature, art, architecture and music.[15] It is high time for a thorough reappraisal of Smend's theory.

[13] Andreas Werckmeister, *Musicalische Paradoxal-Discourse* (Quedlinburg, 1707), pp. 92–5, to which Ulrich Meyer refers in 'Zum Problem der Zahlen in Johann Sebastian Bachs Werk', *Musik und Kirche* 49 (1979), 70.

[14] Herbert Anton Kellner, 'Welches Zahlenalphabet benützte der Thomaskantor Kuhnau?', *Die Musikforschung* 33 (1980), 124,.

[15] The exception is Walter Blankenburg's article 'Zahlensymbolik' in the *Supplement* (1979) to *Die Musik in Geschichte und Gegenwart*, which in any case leans heavily on Smend's work.

1

Friedrich Smend

Smend sets out the evidence for Bach's knowledge and use of the number alphabet most fully in the introduction to the third volume of *Kirchen-Kantaten* (1947),[1] which begins:

Picander's *Ernst-, Schertzhaffte und Satyrische Gedichte* (Leipzig 1732, Part 3) contains the following felicitation:

> On the occasion of the D. and T. wedding. 1 June 1730.
> *Paragramma Cabbalisticum trigonale.* Sirach 26: 13–15.

Bey	294	Ein	151
dem	103	freundlich	653
Daumischen	663	Weib	294
und	311	erfreuet	772
Thymischen	944	ihren	340
Hochzeits	904	Mann	261
Festin	533	und	311
wolte	607	wenn	428
dem	103	sie	231
Herrn	448	vernünfftig	1075
Bräutigam	724	mit	313
und	311	ihm	159
Jungfer	563	umgehet	572
Braut	557	erfrischet	805
beyden	410	sie	231
wahre	436	ihm	159
Liebe	144	sein	322
wahre	436	Hertz.	694
Beständigkeit	874	Ein	151
wahre	436	Weib	294
Treu	568	das	182

---

[1] Smend, *Kirchen-Kantaten* III (1947), 5–21.

reichlich	408	schweigen	638
Auskommen	804	kan	147
und	311	das	182
alles	319	ist	406
vergnügende	866	eine	166
Wohl	438	Gabe	47
nebst	470	Gottes.	699
folgenden	442	Ein	151
aus	382	wohlgezogen	984
der	178	Weib	294
heiligen	341	ist	406
Schrift	643	nicht	368
ein	151	zu	510
alter	425	bezahlen.	527
Teutscher	986	Es	186
und	311	ist	406
naher	296	nichts	539
Befreundter	686	liebers	468
beständigst	930	auf	232
anwünschen	943	Erden	284
	———	denn	207
	20699	ein	151
		züchtig	815
		Weib	294
		und	311
		nichts	539
		köstlichers	1013
		denn	207
		ein	151
		keusches	679
		Weib	294
		———	
			20699

(See Appendix 4 page 146.)

The words and numbers are here employed in a game. Each letter has a numerical value, and therefore every word can be expressed as a total of its letter-numbers. Consequently the number placed beside each word here represents its total. The point of arranging the words and numbers in adjacent columns, since the numbers in each column add up to the same grand total, is that the congratulator means exactly the same thing with the good wishes in his own words as is expressed in the biblical text alongside. This form of self-expression is an age-old tradition, regularly practised in the Cabbala, but also found in other sources. In every instance a puzzle has to be solved. In this particular case, Picander has made it exceptionally difficult for the bridegroom, which prompts the conclusion that they must often have played such riddling games with each other. For he does not use the number alphabet customary in such games; the recipient has first of all to work out the numbers corresponding to each letter. That need not trouble us here: there is something else that has much greater importance for us.

In Bach's first decade as Thomas-Kantor in Leipzig, Picander was his closest collaborator. Moreover, unquestionably Bach knew the volume of poetry containing our paragram; for it also contains the texts of several of his compositions. That is enough in itself to suggest that Bach too was familiar with number games of this type. Indeed, we have good reason to be sure that such was the case, for the number alphabet was very popular at that period as a means of interpreting literary and even biblical texts: a given word in the text might be interpreted according to the numerical value discovered in it; alternatively, a number in the text might be understood to stand for a word – for example, a proper noun – when the letter-numbers of that word added up to that number. When Bach opened, for example, the *Biblische Erklärung* of Johannes Olearius that stood in his book cabinet, he found there, in the exegesis of Revelation 13:18, the number 666, which that verse cites, interpreted according to the above method. '*Lusus ingenii*' or 'intellectual perambulations' are the terms coined by Johann Jacob Schmidt for this preoccupation with numbers, in his book *Biblischer Mathematicus*, published in 1736, that is, in the very year that Bach composed the 'Sanctus' of the *B minor Mass*.

Picander's use, in the wedding felicitation quoted above, of a key other than the one commonly used is quite exceptional. The general practice, among those who gave each other such puzzles to do, was to stick to the traditional number alphabet:

A = 1	E = 5	I. J = 9	N = 13	R = 17	W = 21
B = 2	F = 6	K = 10	O = 14	S = 18	X = 22
C = 3	G = 7	L = 11	P = 15	T = 19	Y = 23
D = 4	H = 8	M = 12	Q = 16	U. V = 20	Z = 24

But Bach, like other great minds, enjoyed the setting and solving of puzzles. Some of these puzzles have survived, and the study of them is well worth while.

Smend then moves straight on to show how Bach made use of this 'traditional' number alphabet. His first example concerns the inscription on a goblet found in the Eisenach museum and allegedly presented to Bach by two of his pupils. His next example is of the *Canon a 4 voce* (BWV 1073) written in 1713 for his second cousin Johann Gottfried Walther, into which, according to Smend, Bach incorporated his own surname as the number of bars:

$$B \quad A \quad C \quad H = 14$$
$$2 + 1 + 3 + 8$$

and Walther's surname as the number of sounding notes:

$$W \quad A \quad L \quad T \quad H \quad E \quad R = 82.$$
$$21 + 1 + 11 + 19 + 8 + 5 + 17$$

Smend points out that Bach's full name is exactly half that of Walther's surname:

$$J. \quad S. \quad B \quad A \quad C \quad H = 41.$$
$$9 + 18 + 2 + 1 + 3 + 8$$

He gives many further examples and towards the end of the introduction writes the following summary:

We have now acquainted ourselves with a small portion of Bach's number symbolism. To begin with the language spoken here is totally foreign to us moderns. First and foremost, some readers will have started to ask by now what all this has to do with Bach's cantatas, which are, after all, the subject of these volumes. The immediate answer to that is that these intellectual games are entirely serious. The humour that Asmussen quite rightly detects here is anything but a joking matter.[2] In the last of our examples we found the alphabet-numbers intermingled with the sacred numbers. Bach added the following motto to another of his puzzle-canons *Christus Coronabit Crucigeros*. Picander himself, in publishing his wedding paragram, was not intending to disseminate a joke: he used a biblical text, and the paragram appears in the 'serious' section of his book of poems . . . If Bach uses the number alphabet in the pieces we have looked at, then we have to reckon with his having done it in the case of his sacred compositions too.

There is one further thing to be said: When Bach uses the number alphabet in his compositions, it is by no means always a matter of his own name alone, although that often occurs. Words of a quite different kind, words of a religious and theological nature, are regularly to be found also. We will do well to consider only a small number of these, in order to see our way clearly. CHRISTUS is expressed by the number-symbol 112, CREDO by 43. The 'Credo' of the *B minor Mass*, in its original form, numbers 784 (i.e. 7×112) bars; the sacred name of CHRISTUS is invoked 7 times therein. In the chorus 'Credo in unum Deum' in the same work, the word CREDO appears 43 times. The same chorus, plus the following movement 'Patrem omnipotentem', amounts to a total of 129 (i.e. 3×43) bars; i.e. Bach's setting of the first article of faith, in the very number of its bars, states: CREDO, CREDO, CREDO. That means: there is no true belief in God outside belief in the Trinity. And Bach makes this affirmation at the very period when Deism was beginning to flourish. It is the Crucified and Risen Christ that stands at the very heart of this faith. The 7 chorale stanzas of the cantata 'Christ

---

[2] On 22 May 1943 Smend included his friend Hans Asmussen's comments in a letter to Jansen, to which Jansen replied a week later: 'What Asmussen says is very fine, but doesn't touch the heart of the problem, in my opinion. I think that Bach did all that only because he needed and was looking for *connections*. It was a matter of fundamental indifference to him, whether posterity one day got to the bottom of his "science" or not.'

lag in Todesbanden' (No. 4) amount to a total of 387 (i.e. 9×43) bars. 9 (3×3) signifies Faith, but 43 stands for CREDO. When we celebrate Easter, it is a celebration of our faith, and nothing else.[3]

Friedrich Smend gives little historical evidence to support his statements. His introduction passes rapidly from an example of a paragram[4] using a milesian alphabet, via general remarks about the existence and character of number alphabets in the eighteenth century and statements on Bach's knowledge of number alphabets, to musical examples of Bach's use of the natural-order number alphabet in his compositions.

Among the general remarks about the number alphabet are Smend's statements on the character and existence of the paragram. Most of his claims have to be taken on trust as he does not support them with references to primary or secondary sources. The most serious omission is an example of the natural-order alphabet from the seventeenth or eighteenth centuries. It is very odd that he could find a contemporary example of the 'exceptional' trigonal alphabet ($A = 1$ to $Z = 300$: see Appendix 1) and yet fail to reproduce an example of the 'traditional' natural-order alphabet.

His statements on Bach's knowledge of the number alphabet begin with a primary source that Bach undoubtedly knew: Picander's paragram of 1730 published in 1732. But from this one can infer only that Bach knew of a trigonal alphabet after 1732 and not, as Smend seems to imply by his second musical example of the 1713 canon, that Bach was familiar with number alphabets before 1732. Smend next implies that Bach was influenced in some way by Schmidt when he wrote the 'Sanctus' of the *B minor Mass*. It is thought today that the 'Sanctus' was composed in 1724 and not in 1736,[5] but, as Bach could have been influenced by many books he read which describe cabbalistic *gematria*, Smend's redundant comment is not affected by the redating. His remarks about Olearius' *Biblische Erklärung* are similarly irrelevant to his argument, as he makes no attempt to show when Bach acquired his copy, or whether he had read the tiny fragment on Revelation 13:18.

Smend's statements on Bach's use of the number alphabet are

---

[3] *Kirchen-Kantaten* III (1947), 17–18 and 21.

[4] I shall use the word paragram as a shortened version of paragramma to refer to the form used in Picander's example of the *Paragramma Cabbalisticum trigonale*.

[5] Smend's edition of the *B minor Mass* for the Neue Bachausgabe was published in 1954 (score) and 1956 (critical commentary). On p. 171 of the critical commentary Smend dates the 'Sanctus' as between 1735 and 1737. In 'Zur Chronologie der Leipziger Vokalwerke J. S. Bachs', *Bach-Jahrbuch* 44 (1957), 77, Alfred Dürr dates the 'Sanctus' as 25 December 1724, and, after taking issue with Smend's dating, Georg von Dadelsen on p. 150 of *Beiträge zur Chronologie der Werke Johann Sebastian Bachs* (Trossingen, 1958) also proposes that the 'Sanctus' was written towards the end of 1724.

devastatingly authoritative. He uses sentences such as 'When Bach uses the number alphabet in his compositions, it is by no means always a matter of his name alone' and 'Words of a quite different kind, words of a religious and theological nature are regularly to be found also' as a foundation on which to build detailed interpretations, of which the following are typical: 'CHRISTUS is expressed by the number-symbol 112, CREDO by 43 . . .' 'The chorus "Credo in unum Deum" . . . plus the following movement "Patrem Omnipotentem" amounts to a total of 129 (i.e. 3 × 43) bars; i.e. . . . . CREDO, CREDO, CREDO. That means: there is no true belief in God outside belief in the Trinity.' Yet Smend provides no historical evidence to show that the natural-order number alphabet was ever used in conjunction with sacred numbers. He thought his musical examples, which attempt to demonstrate Bach's use of the natural-order number alphabet, proceeded logically from his historical evidence, but this is not the case. He acknowledges that Picander used the trigonal and not the natural-order alphabet, but omits the fact that Olearius and Schmidt both use the Hebrew milesian number alphabet.

Smend neither gives an example of the existence in the eighteenth century or otherwise of the Latin or German natural-order alphabet, nor provides any evidence for Bach's knowledge of it. One must therefore query his examples and interpretation of Bach's use of the natural-order alphabet, and, furthermore, his wisdom in basing a complete analytical theory upon it.

SMEND'S SOURCES

Picander's *Paragramma Cabbalisticum trigonale*

A more careful look at Picander's *Ernst-, Schertzhaffte und Satyrische Gedichte* shows that under the heading *On the occasion of the D. and T. wedding. 1 June 1730. Paragramma Cabbalisticum trigonale*, and beneath the parallel columns of figures quoted by Smend there is a lengthy poem. Its eighty lines use ideas generated by the paragram. One wonders whether Smend saw the poem and considered it irrelevant, whether wartime library evacuations prevented him from checking the original, and whether, had he known the poem, it would have altered his interpretation of the paragram.[6]

Close study of the paragram form leaves no doubt that Smend misunderstood Picander's example. Some of his statements may be partially true, but his generalisations are misleading. For example, it is true that there is a relationship between the paragram formulæ used by

---

[6] Smend was familiar with the five poetry volumes by Picander, and knew the third volume as early as 1928, when he quoted it in connection with the published text of Bach's

the early cabbalists and those used by eighteenth-century paragrammatists, but Smend goes no way towards explaining the difference in
function and meaning between them. Some of his statements are totally
wrong. The trigonal alphabet, for example, is far from being exceptional.
Of the 5800 paragrams I have so far discovered over 5000 make use of the
trigonal alphabet. Had Smend known of these paragrams he would not
have ventured the unnecessary and unlikely suggestion that by using the
trigonal alphabet Picander was making his game with the bridegroom
exceptionally difficult.

Johann Olearius' *Biblische Erklärung*

The passage to which Smend refers is from the fifth volume of Olearius'
commentary *Biblische Erklärung* (1681). Olearius' comment on the
number 666 from Revelation 13:18 appears in the first column of page
1973:

Six. χ§ς. Some seek it [the meaning of the number] in the Hebrew רומיית, some in
the Greek ἐκκλησία 'Ιταλικα, some in the Latin *Latinus*, while Irenæus for one,
sees the [Greek] word λατεῖνος in [the city of] *Latium*, where the Latin language,
the Latin version of the Bible and the authority of Latin Bulls are in everyday use,
and yet others in the German, which is doubtful. See the commentary by D.
HoeCom and D. Calov, *Explicatio D Lucii*, page 839, on the threefold power in
Heaven, Earth and Hell, according to Cotterius, in a triple six-part measure.
N.B. For more details, see the *Hand-Buch Art* 116, page 1676, VICarIUs fILII
DeI. The word Romiith and Lateinos will suffice us. And even if we should fail to
find the name or the word, the thing itself is quite clear of which Daniel 12 and II
Thessalonians 2 are the chief witness, and which is discussed in the *Hand-Buch
Art* . . .[7]

Here Olearius cites five examples of the interpretation of the number
666.

i) The Hebrew word רומיית (Romiith):

ר – Res	= 200
ו – Waw	= 6

St Mark Passion in his article 'Bachs *Matthäus-Passion*', *Bach-Jahrbuch* 25 (1928), 1–95,
reprinted in *Friedrich Smend: Bach-Studien: Gesammelte Reden und Aufsätze*, ed.
Christoph Wolff (Kassel, Basel, 1969). See also p. 28 below.
[7] Johann Olearius, *Biblische Erklärung. Darinnen nechst dem allgemeinen Haupt-Schlüssel
Der gantzen heiligen Schrifft*, 5 vols. (Leipzig, 1678–81), V (1681), 1973. The title-page of
the original edition reads: *Biblischer Erklärung* . . . The Latin of lines 5 and 6 might also
be translated as: 'See the commentary by D. HoeCom, D. Calov and D. Luci, *Explicatio*,
p. 839.'

מ – Mem   = 40
י – Yod   = 10
י – Yod   = 10
ת – Taw   = 400
            ———
            666
            ———

ii) The Greek words ἐκκλησία Ἰταλικα (Ecclesia Italica):

ε – Epsilon   =   5
κ – Kappa   = 20
κ – Kappa   = 20
λ – Lambda   = 30
η – Eta   =   8
σ – Sigma   = 200
ι – Iota   = 10
α – Alpha   =   1

I – Iota   = 10
τ – Tau   = 300
α – Alpha   =   1
λ – Lambda   = 30
ι – Iota   = 10
κ – Kappa   = 20
α – Alpha   =   1
               ———
               666
               ———

iii) The Greek word λατεῖνος (Lateinos), which appears in Irenæus' treatise *Against Heresies* (*c.* 180 AD):

λ – Lambda   = 30
α – Alpha   =   1
τ – Tau   = 300
ε – Epsilon   =   5
ι – Iota   = 10
ν – Nu   = 50
ο – Omicron   = 70
ς – Sigma   = 200
               ———
               666
               ———

iv) An unspecified German attempt, which does not convince Olearius; and

v) A number phrase, VICarIUs fILII DeI (substitute of the Son of God), whose Roman numerals add up to 666:

$$V + I + C + I + V + I + L + I + I + D + I = DCLVVIIIIII = 666.$$

Olearius' five examples of the prophetic number 666 have little in common with Picander's paragram except that the first three use a number alphabet, albeit milesian rather than trigonal. There are 7215 pages in the five volumes of Olearius' *Biblische Erklärung*, and, unless Bach was looking specifically for a comment on Revelation 13:18, he may well have missed this quarter-column fragment. Nevertheless, it is interesting to see these interpretations included in a reputable theological book owned by Bach.

Johann Jacob Schmidt's *Biblischer Mathematicus* (1736)

The passage from *Biblischer Mathematicus*, which Smend quotes in *Kirchen-Kantaten* III, comes from the first chapter, in a section on the meaning of biblical numbers:

The fourth usage or significance is cabbalistic, by which the Jews set so great a store, in as much as they are confident that much is contained in their Cabbala, with the so-called Gematrajia [*gematria*], or geometrical and arithmetical interpretation of Scripture, in which they take the numerical values of letters, words or sayings in Holy Scripture, and from that produce I know not what in the way of arcana and curiosities, but depart blasphemously in many respects from the purposes of the Holy Spirit. As when, for instance, they attempt to prove that the world will endure 6,000 years, in as much as in Gen. 1:1 א (Alep) signifies 1,000, and is to be met with six times altogether, the last occasion being in the last verse of the last chapter of the Second Book of Chronicles (which is the last book in the Hebrew Bible). Or when they explain one word by another, the letters of which amount to the same, in numbers, as the letters of the first word; for example, the words שילה יבא , '[until] Shiloh, or the Hero, come' (Gen. 49:10) which add up to 358 in numbers, by the word משיח, which comes to the same total. Similarly, the word צמח (Zech. 3:8) by מנחם, 'a comforter', both of which add up to 138 in numbers.

Yod	10	Mem	40	Sade	90	Mem	40
Bet	2	Shîn	300	Mem	40	Nun	50
Alep	1	Yod	10	Het	8	Het	8
		Het	8			Mem	40
Shîn	300				138		
Yod	10		358				138
Lamed	30						
He	5						
	358						

666

So long as devices of this kind are taken for harmless *lusus ingenii*, or mere intellectual perambulations or games, as the late Luther says, there is no reason why they should be rejected out of hand. But if anyone wished to do as the cabbalists do, and carve out of them articles of faith and arcana, and assert the same, then he would fall into foolish error and sheerly superstitious or even godless ways.[8]

Schmidt is describing a means of biblical exegesis that has its roots in Jewish cabbalism, and his examples show that the milesian alphabet was still known in eighteenth-century Germany. This form of exegesis, using words from the Bible and the Hebrew milesian alphabet has little in common with Picander's paragram and poem. Moreover, in his 'intellectual perambulations' Luther does not use a number alphabet,[9] and Smend's use of Luther's phrase, which he attributes to Schmidt, is therefore both inaccurate and misleading.

Balthasar Raith's unnamed grammar

Smend wrote in *Kirchen-Kantaten* III:

'The practice of using number equivalencies is also a distinctive feature of the Cabbala, where things which have an equal number value are supposed to explain one another by cross reference.' Thus read a commonly used grammar book by Balthasar Raith from shortly before Bach's time.[10]

and:

Balthasar Raith said: 'where things which have an equal number value are supposed to explain one another by cross reference'. This means that the four constantly repeated leading tones of the canon are saying nothing other than BACH.[11]

Balthasar Raith (1616–83) was born in Tübingen, where he later studied. After some years as a Lutheran pastor in Derindingen he returned to Tübingen as a Professor of Theology at the University. Zedler's *Lexicon* lists eleven books and six tracts by Raith, none of which are grammars. An extensive search revealed that the book to which Smend was referring was Wilhelm Schickard's *Horologium Hebraeum*, edited by Raith.[12] *Horologium Hebraeum* is a Hebrew grammar written

---

[8] Johann Jacob Schmidt, *Biblischer Mathematicus* (Züllichau, 1736), p. 10.

[9] *D. Martin Luthers Werke. Kritische Gesamtausgabe* (Weimar, 1883–), X.I,1, 'Kirchenpostille 1522', 422–31. See also Ulrich Meyer, 'Zahlenalphabet bei J. S. Bach?', 16.

[10] Smend, *Kirchen-Kantaten* III (1947), 8.

[11] Ibid., 10, referring to puzzle-canon, 'F A B E Repetatur' (BWV 1078).

[12] Wilhelm Schickard, *Horologium Hebraeum* (Tübingen, 1614). Many editions of *Horologium Hebraeum* were made after Schickard's death, including those by Raith,

in Latin and paginated in the Hebrew manner from the back towards the front. Schickhard was a Professor of Hebrew at Tübingen and died of the plague in 1635.

The phrases cited by Smend are from Schickhard's original, and were not added by Raith. They appear near the beginning of the book, in the third section 'Numeri' of the second chapter 'De Scriptione'. Having described the common Hebrew milesian number alphabet Alep = 1 to Taw = 400, Schickhard makes three points about the use of Hebrew numerals, the third of which reads:

The practice of using number equivalencies is also a distinctive feature of the Cabbala, where things which have an equal number value are supposed to explain one another by cross reference. See the passage Gen. 49:10, יבא שילה Schilo will come, and משיח, Messiam, both of which equal 358, which method of interpretation they call *gematria*.[13]

Although this example was also given by Schmidt in 1736, he was quoting Hocker's *Mathematische Seelen-lust* and not Schickhard.[14] Yet again Smend seems to have misunderstood his sources. The sentence he attributes to Raith describes a means of interpreting the Bible using the Hebrew milesian alphabet: it does little to support Smend's technique of musical analysis using the Latin natural-order number alphabet.

Although *Kirchen-Kantaten* III contains the most thorough presentation of his case for Bach's use of the number alphabet, Smend does in fact discuss the number alphabet in three other places: *Luther und Bach* (1947), pages 15–26, *Kirchen-Kantaten* IV (1947), pages 5–21, and *Johann Sebastian Bach bei seinem Namen gerufen* (1950). The most informative source given in these works for the natural-order number alphabet is Peter Friesenhahn's *Hellenistische Wortzahlenmystik im neuen Testament*, and in *Luther und Bach* Smend's argument for the use of the natural-order number alphabet appears to hang upon Friesenhahn's work:

Finally, the number alphabet also plays a role. In his book *Hellenistische Wortzahlenmystik* (Leipzig, 1935), Peter Friesenhahn has uncovered some strange material relating to the New Testament. While his work, naturally, is

which were published in 1663, 1670 and 1682 as the 13th, 14th and 15th editions respectively. The latest one I have seen, *Editio Nova* (Tübingen, 1714), is edited by Georg Cottam. *Horologium Hebraeum* was also published under the title *Institutiones Linguae Ebraeae*. I am grateful to Dr Walther Dehnhard (Wiesbaden), Dr Stefan Kubów (University Library, Wrocław) and Erika Rother (Deutsche Staatsbibliothek, East Berlin), who independently directed me to Schickhard.

13 Wilhelm Schickhard, *Horologium Hebraeum*, 14th edn (Tübingen, 1670), p. 19.
14 Johann Ludwig Hocker, *Mathematische Seelen-lust*, 2 vols. (Crailsheim, Frankfurt, 1712–15), I, 89. Nor does Hocker quote Schickhard: he quotes works by the theologians Glassius and Pfeiffer as his sources for this example.

based on Hellenism and the Greek alphabet, the Latin alphabet (A = 1; B = 2; . . . I and J = 9; U and V = 20; . . . Z = 24) is standard for the Western World. The total produced by adding up the letter-numbers of a word gives a number which can stand for the word: Christus = 112, Credo = 43. Similarly with Bach, whose name is represented by the number 14.[15]

Friesenhahn's work is a general survey of the many mystical interpretations of numbers. In a chapter entitled 'Schriftzeichen und Zahlzeichen' he describes the Greek milesian number alphabet, then turning swiftly to the Greek natural-order alphabet and the innovative work of Wolfgang Schultz.[16] Greek poetry is a far cry from Bach's music, and it is hard to tell what caused Smend to make a link between Schultz's Greek number alphabets and Bach.

Rather than showing that Smend knew more than he wrote, a closer look at his sources has indicated that he was not even aware of their full content. They show that in seventeenth- and eighteenth-century Germany the Latin trigonal and the Greek and Hebrew milesian alphabets were used in books of poetry, biblical exegesis and Hebrew grammar. They do not show, as Smend thought, that the Latin natural-order was the usual number alphabet, nor that there was one common interpretation of the use of number alphabets. The only example Smend gives of a natural-order alphabet is of a Greek alphabet coming from a secondary source. It would be presumptuous to suggest that it was solely on account of wartime library evacuations that a respected scholar was unable to check source references. These academic *faux pas* are, however, surprising and mysterious.

SMEND AND NUMBER SYMBOLISM

The Neue Bachgesellschaft

Friedrich Smend's father, Julius Smend (1857–1930), was a theologian and musicologist. While a Professor of Theology at the Universities of Straßburg (from 1893) and Münster (from 1918) he pursued his interest in Lutheran Church music,[17] writing nearly two hundred articles for the

---

[15] 'Luther und Bach', *Bach-Studien*, pp. 159–60. Although *Luther und Bach* and *J. S. Bach bei seinem Namen gerufen* were originally published as monographs, references will be given only to the later, more widely available reprint edition.

[16] Peter Friesenhahn, *Hellenistische Wortzahlenmystik im neuen Testament* (Leipzig, Berlin, 1935), pp. 83–4. See also Wolfgang Schultz, *Rätsel des hellenischen Kulturkreises*, Mythologische Bibliothek Vol. III, 2 vols. (Leipzig 1909–10 and 1912), I; and Dornseiff, *Das Alphabet in Mystik und Magie*, pp. 97–8 for a critique of Schultz's theory.

[17] Riemann, *Musik Lexicon*, Personenteil (1961), s.v. 'Smend, Julius'.

journal *Monatschrift für Gottesdienst und kirchliche Kunst*, which he founded with his colleague in Straßburg, Friedrich Spitta (1852–1924), the younger brother of the illustrious Bach scholar Philipp Spitta (1841–94).[18]

Julius Smend and Friedrich Spitta were closely involved with the Neue Bachgesellschaft: Spitta was connected with the society from its inception in 1901, and was one of twenty members of the advisory board;[19] Smend was its director from 1905 and president from 1925. In 1901 the society declared:

> The purpose of the Neue Bachgesellschaft is to create, through the works of the great German composer Johann Sebastian Bach, a force which will reinvigorate the German people and those nations accessible to serious German music.[20]

In 1907 the declaration was amplified by the words 'and in particular to make it possible for those works he wrote for the church to be used in divine service'.[21] This added phrase reflects a view of Bach first espoused by Philipp Spitta and typified by his description of Bach as 'Germany's greatest church composer'.[22] Ulrich Siegele considers that pressure to include the new phrase, which he describes as 'the theologisation of the Neue Bachgesellschaft', came from, among others, the two Straßburg theologians.[23] The society was wholly successful in its purpose. It moulded a popular view of Bach which soon resulted in superlative descriptions of the theological qualities of his music, the most extravagant of which must be Bishop Nathan Söderblom's oft-quoted epithet, 'Bach – the fifth evangelist'.[24]

Friedrich Smend was born on 26 August 1893 into a world where a

---

18   *The New Grove Dictionary*, s.v. 'Smend, Julius', by Hans H. Eggebrecht.
19   The Neue Bachgesellschaft was formed in January 1900, on the day that the last volume of Bach's complete works was issued and the former Bachgesellschaft, whose aim had been to publish all of Bach's works, was dissolved.
20   See the preface to *Das 1. deutsche Bachfest in Berlin 21. bis 23. März 1901: Festschrift* (Leipzig, 1901).
21   *Drittes deutsche Bach-fest zur Einweihung von Johann Sebastian Bachs Geburtshaus als Bach-Museum: Fest- und Programmbuch* (Leipzig, 1907), p. 8. The 1907 Bach festival was held in Eisenach.
22   Spitta, *Johann Sebastian Bach*, I, p. xix of the preface. This phrase does not appear in the preface to the English edition of 1884.
23   Ulrich Siegele, 'Johann Sebastian Bach – "Deutschlands größter Kirchenkomponist". Zur Entstehung und Kritik einer Identifikationsfigur', in *Gattungen der Musik*, ed. Hermann Danuser (Laaber, 1988), p. 68.
24   There seems to be no written source for Söderblom's statement. It was first quoted in a sermon given by Julius Smend on 5 June 1921 at the service celebrating the ninth Bach festival in Hamburg, and published in *Bach-Jahrbuch* 18 (1921), 6. A similar remark by Söderblom occurs in 'Gustav-Adolf-Rede in der Domkirche von Uppsala vom 6. November 1920', *Die Eiche: Vierteljahrsschrift für soziale und internationale Arbeitsgemeinschaft* 9 (1921), 15–20, where on p. 16 he writes: '. . . the Passion music of Johann Sebastian Bach, which I call a fifth gospel [Evangelium], a revelation of the mystery of God . . .'

grounding in theology was a prerequisite for the understanding of Bach's music. In 1912 he entered the University of his home town Straßburg to read theology. His studies were interrupted by the First World War, but by 1921, after periods at the Universities of Tübingen, Marburg and Münster, he had successfully completed his training and gained a licentiate in theology with a dissertation on the conversion of St Paul. After two years on the academic staff of the University library in Münster, he moved in 1923 to the Prussian State Library, Berlin.[25] He remained there throughout the enormously difficult period of the Second World War, and was responsible for the evacuation of part of the library's collection, including the Bach manuscripts, to safer areas of the country. Something of the anguish experienced by the scholarly community at this time can be read in a letter Walter Blankenburg wrote to Smend in 1941.[26] After the war Smend decided to leave the library and accept a position as Lecturer in Liturgy and Hymnology at the *Kirchliche Hochschule* in Berlin, where he remained until his retirement in 1958. During his time there he was appointed Director of the college library (in 1946), Professor (in 1949), and Rector (for the academic year 1954–5). He died in Berlin on 10 February 1980 after a long illness.[27]

Smend's training as a theologian and his subsequent contribution to Bach studies follows the pattern set by his father.[28] He wrote more than forty musicological books and articles besides works on theology and librarianship.[29] This study concentrates on the content of only four works published between 1947 and 1950.

Smend's number-symbolism file

Smend's number-symbolism file is among the working papers and books which were deposited after his death in the Music Department of the Staatsbibliothek, Preußischer Kulturbesitz in West Berlin.[30] The contents of the file are described in Appendix 2. Picander's paragram,

[25] I.e. the Deutsche Staatsbibliothek in what is now (1990) East Berlin.

[26] 'How right you are to urge the removal of Bach's manuscripts from the Staatsbibliothek for the duration of the war has been proved by the example of the Landesbibliothek in Kassel. It got 60–80 incendiary bombs that night, of which about 50 were extinguished, but the rest were enough to as good as totally destroy the library. About an eighth of the holdings were saved, i.e. about 50,000 volumes. What an image of the greatest distress! Fortunately the most valuable manuscripts had previously been put in a safe place.' (Part of a letter dated 24 October 1941; see Appendix 2, p. 140 below.)

[27] *The New Grove Dictionary of Music and Musicians*, s.v. 'Smend, Friedrich', by Hans H. Eggebrecht.

[28] Smend, *Bach-Studien*, p. 63, footnote 58.

[29] Rudolf Elvers, 'Bibliographie Friedrich Smend', *Festschrift für Friedrich Smend zum 70. Geburtstag* (Berlin, 1963), pp. 98–100.

[30] I am grateful to Dr Rudolf Elvers who gave me permission to read the uncatalogued number-symbolism file and to Dr Günther Klein who oversaw my reading in Dr Elvers' absence.

excluding the poem, is the only eighteenth-century primary source in the file which mentions a number alphabet; the only secondary source is Peter Friesenhahn's article 'Sprechende Zahlen – ein verschollenes Geheimwissen'.[31] There are no further paragrams or other forms using number alphabets, and no examples of the all-important Latin or German natural-order alphabet. The file also lacks notes or references to Olearius' *Biblische Erklärung*, Schmidt's *Biblischer Mathematicus* and Raith's edition of Schickhard's *Horologium Hebraeum*.[32]

A clear picture of the evolution of the final stages of Smend's theory of number symbolism can be drawn from material in the surviving correspondence between Friedrich Smend and Martin Jansen. The exceptionally clear thought and phraseology of each letter are indicative of the time Smend and Jansen committed to their exchange of ideas. There are forty-six extant letters, thirty-one in Smend's file, dating from 17 February 1940 (although reference is made to a letter of 1 May 1939) to 20 June 1943, and seventeen in a collection of Jansen's letters (recently deposited in the Deutsche Staatsbibliothek in East Berlin), dating from 1 February 1943 to 13 December 1943.[33] Two of the latter are duplicate copies of letters in Smend's file. (Both Smend and Jansen often kept carbon copies of their typewritten letters.) Appendix 3 gives the date, form and length of each letter and also indicates those which are missing.

Although the last extant letter is from 13 December 1943, Jansen's death was not until the end of September 1944. The final letters were probably handwritten without carbon copies and have not survived, but it is possible that further letters still exist among Smend's uncatalogued papers.

Friendship with Martin Jansen

Martin Jansen was born on 1 November 1885 in Dremmen (in the Rhineland, north of Aachen and north-west of Jülich) and grew up in Berlin.[34] After school he trained as a teacher and took a job in the province of

---

[31] Peter Friesenhahn, 'Sprechende Zahlen – ein verschollenes Geheimwissen', *Velhagen und Klasings Monatshefte* 52 (1938), 417–22.

[32] Olearius' *Biblische Erklärung* is mentioned in a letter of 21 March 1940, but not until April 1943, in either a personal conversation with Jansen or a missing letter to him, does Smend comment on the passage concerning the number 666.

[33] Late in 1986 Dr Wolf Hobohm, of the Zentrum für Telemann-Pflege und -Forschung in Magdeburg, discovered that some of Jansen's papers had survived the bomb that killed him, his wife and one daughter, and in 1987 these were deposited in the Deutsche Staatsbibliothek. I am grateful to Dr Wolfgang Goldhan, who gave permission for the letters to be read, to Frau Bartlitz for invaluable help in deciphering certain handwritten passages, and to Mark Tatlow for reading and noting the letters on my behalf.

[34] I am grateful to Dr Hobohm for the biographical details relating to Martin Jansen. Much of the personal information about Jansen was given to him by Jansen's surviving daughter at a meeting in 1986.

Posen. He was detained in a French prisoner of war camp during the First World War and upon release taught in Bromberg. In 1922 he moved to Magdeburg, where he worked as a middle school-teacher in the Peter-Paul School until his death on 28 September 1944.

Jansen was a practical musician. In 1923 or 1924 he founded the Magdeburg Madrigal Choir, which was to achieve considerable renown for its performances under Jansen's direction of major choral works with orchestra. A project which occupied him for many years was the preparation of Bach's *St Matthew Passion*, performed with the comparatively small forces of twenty-eight singers and twenty-eight instrumentalists.[35] Perhaps his most important public concert was in the Old Military Church in Berlin on 31 March 1935 to celebrate the 250th anniversary of Bach's birth; his most influential publication was his article for the *Bach-Jahrbuch*, 'Bachs Zahlensymbolik, an seinen Passionen untersucht'.[36]

By 1940 Jansen's relationship with Smend went far beyond professional collaboration. After meeting Jansen's surviving daughter in 1986 Wolf Hobohm wrote that 'Martin Jansen was not the *collaborator* of Friedrich Smend . . . He was perhaps his best friend, and certainly his best partner in discussion over a period of many years.'[37] Their most usual form of address in the letters is 'Lieber Freund!', and they sign off with the formal friendliness typical of German letter-writing, 'Stets Ihr M. Jansen', 'Treulichst stets der Ihre Fr. Sm.' or 'Immer der Ihre Fr. Sm.'. Besides small items of personal news, the letters are on the whole concerned with their ongoing discussion of number symbolism in Bach's large-scale compositions. On many occasions they appear to have written in the heat of the moment, trying out speculative ideas with boyish enthusiasm, safe in the knowledge that each would correct the other gently, but firmly.[38]

Their letters frequently show how much the two men appreciated each other's friendship. For example, on 7 February 1942 Smend wrote:

Dear Friend!
I am savouring the peace and quiet of this weekend with gratitude. For days on end I looked forward to talking with you today, and would like to begin by thanking you for having so much sympathetic interest in my thoughts and investigations that you also take a friendly attitude towards my often somewhat

---

[35] The earliest surviving document in Smend's number-symbolism file is a typewritten critique by Smend of Jansen's performance of the *St Matthew Passion* on 24 November 1931. The friendship between Jansen and Smend had probably formed some time earlier.

[36] Martin Jansen, 'Bachs Zahlensymbolik, an seinen Passionen untersucht', *Bach-Jahrbuch* 34 (1937), 98–117.

[37] In a letter to the author dated 18 July 1986.

[38] For example, see the letter of 23 May 1943.

Postcard from Martin Jansen to Friedrich Smend dated 8 June 1943.

turbulent way of expressing myself. You know how much these questions and their solutions mean to me in my heart of hearts. Thank you for making it possible for me to venture to speak my mind to you with complete frankness, with far less anxiety than I would to the general public. You are absolutely right in thinking that putting question marks and exclamation marks in the margin of my manuscripts is the best way of helping me. At the same time I won't forget how much I value your praise, if you can agree with me inwardly. I mean that in the sense of that lovely poem in Goethe's *[West-Östlicher] Divan*: 'It is always safe to put one's case to the knowledgeable man.'

But however warm their friendship, it was inevitable that disagreements would emerge during the course of their joint project. Diverging viewpoints between two friends can be a source of great pain, which was undoubtedly the case in May 1942 when, after a series of misunderstandings, Smend wrote:

Differences with you are all the more painful to me. I have myself, too often, had the experience of going along swimmingly and feeling oneself completely carried away along one particular course; and then of encountering someone else who pours a jet of cold water over one with his scepticism. One recovers from it, of course; but it's not particularly pleasurable. All the less willingly would I cause you displeasure with my scepticism. And yet I can't help it. Your endeavours concerning *The Art of Fugue* completely fail to convince me.

Jansen replied on 6 June 1942:

Very sincere thanks for your letter of 30 May. I don't take our difference of opinion with regard to *The Art of Fugue* as tragically as that. Your comments, even when they argue the opposite case, perhaps especially then, help me to get my thought processes clear and straight; without some of your objections, I would probably have set off along one false track or another. And I'm convinced that you too take what new ideas I convey to you – and only to you! – muddled as they sometimes are, as an incentive to re-examining the views that you formed in earlier days, especially before you knew anything about number symbolism. I don't believe I'm in error if the message I read between your lines is: How can good old Jansen sally into the thoroughly problematical question of *The Art of Fugue* in this frivolous and amateurish way! Well, I'm very conscious of how audacious I'm being, and how shaky the ground is in which my surmises – they're not meant to be any more than that – are sprouting. This is just a private exchange of views with you, not intended for anyone else at all. Nothing certain can come of it, I make too many assumptions for that . . . *Speculations* are all that can be derived from it . . .

It is a mark of the personal maturity of both men that their friendship and their deep commitment to the project survived all these misunderstandings and disagreements.

The correspondence dates from a period of intense national hardship

which affected both the Smend and the Jansen households. The first
extant letter from Smend to Jansen of 17 February 1940 sets the scene:

Dear Friend!

Here I am, troubling you so soon with yet another letter. I am under the doctor
at present; I have such a bad cold that I can't manage to do my work, or the train
journey to get there. You should know that our library is closed at the moment,
because we haven't any coal. But the staff have to go in at least, because a few
rooms are heated. Our department is − 5°, however. And we have to be there by
the hour, in any case, because of course we can't do anything without catalogues
etc. What with the journeys by train (hardly any compartments still have two
doors that shut! one is always half or wholly open! frozen solid!) and the recent
efforts at work, I have caught a thoroughly bad cold. Now I sit at home; there's
not a lot of point in going to bed, either, as we now heat only the dining room, it's
been like that since the beginning of November. So I've wrapped myself up in
blankets and tried to get my splitting, coldy head to take an interest in J. S. Bach.
And it's working at least so so!

They lived with constant uncertainty: Jansen was not called upon to serve
in the war, but he watched and waited anxiously for his son's return;[39]
Smend had been a lieutenant in the First World War, and he feared that
he would be called up again.[40] Both wives had illnesses severe enough to
demand hospitalisation, Frau Jansen in 1942[41] and Frau Smend in 1943.[42]
In 1943 Smend had to evacuate all his working papers and books from the
family home. The Smends were kept awake through air raids,[43] and
physical discomfort was not uncommon.

Systematisation of symbolism

Smend and Jansen's systematisation of numbers in Bach's music must be
understood in this context of enthusiastic enquiry shared by good friends
in physical hardship which often precluded library research. In a letter of
9 February 1940 to an unnamed professor, Smend relates the history of
his work with Jansen:[44]

It was from a practical musician that I received a strong spur, though the decisive
factor was his very intensive study of scores, which extended to theoretical
aspects. It was my friend Martin Jansen from Magdeburg. We had long studied
the score of the *St Matthew Passion* together, essentially with an eye to practical
questions, but then one day some years ago he came to see me with a theory to
expound about the number symbolism of the Passion, which I vigorously resisted

[39] See the letter of 25 March 1943.
[40] See the letter of 8 March 1940.
[41] See the letter of 23 December 1942.
[42] See the letter of 1 November 1943.
[43] See the letter of 3 December 1943, which was written during a night air raid.
[44] Smend also gives an account in *Bach-Studien*, p. 159, footnote 15.

at first. Some of it had long been familiar to me. That the word 'Herr' occurs eleven times in 'Herr, bin ichs?' was something my father had told me. But now it went much further. One cannot obtain any conception of it unless one is presented with all the material in its entirety. Unhappily, in his article on the subject (*Bach-Jahrbuch* 1937), Jansen published only a small selection from his evidence. It would have been far better if he had included the largest possible number of examples, so as to silence the objection that it was all coincidence. In the mean time I myself started to work in the field and arrived at some extraordinary conclusions, but I have not yet made them known, as the work in my case is still in progress.

Smend and Jansen often wondered about the meaning of the frequently recurring numbers they continued to discover in Bach's music. Although they were never short of possible interpretations, both men were keen to move on towards a systematic understanding of Bach's compositional procedures. The development of their thinking can be traced through four documents, the earliest of which is Jansen's article 'Bachs Zahlensymbolik, an seinen Passionen untersucht', published in 1937. It is not possible to know when Jansen wrote it or how long he had to wait for it to be published, but it probably represents the state of his thoughts a few years earlier.[45] He writes:

The phenomena presented in this study provide proof of four techniques. Significant numbers are enciphered:

I.   by repetition of a musical motive, an important word, a phrase [*Wendung*], a movement;
II. in the notes struck [*Anschlägen*] by the continuo part;
III. by the formation of sequences [*Reihenbildung*];
IV. in the notes struck [*Anschlägen*] by the accompanying instrumental parts.

---

[45] Letters expressing frustration with the sluggishness of the editors of the *Bach-Jahrbuch* to publish their articles include those of 22 March 1940 and 7 February 1942. Smend wrote in the latter: 'You complain about the Bachgesellschaft, certainly with justification. One doesn't hear anything more from them at all. I sent in my essay on the *St Mark Passion* for the 1940 yearbook. I received the proofs at Christmas 1940. Then Schering died. The editing of the yearbook went to Schneider . . . the volume will appear in November at the latest. Now of course enormous difficulties have supervened. Whether they will be allowed to have the paper for printing it, I am not sure. The binding is also very difficult, possibly even more difficult than the printing and the permit for the paper. But in my view these are not the crucial obstacles. They lie rather in the unheard-of dawdling on the part of Breitkopf and the society's board, which has been a by-word for decades. I sent the board the manuscript of my edition of "Vom Himmel hoch" in the middle of 1932; Schering had given me very handsome assurances that it would be published. I waited a full seventeen months for confirmation, and wrote eleven times in that period. Only when I wrote a swinish letter, demanding the immediate return of the manuscript, did I get an answer. By return of post they wrote that the thing would appear in print. I am convinced to this day that no one had even looked at the thing; they just said to themselves that they couldn't delay any longer, so they'd best get on with it! That's how it has always been, in the society and at Breitkopfs.'

The significant numbers Jansen describes are numbers such as 10 to represent the Ten Commandments, and 43 to represent the number of days from Maundy Thursday to Ascension Day.[46]

A subsequent systematisation comes in the letter of 9 February 1940 from Smend to the unnamed professor:

So far as the numbers are concerned, Jansen and I now distinguish between three different groups:
1. Representative numbers (the number of the disciples in the Passion);
2. Symbolic numbers in the strict sense (for the Gospel side of the Annunciation the numbers 3, 7, 12. – for the Law side: 10. The latter is not absolutely new; already in Spitta the number of the Commandments is cited as a symbol of the Law);
3. Numbers as quotations. These last are the ones most open to repudiation. The thing is that Bach characteristically uses numbers that refer to biblical passages, especially psalms, which are appropriate to the context. For instance: one has only to start looking for something that might be counted to be struck by the remarkable, metronome-like wind chords in the movement 'Mein Jesu schweigt' from the St Matthew Passion. There are 39 of these chords, spaced regularly through ten bars; I recommend you to look up Psalm 39:10. Bach does not always give the verse, usually the reference to the psalm itself is enough . . .

A further systematisation appears in a handwritten letter from Smend to Jansen of 13 January 1942. Following a lengthy examination of the numerical structure of the B minor Mass, Smend writes:

In the main, I systematise the numbers as follows:

I.   Representative numbers (11 disciples in the Passion);
II.   Chronological numbers (e.g. 70 'Sein Blut komme');
III. 'Symbolic' numbers in the narrower sense (10. 3. 7. 12.);
IV.   Numbers as quotations (Psalms! in Augustine, and from other books of the Bible?).

Here Smend divides their previous second category, symbolic numbers in the strict sense, into two distinct groups, chronological numbers and symbolic numbers in the narrower sense. He continues:

What must be systematised (to summarise it for once) is the way numbers are used in Bach:
  Number of movements, bars, parts,
          of statements of a theme
          of notes in a theme
          of notes in the bass,
          of notes in the instrumental voices in choral passages
  Rhythms, types of bars where words are repeated.
          (something on those lines!)

[46] Jansen, 'Bachs Zahlensymbolik, an seinen Passionen untersucht', 102–4.

Smend's final systematisation is in his essay *Luther und Bach*, published in 1947 after Jansen's death. It abolishes the category of chronological numbers and adds a completely new fourth category, the number alphabet:

(a)   Those numbers cited in the biblical text or in ecclesiastical tradition are the easiest to understand. In the Passion 11 disciples remain loyal to the Lord. 11 is their symbolic number in the context of the Passion. The number 40 in Matt. 4:2 has already been mentioned. Little attention has been paid to the fact that Goethe went into these numbers in some depth, especially the biblical use of the number 40 (*West-Östlicher Divan, Noten und Abhandlungen, Israel in der Wüste*). Chronological numbers and year-dates belong in this category.

(b)   'Symbolic' numbers in the strict sense are of a different nature: 3, 7, 12 represent the Gospel side, 10 the Law side of the Annunciation and teaching.

(c)   It is harder for us to approach the use of numbers in relation to the Psalms. Their number as a whole, and the number of each individual Psalm, is used [to stand] for their contents. But, with the difference in the enumeration of the Psalms, this is where the path of Lutheran theologians departs from the Middle Ages.

(d)   Finally, the number alphabet also plays a role. In his book *Hellenistische Wortzahlenmystik* (Leipzig, 1935), Peter Friesenhahn has uncovered some strange material relating to the New Testament. While his work, naturally, is based on Hellenism and the Greek alphabet, the Latin alphabet ($A = 1$; $B = 2$; . . . I and $J = 9$; U and $V = 20$; . . . $Z = 24$) is standard for the Western world. The total produced by adding up the letter-numbers of a word gives a number which can stand for the word: Christus $= 112$, Credo $= 43$. Similarly with Bach, whose name is represented by the number 14.

In fact Johann Sebastian exploits all these possibilities. The number of movements in the work, of bars in the movement and in the work, of entries of the theme in the fugue, of notes in the theme, in the cantus firmus, in the continuo bass, the repetitions of the most important word in the text, etc., etc. – the possible musical uses of the symbolic number are literally inexhaustible.[47]

THE NUMBER ALPHABET

Henk Dieben

The earliest appearance of the number alphabet in any Smend document is in a letter written to Jansen on 22 March 1943:

I have got the most valuable parts of my library, above all the big Bach edition, away now, to a safer place. Also my manuscripts are no longer in the flat, whose position under the roof is too exposed. So I shall scarcely be able to go on with my studies until the war is over. For the time being we've taken over our bedroom as the only habitable room . . .

---

[47] 'Luther und Bach', *Bach-Studien*, pp. 159–60.

After these depressing news items, something cheering. Last week a Dutch-man (Henk Dieben) was here, who is working on number symbolism in Bach, and wanted to tell Schünemann about it in person, and hear what Sch. thought of it. It's to do with whether he gets a bursary. Schünemann drew me in. And there followed a highly important conversation. I wished you could have been there. Dieben knew your work, also some of mine; e.g. the edition of 'Vom Himmel hoch'.

I can't tell you very much about it in a letter. Dieben takes a different approach from us. He uses a lot of abstract numbers as a way of getting the proportions in order. But alongside that he uses the traditional numerical values of the letters $A = 1$; $B = 2$; etc.; I and J are identical; likewise U and V; hence $Z = 24$. With these values, the total for the sequence of letters Johann Sebastian = 144. This is thus simultaneously 12×12 and the numerical value of the Christian names. And how audacious it seems, as Dieben goes on to transpose numbers, and as a result 144 becomes 441 (21×21). Dates play a rôle, too: 1685; or 1722 (*Well-Tempered Klavier*; year of publication). At all events this introduces new points of view for our work, too. I put Picander's *Paragramma Cabbalisticum trigonale* from volume III of the poems in front of him. He didn't know it. He solved the puzzle in approximately 4 hours, an excellent performance. I must give you a short report on it.

My letter had to be abandoned, because the Music Department has sent its Alphabetical Catalogue away, which made confirmation rather difficult. Today I received the information that the motet you have been looking for is available here, too, only with the unauthentic German text. What a pity! ...

This letter proves that Smend knew of Picander's paragram, but that he had not yet made a connection between it and Bach's compositions. The mathematical wizardry of Henk Dieben persuaded Smend that the paragram belonged in a system of number symbolism. It is a striking fact that it was in the same week as his own study facilities were severely curtailed that Smend first heard of the number alphabet in the context of interpreting the numbers in Bach's music. Jansen's response to this remarkable turn of events was positive:

What you tell me about the young Dutchman is extremely interesting. The business of giving values to letters is historically permissible. It was done in the Middle Ages, and Agrippa too makes use of cabbalisms of that sort.[48]

The number alphabet was, however, a cause of friction. Smend's next letter, of 21 April 1943, reads:

With regard to the number alphabet, we are not yet in complete agreement. It's not really a matter of reading notes (A natural or E flat [*Es*]) as letters [i.e. A or S], and then substituting the numerical value; rather, we start with words BACH $(2 + 1 + 3 + 8 = 14)$, or with written sequences of letters: SDG $(18 + 4 + 7 = 29)$. I enclose as an example a sketch on the canon on Bach's portrait. The solution to

---

[48] See the letter of 25 March 1943.

the puzzle pleases me *very much*. That is the concentrated spirit of number symbolism. I want to publish the thing on its own, since it gives a complete little picture.[49] Do let me know your opinion when you write back. – Things could be worse for us.

Jansen did so, replying: 'It's a marvellous find! I'm really thrilled! My hearty congratulations!'[50] But his acceptance of the technique was not total. In a letter of 20 June 1943 he wrote with cautious enthusiasm:

Your interpretation of 4140 is interesting, to say the least, but it all sounds too rash as yet. Following Dieben's thought processes gives me the uncomfortable feeling that everything is in flux, and an exact interpretation is no longer possible. All sorts of things can be read out of each and every number.

Henk Dieben (1902–56) was a pianist with a special interest in the music of J. S. Bach.[51] By 1943 he had published at least one article on Bach, 'Bach's Kunst der Fuge', which appeared in two parts in the Dutch journal *Caecilia en de Muziek*. In it he mentions number symbolism and proportion, but not the number alphabet. In a later two-part article, however, Dieben uses the number alphabet, but includes no reference to Smend.[52]

In his number-symbolism file Smend mentions Dieben twice. A folder entitled

> *Zahlensymbolik bei Bach*
> (Henk Dieben)
> Speziell für die
> Choralkanons über "Vom Himmel hoch"
> Smend
> 1943.

contains a loose sheet of paper headed 'Henk Dieben', with the address:

> Sonderdankstraat 22
> den Haag (Holland)

beneath which Smend has written out in full Picander's *Paragramma Cabbalisticum trigonale* and a key to the trigonal alphabet, together with the comment: 'The traditional number alphabet $A = 1$, $Z = 24$'. Further

---

[49] It was the sketch on Bach's portrait canon that was to be published in 1950 in a more developed form as *J. S. Bach bei seinem Namen gerufen*.

[50] See the letter of 23 April 1943.

[51] Until recently Dieben's name has not been publicly associated with the number alphabet at all, but in 1985 van Houten and Kasbergen wrote that Dieben was the founder of the study of number symbolism in Holland, although not of the number-alphabet theory specifically. See van Houten and Kasbergen, *Bach en het Getal*, p. 11.

[52] Henk Dieben, 'Bach's Kunst der Fuge', *Caecilia en de Muziek* (1939), 168–71 and (1940), 8–11; and 'Getallenmystiek bij Bach', *Musica Sacra* 5 (1954–5), 21–3 and 47–9.

Friedrich Smend's notes on symbolic numbers from a section headed 'Gesamt Disposition' in his number-symbolism file (written sometime after 1943).

down the page are examples of number-words including Bach as 14 and J. S. Bach as 41. Dieben appears again on some undated handwritten sheets entitled 'Gesamt Disposition' among a collection of unbound papers. In a section entitled 'The symbolic numbers' Smend enumerates the same four categories as in his essay *Luther und Bach*, simply changing the order of the first two. The fourth category here reads:

Alphabet numbers. 2 examples from the Bible. *Gematria* – its significance in Bach was pointed out to me by Henk Dieben. – Use in the secular canon.

Nowhere in his published works did Smend acknowledge Dieben's rôle in the evolution of the number-alphabet theory. Smend's letter to Jansen of 25 April 1943 contains the only reasonable explanation for this curious omission:

The information about the number alphabet which I had from Henk Dieben is indeed of incalculable value to us both. Had we known about it earlier, a lot of associations that we are now beginning to understand would certainly have become clear sooner. On the other hand, I too had something to *give* to the conversation, and did not need to take alone, especially with regard to biblical numbers. Dieben is simply not a theologian, and without any theology at all one will not get far in the great works of Bach.

Friesenhahn's 'Sprechende Zahlen'

The only source in Smend's file to mention the natural-order number alphabet is an article by Peter Friesenhahn, published three years later than his book *Hellenistische Wortzahlenmystik* to which Smend refers in *Luther und Bach* (see page 16 above). It gives examples of the number alphabet used in conjunction with other numerical systems:

The name of a thing, just like every other word, is composed of its individual letters. However, among the Greeks the letters of the alphabet were also numerals, as was also the case among the Romans, the Jews, etc. (the numerals we use today, the so-called Arabic numerals, did not reach Europe until the thirteenth century); and it should be obvious that someone for whom numerals are simultaneously letters will regard letters, vice versa, as numerals. As a result he will involuntarily read a name as being also a number. The Greeks had two different systems for employing letters as numbers, which were in use simultaneously: a simple, old method and a newer and slightly improved one. In the older simple system each of the 24 Greek letters had a numerical value, in accordance with its established position in the alphabet, i.e. the letter A corresponded to the number 1, B to 2, I to 9, Omega to 24 and so on. By applying this simple system the student could read the name 'Zeus', for example, as the number 49 as well ($Z = 6$, $E = 5$, $U = 20$, $S = 18$), and it could also be pointed out to him that this particular number (7×7) is the square, the potentiation, of 7 [the 'newer, slightly improved' method].[53]

Although the earliest record of Smend's use of the natural-order number alphabet for interpreting numbers in Bach's music is March 1943, it is unclear whether he already knew of other uses of the number alphabet. He certainly knew Picander's paragram well enough to produce it within minutes during his impromptu meeting with Henk Dieben. Perhaps he knew Friesenhahn's article and book before 1943, and, on seeing how the number alphabet fitted into his scheme of symbolism in Bach's music, made use of Friesenhahn's work to support his method. But, as Smend freely admits, Friesenhahn was writing about the use of the Greek natural-order alphabet in classical poetry and not about the German natural-order alphabet in eighteenth-century music.

The natural-order number alphabet fitted into the scheme so well that Smend assumed its interpretation would be on the same lines as the interpretation of other symbolic numbers: this hasty assumption caused him to pay less attention than he ought to historical accuracy. Jansen's letter of 20 June 1943 (see page 29 above) shows clearly that Jansen saw the dangers of applying the new symbolic method to Bach's music. He was killed fifteen months later, and one wonders whether the number

---

[53] Friesenhahn, 'Sprechende Zahlen – ein verschollenes Geheimwissen', 418. See Appendix 1 for Friesenhahn's number alphabets.

alphabet would have assumed such an important place in the scheme as a whole had he lived longer. I cannot but think his moderating criticisms would have been immensely valuable in encouraging Smend to be more rigorous in pursuing a historical validation of his method.

THE SMEND–JANSEN WORKING METHOD

Smend was primarily concerned with evidence drawn from the musical score. A glimpse of how highly he regarded the music can be caught from the following comment made in 1926 in response to a statement by Wilhelm Werker:

'Even without Bach's music, the libretto of the *St Matthew Passion* is the best text in the Passion literature, indeed, the finest liturgical drama of all the religious communities known to history.' Even without the music! Oh certainly, we scarcely need it now. As the road began outside music, so it now ends outside it: all is but numerical proportion and geometry.[54]

It is ironic that decades later Smend himself would be implicitly accused of forcing numerical proportion and geometry upon Bach's music as people developed and abused his theory. He tried in vain to prevent this happening, writing in 1947: 'A word of warning at this point: the works of Bach should not be turned into a problem of arithmetic. Number in Bach's compositions should be considered only in association with other structural features.'[55]

When Smend began to work with Jansen their starting-point was the observation of recurring symbolic numbers in Bach's music.[56] In 1940

---

[54] Smend, 'Die *Johannes-Passion* von Bach: Auf ihren Bau untersucht', *Bach-Jahrbuch* 23 (1926), reprinted in *Bach-Studien*, p. 21. Smend's sensitivity to Werker's tone is expressed more strongly in a letter to Martin Jansen (Good Friday, 22 March 1940) in which he tells Jansen that he has been reading Werker again in the last few days. He continues: 'His presumptuous tone is obnoxious (there's no other word for it!). And he's right only in the *most* general sense. His findings in matters of detail are virtually all untenable.'

Smend's abhorrence of certain musicological techniques did not change. In one of his last works, 'Was bleibt? Zu Friedrich Blumes Bach-Bild', *Der Kirchenmusiker* 13 (1962), 180, he writes: 'Dürr and von Dadelsen have studied only the handwriting, but have never looked at *what* is actually written here. The composition, the work of art, the music have not the slightest significance for them. Thus the two of them have declined to give any consideration to all *the* criteria from which can be obtained safe and sure evidence for the provenance and thus the chronology of the manuscripts and of the works of art they contain.'

[55] Smend, *Bach-Studien*, p. 160.

[56] Smend and Jansen frequently referred to the work on symbolism by Arnold Schering. See Arnold Schering, 'Bach und das Symbol', *Bach-Jahrbuch* 22 (1925), 40–63; 25 (1928), 119–37; and 34 (1937), 83–95; reprinted as chapter 2 of *Das Symbol in der Musik* (Leipzig, 1941).

they found it necessary to clarify the meaning of 'symbol'. On 8 March Smend wrote to Jansen: 'I keep on thinking about the concept of "symbol"', continuing a page later:

In the case of real symbols, there is scarcely any room for disagreement. Among 'symbols' in this sense I would understand the marking [*Bezeichnung*] of a spiritual or intellectual content by use of a sign [*Zeichen*] that bears no resemblance to it physically, but which serves to direct the thoughts to the intended content by the application of specific mental processes. If I quote a chorale melody, that melody has not the slightest pictorial similarity to the content of what is meant.

In a letter to Jansen of 30 May 1942, Smend elaborated this opinion. He had been talking to a Dr Fraenger, who considered that Runge's *Symbolkunst* was a typical nineteenth-century misunderstanding:

Runge adopted certain general expressive terms from the tradition, but then attempted to create his own language of symbols. That simply won't do. The essence of *Symbolkunst* is to *adopt* the symbols, and precisely *not* to make one's own symbols, or devise them by elaboration and transformation. And that had been my own opinion for a very long time, [for] I can recognise in Bach only the symbols that were already in use before Bach. 10 = Law; 7 = Holy Spirit, etc., etc. But not 21 = Cross, unless or until it can be proved to me that that is the tradition. I'm not concerned with philology, but with the nature of the symbol altogether. The language of symbols means the speech of tradition! *What* Bach says with it is his affair; but he inherited the words.

However clear Smend's concept of symbol, it was useless without an analytical technique backed up by historical evidence. On 22 March 1940 he writes:

I'm making good progress with number symbolism. There is a problem of the history of theology involved. The great theologians of antiquity all made use of number symbolism. Among them, Augustine is the most important for the Lutherans. I am now studying his number symbolism. There is a lot of important evidence there: 10 for Law, 7 for Grace, the Holy Spirit, etc., 3 for the Trinity (also multiples of 3), 12 for the Church, etc. And complicated combinations as well, that also occur in Bach, $10 = 3 + 7 \ldots$

So using numbers symbolically wasn't a quirk of Bach's, but a very ancient tradition. He is perhaps the last in a line stretching back for centuries.

Augustine and his interpretation of Pythagoras was, in fact, Smend's chief source for the interpretation of number symbols. On 14 April 1940 he wrote to Jansen:

What you added supplementarily, with reference to the number of prophetic books in the Old Testament, does not enter my considerations until or unless I find evidence of it in the Church tradition; for we do not want to pass on our

number symbolism, after all, but traditional number symbolism. Bach stands in
the line of a great and continuous development, after all. That is why it was of
such pre-eminent importance to me to establish that Augustine interpreted psalm
numbers as symbolic numbers.

But his knowledge of the subject went beyond Augustine. When Jansen
related his recent discovery of the works of Cornelius Agrippa, Smend
replied (3 November 1941):

Agrippa of Nettesheim has already crossed my path, too. We shall have to get
to grips with him as well. Ecclesiastical theology is admittedly more important to
me. That was the reason why I took a look at the Augustine material and
collected things that are very important for us. I must send you a separate report
about it sometime.

The haphazard nature of their historical evidence worried Jansen, as the
following passing reference in one of his final letters, dated 9 December
1943, suggests:

You write that 17 was the symbol for blessedness in the early Christian period.
Can't you give quotations or sources for it? It's important to me, because I have
been invited to Heidelberg (Bachverein, Poppen) to give a lecture on number
symbolism.

The letters show that Smend and Jansen had systematised the numbers
in Bach's music before they had ordered their historical sources. In other
words, their understanding of the numbers was based on an analytical
technique which was not founded upon historical evidence. To a certain
extent, however, Smend and Jansen's original objective was reasonable.
There is a wealth of evidence showing that symbolic numbers were used
in the arts in the late Middle Ages, and that various practices persisted
into the eighteenth century. As a widely read man Smend probably knew
much of this evidence. But even more serious than his lax approach to
historical sources was his liberal approach to the interpretation of the
numbers. As the first critic of Smend's number alphabet theory, Jansen
wrote: 'an exact interpretation [of the numbers] is no longer possible'.[57]
Smend did not heed this warning and, in spite of the nature of the
number alphabet, continued to make precise interpretations of the
numbers.[58] In so doing, he inadvertently 'used' them to 'prove' Bach's
piety. Smend was dismissive of Dieben because of Dieben's lack of
theological knowledge;[59] he was not aware that the 'Bachgesellschaft
mentality' was distorting his own perception.

[57] See p. 29 above, referring to Smend's letter of 20 June 1943.
[58] See for example *Kirchen-Kantaten* III (1947), 20 and 21.
[59] See p. 30 above, referring to Smend's letter of 25 April 1943.

Kirchen-Kantaten

In 1947, the same year as *Luther und Bach* appeared, Smend was invited to write programme notes for performances of several Bach cantatas to be given in St Matthew's Church, Berlin-Steglitz, in the context of weekly church services. This project was close to Smend's heart and he willingly accepted. The first group of performances, comprising eight cantatas from Easter to Whitsun 1947, was such a success that a further series was planned. In all there were six cantata series, and for each a booklet was published containing explanatory notes and an introduction by Smend. The six booklets were reprinted in one volume in 1950 with the title *Johann Sebastian Bach: Kirchen-Kantaten: erläutert*, and again in 1966 under the same title. Thus what had been intended as hints (*Fingerzeige*)[60] for a congregation in Berlin became a standard reference work available to a world-wide Bach readership.

Smend's bicentennial booklet *Johann Sebastian Bach bei seinem Namen gerufen* (1950) is his only publication devoted wholly to Bach's use of number symbolism. Conceived in 1943, it was written, unlike *Kirchen-Kantaten*, expressly for Bach scholars.[61] In it Smend gives further convincing illustrations of Bach's use of the number alphabet and of other symbolic numbers, but he does not include much historical evidence to persuade the reader of the validity of his method. In fact, Smend tacitly assumes that his readers will trust his academic integrity when he makes such bold statements as the following:

A particularly popular mode of expression was the use of the number alphabet, or Cabbala as it has become known. It can be demonstrated that Bach was familiar with this, as were others in his circle of friends and colleagues. Essentially this is a matter of assigning the numbers 1 to 24 to the letters of the alphabet.[62]

The trust was clearly forthcoming, and since 1950 *Johann Sebastian Bach bei seinem Namen gerufen* and the prefaces to volumes III and IV of *Kirchen-Kantaten*, in spite of their origins, have been accepted by many as the proof-texts for Bach's use of number symbolism and of the number alphabet.

When Smend authorised the second reprinting of *Kirchen-Kantaten* in 1966, he made no alterations to the text. Nor did he in 1969 when his essays *Luther und Bach* and *Johann Sebastian Bach bei seinem Namen*

---

[60] This description has been taken from Smend's introduction to the reprint edition of *Kirchen-Kantaten* (Berlin, 1966).

[61] See p. 29 above.

[62] Friedrich Smend, 'Johann Sebastian Bach bei seinem Namen gerufen', *Bach-Studien*, p. 187.

gerufen were reprinted in *Friedrich Smend: Bach-Studien*, edited by Christoph Wolff.

Smend's examples are still the foundation text for the theory that Bach used the natural-order number alphabet to incorporate symbolism into his compositions. His evidence, taken from books on poetry, biblical exegesis and Hebrew grammar, shows that number alphabets were used in different ways in the eighteenth century, that some time after 1730 it is extremely likely that Bach saw a poetical paragram using the trigonal alphabet, and that at some unknown point after obtaining Olearius' commentary Bach may have come across examples of Greek and Hebrew milesian alphabets. As we have seen, Smend then maintains that Bach used the German or Latin natural-order alphabet in his compositions. All one should conclude, however, is that Bach probably came across the trigonal and milesian alphabets at some point in his life. No musical application can possibly be deduced from this sketchy historical evidence.

The use of the number alphabet in musical analysis might have died out and become a musicological curiosity had Smend's works not been reprinted, and uncritical writers adapted parts of his theory to their own ends. It is unfortunate that the many valuable aspects of the theory have not been developed more rigorously. If Smend's work is to be the point of departure for a study on the number alphabet, there are only two possible ways forward: either his evidence must be reinterpreted to see what modified musical application can be made, or fresh evidence must be sought in an attempt to find a more solid basis for his musical examples. I have chosen the latter alternative. The results of my research into the history of the number alphabet have yielded a more historically plausible method of interpreting the numbers, which will permit a fresh approach to the question of Bach's conscious incorporation of numbers into his music.

2

Number alphabets

Contrary to the impression given by Smend, there were over fifty different number alphabets in existence in Lutheran Germany. They are variations on approximately twenty basic alphabets and fall into one of three categories: those whose numerical sequences are built on arithmetical series, the milesian alphabet with its altered arithmetical series, and variable alphabets with no regular numerical sequence at all (see Appendix 1). They were used by children in communication games, young ladies in drawing-room diversions, necromancers in magic spells, diplomats in passing state secrets and even by a pastor in predicting the Parousia.

The eclectic nature of many seventeenth- and eighteenth-century number-alphabet sources and the overlapping influences of the developing forms make the task of categorisation more complicated, but gradually a distinction emerges between forms which operate on the premise that the numbers themselves have mysterious properties or powers, and forms which make no such assumption. The only way to unravel the tangle of complex interrelationships is to trace each form to its source. In so doing it becomes apparent that several stem from a common root: the use of number alphabets in ancient Greece.

EARLY NUMBER-ALPHABET FORMS

The characters used for numbers and letters have come to be quite distinct in most languages, although in earlier languages this was not the case. For example, in Greek and Hebrew all the letters of the alphabet can be read as numerals, and in Latin seven letters are used as 'Roman numerals'.

Symbolic numbers and substitutionary number alphabets existed several centuries before Christ. The Jewish scholar Gerhard Gershom Scholem writes:

The use of letters to signify numbers was known to the Babylonians and the Greeks. The first use of *gematria* occurs in an inscription of Sargon II (727–707 BCE) which states that the king built the wall of Khorsabad 16,283 cubits long to correspond with the numerical value of his name.[1]

Another early example of the use of a substitutionary number alphabet is the pseudo-prophetic use of the number-names of Homer's four heroes in the *Iliad* (*c.* 700 BC). It was supposedly foreordained by the numerical superiority of their names that Hector (1225) would kill Patroclus (861), Achilles (1276) kill Hector, and Paris Alexander kill Achilles.[2]

Over the years a belief in the mystical properties of numbers developed, particularly through the influence of the writings of the philosopher Pythagoras (*c.* 582–*c.* 505 BC). Pythagoras was a well-travelled man for his time, having visited Babylon, India and Egypt, and the ideas he met in these different countries influenced the development of his philosophy of number. He wrote:

All things are fittingly ordered according to the nature of numbers; number is the external essence; God is number; number is God.[3]

Towards the end of his life Pythagoras founded a secret cult in southern Italy to search for numerical explanations of the universe.[4] His followers believed that the four elements (fire, air, water and earth) emanated from the first four numbers (I, II, III and IV), an idea taken up in the ninth century AD by the Jewish cabbalists in *Sefir Yezira*.[5] Many numbers were important to the Pythagoreans, and Tobias Dantzig writes that 'It almost seems as if for fear of offending a number by ignoring it, they attributed divine significance to most numbers up to fifty.'[6] It has

[1] *Encyclopædia Judaica*, s.v. 'Gematria', by Gershom Gerhard Scholem. BCE is the Jewish abbreviation for Before the Christian Era, and means the same as the standard abbreviation BC (Before Christ).

[2] Estienne Tabourot, *Les Bigarrures du Seigneur des Accords*, facsimile reprint of 1588 edition, ed. Francis Goyet, 2 vols. (Genève, 1986), I, 132 verso and II, 107 note H. Tabourot misquotes Petrecinus, and gives the figure for Achilles as 1501 and not 1276.

   Using the Greek milesian alphabet (see Appendix 1), Achilles ('Αχιλλευς) comes to 1276 (i.e. $1 + 600 + 10 + 30 + 30 + 5 + 400 + 200$); Hector ('Εκτώρ) to 1225 (i.e. $5 + 20 + 300 + 800 + 100$); and Patroclus (Πάτροκλος) to 871 (i.e. $80 + 1 + 300 + 100 + 70 + 20 + 30 + 70 + 200$) and not 861 as Tabourot gives. Tabourot gives no numerical equivalent for the outright victor, Paris, whose name should, logically, have the greatest value. Paris (Πάρις) adds up to only 391 (i.e. $80 + 1 + 100 + 10 + 200$), and even with Tabourot's addition of the second name Alexander ('Αλέξανδρος), which comes to 521 (i.e. $1 + 30 + 5 + 60 + 1 + 50 + 4 + 100 + 70 + 200$), the total is still only 912. Since Goyet remarks on the discrepancy between Petrecinus' 1276 and Tabourot's 1501 for the name 'Achilles', it is strange that he does not comment upon the inaccuracy of Tabourot's 'Patroclus' and 'Paris Alexander' calculations.

[3] Quoted by John J. Davis in *Biblical Numerology* (Grand Rapids, Mich., 1968), p. 126, and by Eric Temple Bell in *The Magic of Numbers* (New York, London, 1946), p. 85.

[4] Davis, ibid., p. 108.   [5] Ibid., p. 127.

[6] Tobias Dantzig, *Number, The Language of Science* (New York, 1959), p. 39. Quoted in Davis, ibid., p. 108.

also been said that the Greek natural-order number alphabet was invented by Pythagoras.[7]

Other Greek philosophers took up aspects of Pythagoras' ideas about number, including Plato (427–347 BC).[8] His influence was considerable, both through the residual effect of Greek philosophy on Western thought, and more directly through the conscious revival of his work particularly associated with the Platonic Academy, founded by Marsilio Ficino (1433–99) in Florence. As will be seen later, Neoplatonism was to have an important place in the development of cabbalism through the work of Pico della Mirandola and Johannes Reuchlin.[9]

Scholem explains how *gematria* was introduced in Israel:

The use of *gematria* (τὸ ἰσόψηφον) was widespread in the literature of the Magi and among interpreters of dreams in the Hellenistic world. The Gnostics equated the two holy names *Abraxas* ('Αβράξας) and *Mithras* (Μίθρας) on the basis of the equivalent numerical value of their letters (365, corresponding to the days of the solar year). Its use was apparently introduced in Israel during the time of the Second Temple [520–515 BC], even in the Temple itself, Greek letters being used to indicate numbers (Shek. 3:2).[10]

Jewish and later Judæo-Christian culture did not repudiate Pythagorean thought with its use of various *gematria*. Evidence of the continued knowledge of *gematria* can be seen in the writings of the Church Fathers. At that time, when fundamental Christian doctrines were being challenged by Gnosticism, Irenæus, Bishop of Lyons, wrote his book *Against Heresies* (*c*. AD 180) in response to Gnostic threats.[11] It contains a section dealing specifically with *gematria*, which Irenæus traces back to the Greeks, recommending that it be given no place in Christian hermeneutics:

This very thing, too, still further demonstrates their [the Gnostics'] opinion false, and their fictitious system untenable; that they endeavour to bring forward proofs of it sometimes through means of numbers, and the syllables of names, and sometimes also through the letters of syllables, and yet again through those numbers, which are, according to the practice followed by the Greeks, contained in different letters: this I say, demonstrates in the clearest manner their overthrow and confusion, as well as the untenable and perverse character of their professed knowledge.[12]

---

[7] Davis, ibid., p. 127. See also Athanasius Kircher, *Arithmologia* (1665), p. 226. Quoted on p. 50 below.

[8] Particularly in the *Timæus*. See Christopher Butler, *Number Symbolism* (London, 1970), pp. 11–19.

[9] See p. 42 below.

[10] *Encyclopædia Judaica*, s.v. 'Gematria'. Shek. 3:2 refers to chapter 3, verse 2 of the Talmudic tractate *Shekalim*.

[11] *The History of Christianity*, A Lion Handbook (Berkhamsted, 1977), p. 77.

[12] Irenæus, *Against Heresies*, 2.24.3. Quoted in Davis, *Biblical Numerology*, p. 130.

Irenæus' attempt to purge the Christian Church of this practice failed. The continuing fascination of the mystical power of numbers can be seen two centuries later when Augustine of Hippo (354–430) discussed the meaning of several biblical numbers. Augustine was directly influenced by Plato, explicitly recalling in his *Civitas Dei XII* Plato's numerical principles:[13]

We do not despise the science of numbers, which, in many passages of Holy Scripture, is found to be of eminent service to the careful interpreter. Neither has it been without reason numbered among God's praises 'thou hast ordered all things in number and measure and weight' (Wisd. 11:20).[14]

There are two particular numbers in the New Testament that have attracted the attention of lovers of *gematria*: 666 from Revelation 13:18 and 153 from John 21:11.[15] Already by Augustine's time there had been many serious attempts to interpret the number 666 as if it were *gematria*. The dispute over whether it is an example of *gematria* or not continues today. John J. Davis writes:

Some texts represent the number 666 by the letters *chi xi sigma*. This, according to some, is the final proof of the fact that *gematria* was used by Bible writers. In answer to this assertion it should be pointed out that not all texts contain this reading. Some manuscripts have the number written out and some contain the variant reading 616 instead of 666. Even if the original reading was *chi xi sigma* it cannot be proved that the number *per se* contained mystical or symbolical values. One only has to view the multitude of attempts to identify the Anti-Christ on the basis of this number to see the futility of exegesis based on *gematria*.

In antiquity Nero was considered a likely candidate for the Anti-Christ because his name, when written with Hebrew characters, had a numerical value of 666.[16] Irenæus in *Against Heresies* writes that the term *lateinos* was a possible identification because it had a numerical value of 666, although he does not seem to adopt the idea. His comment on this number is interesting and instructive:

It is therefore more certain, and less hazardous, to await the fulfilment of the prophecy, than to be making surmises, and casting about for any names that may present themselves, insomuch as many names can be found possessing the number.[17]

In *Arithmologia* (1665) Athanasius Kircher gives the names of twelve different men considered at one time to have been the fulfilment of the number. Davis includes some more recent examples, even the name of the Ku Klux Klan, proposed in 1924.[18]

---

[13] Butler, *Number Symbolism*, p. 25.   [14] Ibid., p. 24.   [15] Ibid., pp. 24–8.
[16] Davis, *Biblical Numerology*, p. 127.
[17] Ibid., pp. 144–5. The original appears in Irenæus, *Against Heresies*, 5.30.
[18] Davis, ibid., p. 145. See also Frederick Dunning, 'Ku Klux Fulfills the Scripture', *The Christian Century* 41 (1924), 31.

Gematria is also one of the many techniques favoured by cabbalists. Since Smend put forward his theory in 1947, those making use of it have frequently treated the terms cabbalism and Cabbala too loosely. It is therefore important to define cabbalism clearly before moving on to consider other eighteenth-century number alphabet forms.

CABBALISM

Definitions and early history

Scholem's definition of Cabbala, or Kabbalah as he spells it, reads:

'Kabbalah' is the traditional and most commonly used term for the esoteric teachings of Judaism and for Jewish mysticism, especially the forms which it assumed in the Middle Ages from the twelfth century onward. In its wider sense it signifies all the successive esoteric movements in Judaism that evolved from the end of the period of the Second Temple and became active factors in the history of Israel.[19]

He explains that it was during the twelfth and thirteenth centuries that the use of *gematria* was particularly developed, one manuscript (Ms. Oxford 1822) listing seventy-five different forms.[20] Cabbalism was not wholly reserved for Jewish mystics, however:

From the late fifteenth century onward, in certain Christian circles of a mystical and theosophical persuasion, a movement began to evolve with the object of harmonizing kabbalistic doctrines with Christianity, and, above all, of demonstrating that the true hidden meaning of the teachings of the Kabbalah points in a Christian direction. Naturally, such views did not meet with a friendly reception from the kabbalists themselves, who expressed nothing but derision for the misunderstandings and distortions of kabbalistic doctrine of which Christian Kabbalah was full; but the latter undeniably succeeded in arousing lively interest and debate among spiritualist circles in the West until at least the middle of the 18th century. Historically, Christian Kabbalah sprang from two sources. The first was the christological speculations of a number of Jewish converts, who are known to us from the end of the 13th century until the period of the Spanish expulsion . . . [The second] was the Christian speculation about the Kabbalah that first developed around the Platonic Academy endowed by the Medicis in Florence and was pursued in close connection with the new horizons opened up by the Renaissance in general.[21]

---

[19] *Encyclopædia Judaica*, s.v. 'Kabbalah', by Gershom Gerhard Scholem.
[20] *Encyclopædia Judaica*, s.v. 'Gematria in Kabbalah', by Gershom Gerhard Scholem.
[21] Ibid., s.v. 'Kabbalah – The Christian Kabbalah', by Gershom Gerhard Scholem. Scholem's comprehensive bibliography of cabbalistic works *Bibliographia Kabbalistica* (Leipzig, 1927) lists many interesting volumes by Christian cabbalists in the sixteenth, seventeenth and eighteenth centuries.

Pico della Mirandola (1463–94) was the founder of the Florentine Christian cabbalist school, whose aim was to gain a fuller understanding of Pythagoras, Plato, the Orphics and Catholic doctrine by means of the Cabbala.[22] Johannes Reuchlin (1455–1522), uncle of the great reformer Philipp Melancthon, was the first Gentile to write books on the Cabbala. He was a Hebrew scholar and, influenced by Pico della Mirandola, wrote two seminal works on Christian cabbalism, *De Verbo Mirifico* (1494) and *De Arte Cabalistica* (1517). Pico's and Reuchlin's studies attracted much attention. Pico justified his cabbalistic research to suspicious fellow Christians by claiming that 'no science can better convince us of the divinity of Jesus than magic and the Kabbalah'.[23]

By the end of the fifteenth century the respectable reputation formerly enjoyed by Christian cabbalism was diminishing. It had been tarnished by men experimenting with practical cabbalism (Cabbala Practica), a typical product of which is Cornelius Agrippa of Nettesheim's (1486–1535) *De Occulta Philosophia*, written in 1510, but not published until 1531.[24]

Christian cabbalism and the Reformation

The contemporaries Martin Luther (1483–1546) and Cornelius Agrippa of Nettesheim (1486–1535) both knew about cabbalism, but they applied their knowledge differently. While Agrippa was pushing forward the frontiers of practical cabbalism Luther was challenging the frontiers set by the Roman Church.

Luther's close study of the biblical text as he translated it into German resulted in a series of commentaries. Among these is his commentary on Luke's gospel published in 1522. As stated on page 15 above, his discussion of Luke 2:36–7 makes use of a form of cabbalistic *gematria* which does not include the number alphabet.[25] Twenty years later Luther was less tolerant of customs associated with the Jews. In his essay *Vom Schemhamphoras und vom Geschlecht Christi* (1543) he describes a technique which uses the Hebrew milesian alphabet in order to demonstrate how misguided Rabbinical traditions were. He comments that it is forbidden for 'us Christians' to believe in the technique although 'we may read it to see what Devil's work they [the Jews]

---

[22] Ibid.
[23] Ibid. The Jewish convert Elchanon Paulus used cabbalist techniques in this way in *Mysterium novum, ein new . . . beweiss nach der Hebreer Cabala, dass aigentlich der Name und Tittel des Herrn Jesus Christi, Gottes Sohn, in dem fürnembsten Propheceyungen von Messia, verdeckt inn den Hebräischen Buchstaben bedeutet ist* (Wien, 1582).
[24] *Encyclopædia Judaica*, s.v. 'Trithemius, Johannes' by Godfrey Edmond Silverman.
[25] See footnote 9 on p. 15 above.

practise'.[26] Luther wrote little else about *gematria*, although he certainly knew more about cabbalistic techniques than he wrote, as the following incident shows.

The Reformation was gathering pace. Luther left his monastery in 1517, and by 1522 one of his closest friends, Michael Stiefel, had done the same. In 1520 Luther had written a tract declaring that he believed the Pope to be the Anti-Christ.[27] Perhaps as a gesture of solidarity with Luther, Stiefel began to experiment with number alphabets to see if it could be shown by this means that Pope Leo X was the Anti-Christ. Stiefel succeeded by using the Latin number-letters,[28] thus:

$$\text{Leo DeCIMVs} = \text{MDCLVI}.$$

The Roman numerals add up to 1656 and not 666, so Stiefel adjusted the total by withdrawing M (1000) as it stands for *Mysterium*, and by adding X (10) as there are ten letters in the phrase *Leo Decimus*!

Stiefel's experiments did not stop at this point. He began to be absorbed by the arithmetic involved, devising the trigonal number alphabet and gradually coming to believe in the power of numbers. He became convinced that a divine mystery was being revealed through his arithmetical experiments, and in 1532 his anonymous publication *Ein Rechenbüchlin Vom End Christ. Apocalypsis in Apocalypsin* disclosed the day and hour of the Second Coming of Christ. Unfortunately Stiefel was the pastor of a church in Lochau (between Wittenberg and Torgau) and a persuasive leader. At eight o'clock on the morning of 18 October 1533 Michael Stiefel and his faithful flock gathered together in the church to await the end of the world. It takes little to imagine the dismal scene that followed. Stiefel was put under house arrest, then summoned to the Wittenberg Consistory, where he received solemn admonitions and was spared far worse punishment only because he was a friend of Martin Luther. Two years later he was given a new pastorate in Holzdorf, and encouraged to channel his arithmetical energies into studying for a mathematics degree at the University of Wittenberg.[29] This colourful character appears later in the history of the number alphabet, not as a

[26] Meyer, 'Zahlenalphabet bei J. S. Bach?', pp. 15–16. See also Walther Linden, *Luthers Kampffschrifften gegen das Judentüm* (Berlin, 1936).

[27] 'Adversus execrabilem Antichristi bullam' (Wittenberg, 1520). See Joseph E. Hofmann, 'Michael Stifel (1487?–1567): Leben, Wirken und Bedeutung für die Mathematik seiner Zeit', *Sudhoffs Archiv* 9 (1968), 2, note 3.

[28] I am following a differentiation made by Harsdörffer on p. 33 of the second volume of his *Erquickstunden* (Nürnberg, 1651) between letter-numbers (*Buchstabzahlen*) and number-letters (*Zahlbuchstaben*), which states that in German compound-words, the last word says what a thing *is* and the first says what it is *like*. In this way he uses the term number-letters to describe Roman numerals and the term letter-numbers to describe numbers generated from number alphabets to signify words. See p. 73 below.

[29] Michael Stiefel, *Ein sehr Wunderbarliche Wortrechnung* (Nürnberg?, 1553), A3 verso – A4 recto.

Wollen aber die Juden glauben/ daß diese Manier etwas zu beweisen gültig sey/ so ist ihnen leichtlich dadurch darzuthun/ daß JEsus Christus/ der wahre verheissene Messias/ und nicht ein frembder/ sondern der ewige GOtt sey/ dann im Buch Zeror hammor stehet fol. 37. col. 2. in der Parascha Vajeze, also geschrieben: משיח עולה ממני שרו וגו כלל עליל שווא עולם איר מלת das ist/ Das Wort משיח Meschiach (das ist/Messias/) machet an der Zahl 358. und darinnen wird das Wort שילה Schiloh, (dessen Gen. 49. 10. Meldung geschiehet/ dadurch der Messias verstanden wird/) begriffen/ welches so viel an der Zahl als השם Haschém, (welches bey den Rabbinen auch Gott bedeutet/ nemlich 345.) auswirfft. Auff solche Weise könte auch behauptet werden/ daß durch das gedachte Worte Schiloh Gen. 49. v. 10. JEsus zu verstehen sey/ dieweil die Worte עד כי יבא שילה ad ki jávo Schiloh, das ist/ biß daß der Schiloh oder der Held kommet/ eben so viel an der Zahl/ als ישוע בן Jeschúa ben David, das ist/ JEsus der Sohn Davids/ nemlich 462. machen. Und daß die Worte Esa. 9. v. 6. פלא יועץ אל גבור Pele, joëz, Elgibbor, das ist/ wunderbar/ Rath/ starcker GOtt/ JEsum Christum bedeuten/ dieweil dieselbe eine gleiche Zahl mit den Worten ישוע בן אלהים Jeschúa ben Elohim, das ist/ JEsus/ der Sohn GOttes haben/ welche in 529. bestehet. Wie auch/ daß die Worte Psal. 72. v. 17. ינון שמו Jinnon Schemó, das ist/ Sein Nahme wird von Kind zu Kind fortgepflantzet werden/ auff Christum zielen/ dieweil derselben Zahl/ nemlich 462. mit der Zahl der obgedachten Wörter ישוע בן Jeschúa ben David, das ist/ JEsus der Sohn Davids/übereinkommen; dergleichen Exempel mehr gegen die Juden hicher gesetzet werden könten. So wenig aber/ als sie diese vor bündig und unverwerfflich annehmen/ eben so wenig auch seynd ihre Beweise/ die sie solcher gestalt gegen die Christliche Religion herbey bringen/ zu achten.

Examples of *gematria* from Johann Andreas Eisenmenger's *Entdecktes Judenthum* (1700). His *gematria* on Gen. 49:10 is more elaborate than that given by Schmidt in *Biblischer Mathematicus* (1736).

humiliated prophet, but as the reformed and repentant founder of the poetical paragram.

The official Lutheran reaction to Stiefel's prophecy shows clearly that this kind of activity was not welcome. Belief in the power of numbers was unacceptable in reformed circles, and by 1532 *gematria* was not part of Luther's method of interpreting the Bible. Yet cabbalistic practices did not disappear.

Cabbalism in eighteenth-century Lutheran society

Luther's fierce antipathy towards the Jews set an example for Lutheran Christians, who understandably became cautious when dealing with their Jewish neighbours. As Lutheranism grew from the insecurity of its infancy into an integral part of German society, however, scholars began to reassess Luther's writings, and question some of his more outrageous opinions in the light of his work as a whole. In this way his earlier tracts, with their passion for evangelism among the Jews, became the accepted model rather than his later anti-semitic writings. Furthermore, with the rising Jewish population of eighteenth-century Germany, it was becoming increasingly important to help the Lutheran believer understand the Jews and their customs. Typical of books written to this end are Johann Andreas Eisenmenger's *Endecktes Judenthum* (1700), Johann Müller's *Judaïsmus* (1707), of which Bach had a copy, and Johann Jacob Schudt's *Jüdische Merckwürdigkeiten* (1714).

Müller, a Lutheran pastor in Hamburg, devotes a complete section to cabbalism in *Judaïsmus*. Having discussed the Christian cabbalists Johannes Reuchlin and Pico della Mirandola, he writes:

Indeed, the whole Pythagorean and Platonic philosophy is to be found therein, and there is no quarrel that we Christians have with the Jews wherein they may not be converted and persuaded by reference to the Cabbala.[30]

Müller then defines the Cabbala, dividing it into two distinct parts, Cabbala Practica and Cabbala Speculativa:

III.   Division of the Cabbala, and what part of it is *Speculativa*
. . . Elchanon Paulus, a baptised Jew, has written an entire book on this subject, wherein he presents 75 proofs, all drawn from letters and numbers in the manner of the cabbalists, that Jesus is the true Messiah . . .[31]
IV.   That which is *Cabbala Practica*
The *Practica* and real Cabbala consists in this, that something real is accomplished with words and verses of Holy Scripture in an outward *Objectus*. This Cabbala is packed full of arcane arts, great idolatry, superstitions, deception and magic art: Luther writes thereof in *Tom. 8. Jen* in the book of *Schemhamphoras fol. 127*.[32] 'There is as much idolatry and magic in a Jew as there is hair on nine cows, that is, without end and without number, as the Devil their god is full of lies.' . . .
VI.   To what end the Cabbala was invented and used
Reuchlin, in *De Cabbala* and also in *De Verbo Mirifico*, ventures that the Jews did not primarily seek religion therein, but may have accomplished wondrous secret matters therewith, foretold things to come, and in particular consorted with spirits. Hence certain others who were not Jews took the Cabbala for magic; and that is true if it is said of the Cabbala Practica. But we Christians use the Cabbala above all for the purpose of convincing and converting the Jews, for they are much more readily to be won with cabbalistic *speculationes* than with the clear grounds and words of Scripture. On this matter one may read *Ludovicus Carret*, a foreigner, in his book *De Visionibus Dei*, for he was formerly a Jew but, through

---

[30] Johann Müller, *Judaïsmus oder Judenthum, das ist ausführlicher Bericht, von des Jüdischen Volkes Unglauben, Blindheit und Verstockung* (Hamburg, 1707), p. 41.
[31] Ibid., p. 42. Johann Henning also refers to Paulus' book (see p. 82 below and also footnote 23 on p. 42 above).
[32] This refers to the essay 'Vom Schemhamphoras' on p. 127 of volume VIII of the Jena edition of Luther's works, published in 8 volumes (1560–2). Bach owned this edition. See R. A. Leaver, *Bachs theologische Bibliothek* (Stuttgart, 1983), pp. 56–7.

The final page of Johann Müller's *Judaïsmus* (1707), containing his discussion of the acceptable and unacceptable uses of cabbalism.

cabbalist *meditationes*, was moved by the Holy Trinity and Our Lord the Messiah to give the more approval to the divine teaching in Holy Scripture.[33]

Müller follows Pico in arguing that Cabbala Speculativa should be used as a cross-cultural bridge between Jews and Christians. At this point he does not make it clear whether he believes a Christian should use Cabbala Speculativa in any other way. On the final page of the book, however, in a section entitled 'Contentious questions concerning Jews, which occur among Christians in everyday life and conversation and are called *Casus Conscientiæ* or questions of conscience', Müller writes:

Of the Use of the Jewish Cabbala: May Christians admit with a good conscience that the Cabbala is used among them?

The true nature of the Jewish Cabbala is treated above in the *Prolegomenis*.

[33] Müller, *Judaïsmus*, p. 45.

But when a question is asked about its use among Christians, a certain distinction must be made in answering. (1.) The Cabbala is either like faith in that it is founded on significant thoughts, or it is idolatrous, magical and superstitious. Thus Reuchlin relates (*lib. 3 de Cabbala*) that the cabbalists take the first and the last letters of the first chapter of the Book of Genesis, write them on undressed parchment and hang them about a man's neck as a sure means of warding off every kind of danger thereby. (2.) A distinction should also be made between the interpretation of Holy Scripture and its true meaning on the one hand, and the allusion to individual letters, words and verses from Scripture on the other: Cabbala consists of such allusion, substitution, numeration and transformation. (3.) It is one thing, moreover, to observe how the Cabbala has been used by others, but it is another matter to use the Cabbala for new enquiry into Scripture and to ransack it in the manner of the cabbalists for the sake of curiosity. With this distinction understood, the answer is, briefly: if one uses the Cabbala not in order to interpret Scripture but only in order to allude to it in an ingenious manner, so long as this is not idolatrous or magical but similar to Christian faith, in like manner as it has already been done by others, and so long as one does not ransack Scripture in the manner of the cabbalists for idle curiosity, then it can well be done without offence to the conscience.[34]

Here Müller is not writing exclusively about the use of *gematria*, but of the many different cabbalistic forms of biblical interpretation. Furthermore, his major concern is not with the forms or techniques themselves, but rather with the way in which they are employed. Müller makes a clear division between those practices he considers to be magical and superstitious, and those he considers acceptable for a Lutheran Christian: his readers should not construct false doctrines or creeds as a result of dabbling in cabbalistic techniques, but rather use them as an aid to meditation on the biblical text.

The popular Leipzig weekly *Unschuldige Nachrichten von Alten und Neuen Theologischen Sachen* frequently made passing references to cabbalism, as if the readership were conversant with its concepts, and one full-length article 'Systema der Cabbalistischen Philosophie' was published in July 1702.[35]

Johann Jacob Schmidt's comments in *Biblischer Mathematicus* (1736), quoted by Smend (see pages 14–15 above), concur with Müller's view:

So long as devices of this kind are taken for harmless *lusus ingenii*, or mere intellectual perambulations or games, as the late Luther says, there is no reason

---

[34] Ibid., p. 1222. I am grateful to the Revd Dr Robin Leaver for drawing my attention to this page. The idolatry, magic and superstitions here probably refer to the trend of using alchemistic symbolism in the Christian Cabbala, which began as early as the late sixteenth century and gave 'an oddly original character to the final stages of its development in the seventeenth and eighteenth centuries'. See Scholem's article 'Kabbalah – The Christian Kabbalah' in *Encyclopædia Judaica*.

[35] *Unschuldige Nachrichten von Alten und Neuen Theologischen Sachen* (July 1702), 672–8.

why they should be rejected out of hand. But if anyone wished to do as the cabbalists do, and carve out of them articles of faith and arcana, and assert the same, then he would fall into foolish error and sheerly superstitious or even godless ways.[36]

The entry under 'Cabbala' in the major encyclopædia of the period, Zedler's *Universal Lexicon* (1732–52),[37] also concurs with Müller, as do comments by Johann Ludwig Hocker in *Mathematische Seelen-lust* (1712), Salomon Glass in *Philologiæ Sacræ* (1700) and Johann Jacob Schudt in *Jüdische Merckwürdigkeiten* (1714). The following comment by Hocker, however, suggests that the Pythagorean view was still lurking in the minds of some Lutheran readers: 'No number in itself has any power or effect.'[38]

Unfortunately one cannot know whether Bach ever read the relevant pages in his copy of Müller's *Judaïsmus*. However, since there is a consensus in the printed sources, some of which will have moulded Bach's thinking either directly or indirectly, it is not unreasonable to infer that he and many of his contemporaries viewed cabbalism similarly.

CABBALA PRACTICA

According to Zedler, practitioners of Cabbala Practica believe that by calling up spirits through the use of heavenly names and other superstitious things, they can drive out sickness, extinguish fires and perform other wonders.[39] Although number alphabets are not central to practical cabbalism, certain sixteenth-century authors, including Trithemius, Agrippa and Paracelsus, found them useful.

It seems that the brilliant Benedictine monk Johannes of Trittenheim (Trithemius) (1462–1516) was the first person to develop the use of number alphabets for Cabbala Practica and magic. He was a prolific writer and has recently been hailed 'Father of Bibliography'.[40] In 1499 he produced his most controversial work under the uncontroversial title *Steganographia* ('covered writing'). Among its eight volumes is one (volume VI) devoted entirely to magic and witchcraft. *Steganographia* caused such a furore that by 1506 Trithemius was *persona non grata* in the monastery at Spanheim and was transferred to Würzburg. *Steganographia*

---

36 Johann Jacob Schmidt, *Biblischer Mathematicus* (Züllichau, 1736), p. 10.
37 Zedler, *Großes vollständiges Universal Lexicon*, s.v. 'Cabala, Cabbala, Cabalistæ'.
38 Hocker, *Mathematische Seelen-lust*, I, 97.
39 Zedler, *Lexicon*, s.v. 'Cabala, Cabbala, Cabalistæ'. See also Müller's definition on p. 45 above.
40 The bibliographer Theodore Besterman coined this title for Trithemius. See David Kahn, *The Codebreakers: The Full Treatment of the History of Codes and Ciphers* (London, 1966), p. 131.

was not printed until 1606, although manuscript copies had been widely available beforehand in response to public interest,[41] and in 1609 it was placed on the Index of Prohibited Books compiled by the Roman Catholic Church. It remained there for 200 years, in spite of being reprinted many times until 1721. Trithemius became one of the main figures in occult science and his work greatly influenced the other notorious occultists Cornelius Agrippa and Paracelsus. It has been said that popular imagination created the legendary character of Faust from the combined reputations of Trithemius, Agrippa and Paracelsus.[42]

Later authors published some of the alphabets used by these men. One example appears in Tabourot's *Les Bigarrures du Seigneur des Accords* (1583) in Chapter Twelve 'On number-letters and number-verses', where he describes the Greek and Latin milesian alphabets and shows how they can be used for divination, giving the example of the Greek victors (see page 38 above). He continues that he has seen an Italian using number-names similarly to determine on which side of the body a person will be wounded, odd numbers indicating a wound on the right side, and even numbers a wound on the left. He then adds that Cornelius Agrippa used a different alphabet, which is

just as much chance and fantasy as reading dice:

3	3	24	25	3	3	8	15	15	15	22	23	15	8	13	22	22	9	5	5	8	3	3
A	b	c	d	e	f	g	h	i	k	l	m	n	o	p	q	r	s	t	v	x	y	z

To arrive at his opinion he [Agrippa] wrote down a name and took the numbers given, then divided by five; depending whether the remainder was odd or even, his judgement was made on the basis already stated. He also used this method for marriages by dividing the numbers by nine. To discover whether the husband or wife would be the first to die, he divided by seven . . .[43]

Eighty years later, in *Arithmologia* (1665), the Jesuit Athanasius Kircher presented a comprehensive survey of all the different number alphabets known about from ancient times, putting side by side alphabets used for divination, magic, prophecy and cryptography. He describes Syrian, Chaldean, Arabic, Coptic, Greek and Latin number alphabets, gives a historical survey of twelve interpretations of the biblical number 666, discusses the cabbalistic use of *gematria* and comments on the unsavoury character of geomancy, tracing it back to Pythagoras.[44] There is a fearless objectivity in Kircher's discussion:

[41] Kahn, ibid., pp. 131–3.
[42] *Encyclopædia Judaica*, s.v. 'Trithemius', although on p. 131 of *The Codebreakers* Kahn states that Trithemius 'knew the original Dr Faustus well enough to consider him a charlatan'.
[43] Tabouret, *Les Bigarrures*, I, 131–3.
[44] Athanasius Kircher, *Arithmologia* (Rome, 1665), pp. 226–9. Chapters 2 'De Cabbala Pythagorica' and 3 'De Rota Vite et Mortis' of Part 5 'De magicis Amuletis'.

It was the Pythagorean priests, complete charlatans to my mind, who made the first [number] substitutions, using an alphabet of Latin letters for the Latins, Italian for the Itali, Greek for the Greeks and Arabic for the Arabs, in other words misusing various alphabets. Cathanus Magus in his absurd work *Geomantia* gives us this example:

A	B	C	D	E	F	G	H	I	K	L	M	N	O	P	Q	R	S	T	V	X	Y	Z
1	3	22	24	22	3	7	6	20	1	10	23	12	8	13	27	13	9	8	2	6	3	4

In this alphabet you find a number value of the individual letters which certainly has no sense to it whether discovered by man or God. For what conceivable reason is 1, the very essence of unity, used as a substitute for the letter K, and then used again for the letter A? Why is 8 used for the letter O, 12 for the letter N and so on with the rest? Cornelius Agrippa noticed the absurdity of all this and decided that a system should be established which would be closer to the truth. He arranged his own Onomatomantic, or rather Onomantic, alphabet using a different set of number substitutes and we find what follows.

A	B	C	D	E	F	G	H	I	K	L	M	N	O	P	Q	R	S	T	V	X	Y	Z
1	2	3	4	5	6	7	8	9	10	20	30	40	50	60	70	80	90	100	200	300	400	500

He claims that this is a divinely inspired discovery of the Pythagoreans and praises the philosopher Alexander because he taught a method by means of which the numbers derived from the letters could be used to discover horoscopes and prophetic stars; also of a husband and wife which would die first or outlive the other. Since these ideas have no sound basis of reason whatsoever and could be quite properly laughed at even by schoolboys it is wholly appropriate that all true Christians should keep well clear of them as if they were the senseless, stupid, blasphemous works of Satan himself.[45]

Kircher then quotes a variable alphabet devised by Agrippa (similar to the one quoted by Tabourot) and asks why B, F and Y should all equal 3, C and E both equal 22 and P and R both equal 13. He finds the alphabet ridiculous and prefers the Latin milesian. He also asks how one can divine who is to die first when names such as Mary and Stephen have different numerical totals in different cases and languages, for example, Maria, Mariæ and Mariam, and Stephano, Stephanum and Estienne. Kircher's view of the absurdity of geomancy concurs with the rejection of the power of numbers expressed in seventeenth- and eighteenth-century Lutheran books on cabbalism. In fact the Lutheran journal *Unschuldige Nachrichten* had condemned Cornelius Agrippa's works in 1701,[46] and in 1702 placed them on a list of atheistic writings.[47]

Another group of people who have made use of number alphabets in a superstitious manner are the Rosicrucians and their successors the

---

[45] Ibid., p. 227.   [46] *Unschuldige Nachrichten* (March 1701), 84.
[47] Ibid. (April 1702), 358.

Freemasons.[48] A revival of interest in the Rosicrucian movement, otherwise known as the Order of the Great White Brotherhood, was engendered by the publication of *Fama Fraternitatis* between 1610 and 1616. It is not known for certain who wrote this tract, which gives an account of the origins of the order, but Johann Valentin Andreæ, Simon Studion and Francis Bacon have all been suggested as possible authors.[49] *Fama Fraternitatis* recounts the journeys of Christian Rosenkreuz, who is supposed to have been born in 1378 and to have lived for 106 years. Rosenkreuz is generally understood to have been a fictitious character, and Paracelsus (1493–1541) is more commonly regarded as the founder of the order, although many consider that its origins lie much earlier. Practising Rosicrucians today believe that Christ too was a member of the Brotherhood. There is a quantity of early twentieth-century Rosicrucian literature which makes use of the number alphabet, including works by Sir Edwin Durning-Lawrence.[50] More recently the Dutch book *Bach en het Getal* (see page 1 above) has linked Rosicrucianism with Bach studies and the work of Smend.

The society of Freemasons was formed in the eighteenth century and grew rapidly, fulfilling the needs of those who missed 'the mysticism long suppressed by church orthodoxy'.[51] It was first organised in Britain in 1717, in France in 1725 and in Germany in 1735. The initial reaction of the Roman Catholic Church was one of fierce opposition, and to this day Freemasonry is officially condemned. One hundred years ago popular knowledge of masonic number practices was such that Tolstoy could refer to a number alphabet in his novel *War and Peace* (1865–9). Count

[48] There is some dispute over whether Freemasonry historically succeeds Rosicrucianism. Rosicrucians tend to deny any link with the Freemasons.

[49] H. Spencer Lewis, *Rosicrucian Questions and Answers with a Complete History of the Rosicrucian Order*, 15th edn (San José, Calif., 1981), p. 111: and *The New Encyclopædia Britannica*, s.v. 'Rosicrucian'. An interesting juxtaposition of reformed and Rosicrucian interpretations of cabbalistic symbols is seen in the history of an altar tryptych commissioned by Princess Antonia of Wurttemburg. It was completed in 1663 and consecrated in Trinity Church, Teinach in 1673. The Hebrew scholar and theologian Balthasar Raith preached the dedicatory sermon, *Turris Antonia* (Tübingen, 1673), drawing out a Christian meditation from the message in the picture. Ninety years later a man wholly sympathetic with Rosicrucianism, Friedrich Christoph Oetinger, made what is often considered the definitive interpretation of the altar piece, published as *Öffentliches Denckmahl der Lehrtafel der Prinzessin Antonia*, 2 vols. (Tübingen, 1763; reprint edn Berlin, New York, 1977).

[50] The most famous book by Durning-Lawrence in this context is *Bacon is Shakespeare* (London, 1910). On p. 99 Durning-Lawrence shows that the word *honorificabilitudinitatibus* (Love's Labour's Lost) contains the phrase *Hi ludi F. Baconis nati tuiti orbi ist.* With the natural-order alphabet, Bacon's own name [B = 2, A = 1, C = 3, O = 14, N = 13] comes to 33, 'a number about which it is possible to say a good deal'. Sir Edwin Durning-Lawrence's library is held, with its original furniture and a collection of sixteenth- and seventeenth-century English Literature (particularly Bacon and Shakespeare), in the University of London library.

[51] *Encyclopædia Britannica*, s.v. 'Rosicrucian'.

Pierre Bezuhov uses an adapted milesian alphabet to calculate the meaning of the number 666.[52] It is interesting that Rosicrucianism, Freemasonry and other smaller esoteric groups have kept alive, albeit behind closed doors, cabbalistically related practices using number alphabets.

MATHEMATICAL PUZZLES

Mathematical or algebraic puzzles using a number alphabet in some way were not uncommon in Germany in the sixteenth, seventeenth and eighteenth centuries.[53] The earliest example I have come across is at the end of Christoff Rudolff's *Behend und Hubsch Rechnung* (1525),[54] where the puzzle is a series of complex algebraic problems that test the reader's comprehension of the book. The algebraic solutions are eventually decoded using the natural-order alphabet, and the reader thereby discovers that the book was published by *Vulfius Cephaleus Ioanni Iung: Argentorati*. Similar examples appear in books by Schwenter (1636), Harsdörffer (1651) and Colonius (1748). Schwenter quotes from Simon Jacob's *Ein New und Wolgegründt Rechenbuch* (1565),[55] in which the correct solution to the puzzle reveals the date of the book's completion. Harsdörffer's example is more complex and illustrates a means of calculating with letters.[56] It is taken from a *Rechenbuch* by Anton Schultz of Liegnitz.[57] By using a variation of the natural-order alphabet, which gives the letter O the numerical value zero, and Z 23 rather than 24, the reader has to discover which of the buyer or seller of a quantity of wax was correct about its price. Colonius also uses the natural-order number alphabet. His puzzle covers two pages before the reader reaches the solution *Sit Deo Gloria*.[58]

Perhaps the most interesting example for this study is one which appears in the prefatory material of a musical publication. In 1700 the future cantor of St Thomas' Leipzig and Bach's immediate predecessor, Johann Kuhnau, published six programme sonatas for keyboard under the title *Musicalische Vorstellung einiger Biblischer Historien*. In the

[52] Leo Tolstoy, *War and Peace* (Moscow, 1865–9), trans. Rosemary Edmonds (Harmondsworth, 1957; reprint edn 1978), p. 788.

[53] Archer Taylor lists many books dealing with the arithmetical riddle on pp. 141–2 of *A Bibliography of Riddles* (Helsinki, 1939).

[54] Christoff Rudolff, *Behend unnd [sic] Hubsch Rechnung* (Argentorati, 1525), p. 208.

[55] Simon Jacob, *Ein New und Wolgegründt Rechenbuch* (Frankfurt am Main, 1565). This puzzle is quoted on p. 123 of Daniel Schwenter's *Erquickstunden* (Nürnberg, 1636).

[56] Georg Philipp Harsdörffer, *Delitiae Mathematicae et Physicae. Der Mathematischen und Philosophischen Erquickstunden*, 3 vols. (Nürnberg, 1651–3), II (1651), 36.

[57] Anton Schultz, *Arithmetica oder Rechenbuch* (Liegnitz, 1600), p. 253.

[58] Johann Philipp Colonius, *Systema Arithmeticum Speciosum* (Frankfurt am Main, 1748), pp. 807–8.

preface Kuhnau includes a mathematical puzzle to disguise the name of a celebrated musician who had influenced him greatly:

Among others, one Author in particular has, in my *Judicium*, demonstrated something unusual and *admirable*. I will not name him here, lest others who ought also to be mentioned on account of their deserved reputations should be angry with me. But if anyone is so *curieux*, and would be glad to know his name, I will give him an Algebraical *Problema*, by which he may guess it by way of a pastime, or a *Lusus ingenii* (indeed, this entire work of mine is nothing more than such a *Lusus*, as My Lady Muse makes plain on the first engraved plate). But he should first know that I have assigned to each letter the number that falls to it according to alphabetical order: 1 signifies A, 2 B and so on. Secondly, I leave the reader in doubt as to whether I have used 1 or 2 letters too few or too many at the end. The reason for that is to prevent you reaching a conclusion immediately, from the number of letters being obvious. With that proviso, the name will certainly appear when the solution has been correctly worked out. The Algebraical puzzle is as follows: The letters altogether amount to a certain number. The first letter would be a quarter of that number, if it was 4 more. The second is 8 too many, else it would be the 8th of the whole *Aggregatus*. If 1 is added to the third, it is the *Subtriplum* of the first letter. If you subtract 4 from the total made up of the remaining letters, it bears to the aggregate of the preceding 3 letters such a respect as three angles of a Triangle bear to two right angles. The fourth, however, is the *Triplum* of that which precedes it. And if 7 be added to the *Collect* of those 4 letters, then the fifth is the *Radix quadrata* thereof: whereas if 1 be added to the sixth, then it is the *Radix cubica* of the fifth. If you take 2 from the seventh letter and add it to the eighth, then one of these two is the 8th of the whole *Summa* mentioned at the first when it was yet unknown. He who solves this puzzle may pass for half an *Oedipus*; although the *Æquationes* are not of such a nature that you should need to seek refuge in the laborious studies of Cardani, Vietæ and other Algebraists on the *Extractio Radicum*, or in the *Parabola* of the Englander Thomas Backer and the *Regula Centrali* to be found therein.[59]

The puzzle (which he proudly writes was his own unaided work) reveals that the influential musician was Stephani (Steffani).[60] Kuhnau's mathematical puzzle links a natural-order alphabet with two musicians, Kuhnau and Steffani, and a composition well known to Bach, Kuhnau's *Musicalische Vorstellung einiger Biblischer Historien*.[61] As the first link

---

[59] Johann Kuhnau, *Sechs Biblischer Sonaten. Musicalische Vorstellung einiger Biblischer Historien* (Leipzig, 1700; facsimile reprint edn Leipzig, 1973). I am grateful to Professor Ulrich Siegele for drawing my attention to the puzzles by Colonius and Kuhnau.

[60] Agostino Steffani (1654–1728) was a great friend of the philosopher and mathematician Leibniz from at least 1688 until Leibniz' death in 1716. He is remembered as a composer by his chamber duets for two voices and continuo, which he had finished writing by 1702, and for the considerable influence his works had on the development of opera in northern Germany, where he spent most of his life. See *The New Grove Dictionary of Music and Musicians*, s.v. 'Steffani, Agostino', by Colin Timms.

[61] Kellner, 'Welches Zahlenalphabet benützte der Thomaskantor Kuhnau?', p. 125.

made between Bach and a natural-order alphabet, Kuhnau's curious puzzle is significant.

All the examples of mathematical puzzles that I have seen make use of the natural-order alphabet. This is probably because the interest of these puzzles lies not in the alphabet itself, but in the complexity of the algebraical processes required to reach the figures finally decoded with the alphabet.

CRYPTOGRAPHY

True cryptographers of the seventeenth and eighteenth centuries were engaged in safeguarding political secrets of vital importance and their number alphabets were extremely complex. In his comprehensive study of cryptography, David Kahn comments on books by Selenus, Kircher and Schott which contain simple number alphabets among more complex alphabetic forms:

These books shed no new light on polyalphabetics and none on the political cryptography of their day. They are divorced from the realities, and generally content themselves with commentaries on earlier works, chiefly Trithemius, and with describing a few trivial inventions. Neglect justly entombs most.[62]

However, these books brought to popular attention many different alphabetic and numerical codes, polyalphabetics (i.e. codes devised from the concurrent use of many different alphabets) being more common than simple number alphabets. The following game, which appears opposite an example of musical cryptography in Gaspar Schott's *Schola Steganographica*,[63] is a technique of communicating silently over short distances, probably devised for children. The communicators stand within sight of each other and they either move a prescribed number of paces or stand up and sit down a certain number of times. The movements are interpreted through the natural-order number alphabet. The letter C, for example, is signified by the person moving three paces and then pausing, the letter A by one pace and a pause, and so on. Gustavus Selenus (August II of Braunschweig-Lüneburg), the founder of St Michael's school in Lüneburg, where Bach completed his formal education, was also a writer of popular cryptographic books. Although he does not describe the above game, he wrote about many other number devices and puzzles.[64]

It is not clear how widespread such children's games were: it may have

---

[62] Kahn, *The Codebreakers*, p. 154.
[63] Gaspar Schott, *Schola Steganographica* (Nürnberg, 1665), p. 333. Schott gives an almost identical example on p. 191 of his *Joco-seriorum* (Frankfurt am Main, 1667).
[64] See Gustavus Selenus, *Cryptomenytices et Cryptographiæ* (Lüneburg, 1624), pp. 311–423.

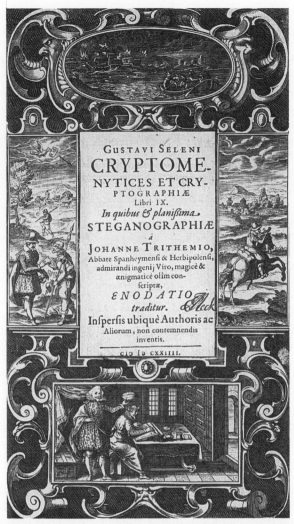

The title-page of *Cryptomenytices et Cryptographiæ* (1624) by Gustavus
Selenus (August II of Braunschweig-Lüneburg).

been fairly common for German children to have used the natural-order
number alphabet as a simple code: if so, Bach may have known about the
alphabet from his youth. And if Selenus' cryptographic techniques and
games were well known in the Braunschweig-Lüneburg region, then
Bach may have come across them when he lived there for a while as a
young man.

This historical survey has uncovered evidence that demands a reassessment of Smend's claims. The sentence from Olearius' *Biblische Erklärung* refers to a scholarly description of five interpretations of the number 666, and does not encourage the eighteenth-century reader to dabble in interpreting the number 666 for himself. Smend uses the phrase 'intellectual perambulations and games'[65] from Schmidt's *Biblischer Mathematicus* to support the eighteenth-century use of number alphabets, and implicitly, the natural-order number alphabet. As we have seen, however, it was first used by Luther to refer to a cabbalistic number process, but not specifically to a number alphabet. Schmidt later adapted it in his comment on the potential abuse of cabbalistic *gematria* using the Hebrew milesian number alphabet. Until it can be proved that the poetical paragram was included in Schmidt's definition of Cabbala Speculativa, one has to assume that Smend was misguided in using the phrase as he did. Furthermore, none of the sources on cabbalism mention the words 'paragram' or 'paragramma', which suggests that the eighteenth-century paragram may not have been cabbalistic at all. Smend did not elaborate upon the link he made between cabbalism and the form used by Picander, writing merely: 'This form of self-expression is an age-old tradition, regularly practised in the Cabbala, but also found in other sources.'[66] The distinction became even more blurred when he linked the 'cabbalistic' number alphabet with 'religious' symbolic numbers traditionally used in the Church, and then went on to suggest that the number alphabet likewise had a religious interpretation.[67] He supported this by pointing out that Picander's paragram was published in the *Ernsthafft* or serious section of the collection of poems.[68]

Other questions, untouched by Smend, have also been raised. Could Bach have been associated with Rosicrucians or Freemasons who were using number alphabets?[69] Most biographers have portrayed him as an eminently respectable Lutheran. If links with either group were established, and Bach had been using a number alphabet cabbalistically, we have to ask whether he would have been allowed to hold his appointment

---

[65] The phrase from Schmidt's original reads 'unverfängliche *lusus ingenii* oder blosse geistliche Spatzieränge und Spiele'.

[66] Smend, *Kirchen-Kantaten* III (1947), 6. See p. 8 above.

[67] Ibid., 20. See p. 9 above.

[68] Ibid., 18. See p. 9 above.

[69] Owing to a lack of sources I have been unable to explore the question of how Henk Dieben came across the number alphabet. It could have been that he heard of number alphabets through Dutch Rosicrucianism or Freemasonry and then subsequently made the connection with Bach through Picander's paragram, although I have no evidence to support this. Nor do I have any evidence to suggest that Smend himself was connected with the Rosicrucians or Freemasons.

in Leipzig at the same time.[70] Similarly, Smend did not mention in his theory the mathematical puzzle or any cryptographic use of the number alphabet, even though his examples chiefly concern Bach hiding his own name in his compositions. Many an outsider reading Smend could be forgiven for thinking that, in concealing his name in music, Bach was indulging in a puzzling game or form of cryptogram. In fact, the evidence suggests that Bach is at least as likely to have used the number alphabet in this way as in any cabbalistic practice.

---

[70] It is disputable whether being a Rosicrucian or Freemason would have been theologically or socially incompatible with active membership of the Lutheran Church in the first part of the eighteenth century.

3

The poetical paragram

Smend's premise that Bach was conversant with number-alphabet practices leans heavily on the fact that Bach knew the poetry volume containing Picander's *Paragramma Cabbalisticum trigonale*: Smend considered Bach's knowledge of the volume 'enough in itself to suggest that Bach too was familiar with number games of this type'.[1] The history of the paragram, however, shows all too clearly that Smend did not know what type of 'number game' the paragram was.

Zedler's *Universal Lexicon* was published in Leipzig from 1732, the same year as the third volume of Picander's *Ernst-, Schertzhaffte und Satyrische Gedichte*, and yet it has no entry under any conceivable variation of the word 'paragram'.[2] The next major German encyclopædia, also published in Leipzig, was Brockhaus' *Allgemeine Encyklopädie* (1838), which contains the following definition:

PARAGRAMMA (παραγραμμα), firstly, that which is written *beside* something else, secondly, that which is written *instead* of something else, whether it be a letter or a word (e.g. Biberius instead of Tiberius, Mero instead of Nero, Hillus instead of Hirlus), and whether the exchange be made in jest or with the intention to deceive. The moderns use the word Paragram improperly, partly for Anagram, partly in order to denominate thereby the cabbalistic use of a word, where every letter has the value of a particular number assigned to it, and conclusions are drawn from the total. – PARAGRAMMATISM is the term used for the act of substituting one letter for another.[3]

The second of the two 'improper' uses of the word could be a description either of Picander's paragram or of traditional *gematria*. The *Oxford English Dictionary* repeats Brockhaus' first meaning, giving the same spoonerism as an example,[4] whereas the French *Grand Dictionnaire*

---

[1] Smend, *Kirchen-Kantaten* III (1947), 7, quoted on p. 8 above.
[2] Johann Heinrich Zedler, *Großes vollständiges Universal Lexicon aller Wissenschafften und Künste* (Leipzig, Halle, 1732–52).
[3] F. M. Brockhaus, *Allgemeine Encyklopädie der Wissenschaften und Künste* (Leipzig, 1838), s.v. 'Paragramma'.
[4] *The Oxford English Dictionary*, revised edn (1989), s.v. 'Paragram'.

Encyclopédique Larousse describes a paragram as an inability to order grammatical and syntactical forms correctly in spoken language, a kind of neuro-psychological disorder.[5]

No full history of the paragram has ever been written,[6] and so I have undertaken the task in the hope of discovering what the paragram was in early eighteenth-century Germany, how it related to cabbalism and if indeed it came into Müller's category of 'acceptable' Cabbala Speculativa. The material is presented in chronological order beginning with the 'invention' of the paragram by the erstwhile prophet Michael Stiefel.

THE INVENTION AND EARLY DEVELOPMENT
OF THE PARAGRAM

Michael Stiefel

Michael Stiefel[7] (*c.* 1487–1567) was born in Eßlingen, near Stuttgart, where he later became an Augustinian Friar. In 1522 he left the order to become a Lutheran pastor and, notwithstanding the near-disastrous repercussions of his apocalyptic prophecy (see page 43 above), had a fruitful ministry thereafter as mathematician, theologian, hymnodist and paragrammatist. After completing his degree in 1541 Stiefel was appointed to teach mathematics at Wittenberg University. He published over twenty books, of which thirteen are theological, five mathematical and two connected with the number alphabet.[8]

The most influential of Stiefel's mathematical publications was a revised and enlarged edition of Christoff Rudolff's *Coss*.[9] His first mathematical book, *Arithmetica Integra* (1544), has a preface written by one of his friends, Philipp Melancthon, the distinguished theologian and nephew of the Christian cabbalist Johannes Reuchlin. It contains a procedure for extending a magic square which is still considered a masterpiece today.[10]

---

[5] *Grand Dictionnaire Encyclopédique Larousse* (Paris, 1984), s.v. 'Paragrammatisme'.

[6] The preface to Johann Friedrich Riederer, *Catalogus derer Eintausend funffzig Paragrammatum Cabbalisticorum Trigonalium* (Nürnberg, 1719) contains the most recent historical sketch of the poetical paragram.

[7] According to Wolfgang Meretz (in 'Standortnachweise der Drucke und Autographen von Heinrich Schreyber (= Grammateus, vor 1496 bis 1525), Christoff Rudolff (1500? bis 1545?), und Michael Stifel (1487? bis 1567)', *Archiv für Geschichte des Buchwesens*, 1976, 320) mathematicians spell the surname Stiefel with an I and no E (Stifel), theologians spell it with an I and an E (Stiefel) and church musicians spell it with a Y (Styfel).

[8] Ibid., 319–38.

[9] Michael Stiefel, *Die Coss Christoff Rudolffs Mit schoenen Exempeln der Coss* (Königsberg, 1554).

[10] Joseph E. Hofmann, 'Michael Stifel (1487?–1567): Leben, Wirken und Bedeutung für die Mathematik seiner Zeit', *Sudhoffs Archiv* 9 (1968), facing page 1.

A decade before his respectable mathematical publications, however, Stiefel published the first of his number alphabet books. At the beginning of *Apocalypsis in Apocalypsin* (1532) he describes the natural-order and trigonal number alphabets, claiming to have invented the latter.[11] He used the trigonal alphabet in interpreting the prophecy expounded in the accompanying sermon 'Vom End der Welt'. This led to the fiasco of 18 October 1533. As we have seen, Christian charity and the friendship of Martin Luther allowed him a second chance, and he *should have* turned his back on number alphabets for ever. But several years later he experienced a change of heart.

At the end of the original edition of *Coss* (1525) Christoff Rudolff used the natural-order number alphabet in a mathematical puzzle,[12] and it has been suggested that working on Rudolff's book in the 1540s revived Stiefel's interest in number alphabets.[13] In 1553 he publicly declared his renewed interest by publishing, albeit anonymously, *Ein sehr Wunderbarliche Wortrechnung*.[14] Stiefel's long introduction includes a candid acknowledgement of his former errors and a straightforward statement of his intentions for a reformed use of the trigonal number alphabet. He leaves no room for critics to misunderstand him:

Thereafter, when I had come out of the monastery, and was court preacher at Mansfeld, and pondered on these calculations, I came upon the progression that I still use [i.e. the trigonal]. But when I showed it to Doctor Martin [i.e. Luther], and he said to me there was nothing certain therein, I let it be until the year 1532. As I was leading an idle life, curiosity drew me to it again with such force that I issued a little book on the subject. And reckoned unskilfully and absurdly so long until I had misused the numbers of Daniel, in order to find out the day and hour of the Last Day. When men reminded me of the word of Christ, Mark 13, 'Of that day and that hour knoweth no man, no, not the angels which are in heaven, neither the Son, but the Father', then I asked in turn, 'Tell me rather, if then the Son of God also (after his time on earth) still doth not know, and hath not known, the day and the hour, from that day forward when he took his seat at the right hand of God the Father.' And by that I intended to signify that it was not contrary to the word of Christ if men believed that at the end of the world such things would be revealed to the Church of God, and that the numbers of Daniel had not been set forth in vain. But now I confess my error and my sin, in the sight of God and of all the world, which error and sin were all the greater, in as much as I did not heed dear Luther and others who warned me in good faith. And when I came to see how deceived I had been in such reckoning, then was I close to death . . .

---

11 *Ein Rechen Büchlin Vom End Christ, Apocalypsis in Apocalypsin* (Wittenberg, 1532), pp. A4 verso and A5 recto. See Appendix 1 for Stiefel's number alphabets.
12 Rudolff, *Behend unnd Hubsch Rechnung*, pp. 207–8.
13 Viktor Kommerell, 'Michael Stifel: Mathematiker und Theologe 1487–1567', *Schwäbische Lebensbilder* 3 (1942), 520.
14 Michael Stiefel, *Ein sehr Wunderbarliche Wortrechnung* (Nürnberg?, 1553).

Thereafter I was such an enemy of these calculations that I was reluctant to hear them spoken of, and for more than 14 years I renounced them altogether . . .[15]

However, he then decided to experiment with a number alphabet and the anti-papist phrase 'Væ tibi Papa, væ tibi' (see Appendix 4 pages 146–7). Stiefel was in the bath at the time, so he instructed his student apprentice to add the numbers together. The total came to 1260:

I wondered thereat not a little, but I trembled also, because that number was very well known to me, for it is found in two places in the Revelation of St John. I hurried from the bath to look over the number, took the matter into my own hands, and found that the lad had reckoned correctly. And when my conscience tried to tell me that once more I had meddled with vile calculations, I started to consider that the fault was not with the calculations, but with me, for having used them ill and applied them wrongly. And therefore I began to pursue the calculations again, and had the good fortune to find texts that in truth I had not previously had.[16]

The contents of *Ein sehr Wunderbarliche Wortrechnung* are arranged into seven chapters entitled: 'Of the sealed words'; 'Of the sealed words in Daniel'; 'Of Daniel's number 2300'; 'Of the number 666'; 'Of the number 1260'; 'Of Daniel's number 1290'; and 'Of the number 1335'. At the end of the first chapter Stiefel gives four reasons why he considers Latin to be of more value than Greek or Hebrew for these calculations:

First, these secrets of the Beast are worthy of belief and were made manifest and brought to pass in the Latin church and not in the Greek.

Secondly, they are understood to have been revealed and explained among the Latin churches.

Thirdly, the calculations are of service to many more people in the Latin language than in the Greek.

Fourthly, the Latin language has a more consistent orthography than the Greek.[17]

One writer dismissively claims that the true reason for Stiefel's use of Latin was that he knew neither Hebrew nor Greek![18] In the second chapter Stiefel explains the trigonal number alphabet, which he uses throughout the book, once more reassures his readers of the legitimacy of his intentions, and then gives his first example of the newly invented paragram:

2300

Ista est summa summarum

Summa summarum ex Alhpabeto [*sic*]

Ex Alphabeto latino fit Numeris

---

[15] Ibid., pp. A3 verso – [A4 recto].   [16] Ibid., p. B verso.   [17] Ibid., p. B3 verso.
[18] Kommerell, 'Michael Stifel', 513.

Atque est Numerus Danielis
Ecce Summa sacra totius Alphabeti
Sûma audita a Daniele Danielis octauo
Et est summa sacra de coelo signata
Ecce Numerus Triangulorum
Triangulis complet Alphabetum
Et ecce fit pyramis triangulata
Ecce hic Numerus est hoc Alphabetum
Ecce hoc uiginti tribus literis
Et ex hoc numero computatio
Ac computatio literis solis
Solis numeris eisdem annexis
Ecce Alphabetum latinum & certum
Alphabetum latinum in numeris
Hæc ipsa puncta duo millia trecenta
Perficiunt dies Antiochi Epiphanis
Dies Antiochi ac puncta Alphabeti latini
Ea indicant istam progressionem dei
Progressio Computationem[19]

(See Appendix 4 pages 147–52.) Each line of the 'poem' adds up to the same numerical total, in this case 2300. Stiefel composed over 700 number-lines in twenty separate 'poems' for *Ein sehr Wunderbarliche Wortrechnung*.

Although there may be a superficial similarity between the numerical devices he used in 1532 and 1553, Stiefel's application of them in *Ein Sehr Wunderbarliche Wortrechnung* is genuinely different. The new form reflects this change: no longer is *one* meaning held up as *the* interpretation or fulfilment of a biblical number, rather, many different sentences contribute to a broader interpretation, which he offers to his readers as an uplifting meditation. In 1532 Stiefel believed that he had fathomed some of the mysteries of the Scriptures, in a manner that Müller was later to condemn as 'idolatrous, magical and superstitious',[20] whereas in 1553 he used the same technique 'to allude to it [i.e. the Scriptures] in an ingenious manner'.[21] It seems therefore that Stiefel's number-alphabet practices changed from an 'unacceptable' form of Cabbala Speculativa in his prophecy of 1532 into a more 'acceptable' form of Cabbala Speculativa in the meditations of 1553.

---

[19] Stiefel, *Ein sehr Wunderbarliche Wortrechnung*, pp. D2 verso – D3 recto.
[20] Müller, *Judaïsmus*, p. 1222. See p. 47 above.
[21] Ibid.

Johann Hörner

Johann Hörner of Dinckelspühl was a Rosicrucian, philosopher, medical chemist and citizen of Heilbronn.[22] In 1587 he began numerical researches which resulted in his only extant book *Problema Summum, Mathematicum & Cabalisticum* (1619). It is divided into two parts: the first gives the theoretical basis of his version of the Cabbala, and the second describes his practical applications. The preface is addressed to the 'Christianly unprejudiced and arts-loving reader' and includes an apparently rational account of his cabbalistic researches, although in the later 'Protestatio Autoris' Hörner defends his unorthodox theology by arguing that he is writing as a philosopher and not a theologian. Hörner explains that, using Stiefel's trigonal alphabet, the words *Calendarium Gregorianum* come to the total 1583,[23] the year in which the new calendar was introduced (see Appendix 4 page 152). Hörner was overwhelmed and resolved to study the Cabbala in more detail. After much fruitless labour experimenting with the number 666, however, he decided to give up; but this was not the end of the matter. On 27 September 1603 he was working in his laboratory as usual when there was an enormous explosion.[24] He was badly injured and bedridden for at least four months. During his convalescence his attention turned once more to

the cabbalistic word-reckoning that I had worked out 16 years earlier, on the *Calendarium Gregorianum* of the year 1583; before long, moreover, and without trouble I found both the Special and General Names of 666, the number of the Beast; & *per manuductionem* or inner urging of the Holy Spirit, often contrary to my own will and desire, [I found] everything that had previously, for all my application, been quite impossible to devise.[25]

Hörner was right to have warned his readers to be unprejudiced. By this early stage in the preface the tolerance of many a Lutheran Christian would have been severely tested! He continues, writing that his Cabbala is not

the Cossic or Algebraic word-reckoning, which is incomprehensible, vexing and unnecessary for the explanation of the sealed words of the prophets . . . nor an enthusiasm or rapture of the mind, nor a temptation of the feelings [*Gemuth*], nor a *Fatidica revolutio vel visio*, that is, a prophetic revelation or vision of things to come, with the visible apparition of God or the holy angels, by way of images or

[22] Johann Hörner, *Problema Summum, Mathematicum & Cabalisticum* (Nürnberg, 1619), title-page, and Georg Philipp Harsdörffer, *Delitiae Mathematicae et Physicae. Der Mathematischen und Philosophischen Erquickstunden*, 3 vols. (Nürnberg, 1651–3), II (1651), 36.
[23] Hörner, ibid., pp. xxi verso – xxii recto.
[24] Hörner described it as a chemical flash of lightning and a thunderbolt.
[25] Ibid., p. xxii recto.

in another form, in the manner of those divers revelations (whether in dream or waking, namely when the reason is sound) of which Holy Scripture tells us . . .

but that it is 'an interpreter and expounder of the hidden words of the prophets', 'a means or guide to anyone attempting interpretation of the prophetic books of Scripture'.

In the first chapter of Part Two Hörner acknowledges that Stiefel was the first to use the trigonal alphabet in word calculations, but, quoting his *Ein sehr Wunderbarliche Wortrechnung* (1553), he states that Stiefel did not develop the technique far enough. He writes that Stiefel should have used the radical (natural-order) alphabet as well as the trigonal, used it in German as well as in Latin, and taken other parts of the Cabbala as well as other numbers in the Bible. 'In Stiefel's time', he writes, 'it was, however, still too early to know all these things, of which he was only to make the start . . . But even then he must have known that what he accomplished herein was insufficient, and that there was far more to the Cabbala than that.'[26] Yes indeed, but Stiefel did not believe that his numerical meditations of 1553 were a divinely revealed interpretation, nor did he wish to repeat his mistakes of 1532 by developing the Cabbala further.

Hörner considered that he was involved in Cabbala Speculativa, as the title-page to Part Two shows:

Part Two Namely the Cabbalistic Practice or the *Speculum Cabalisticum*, in which it is demonstrated cabbalistically and with some fine examples what Cabbala is, and how it is based on Holy Scripture. With the explanation of certain deeply hidden and sealed words and numbers of Holy Scripture for instruction as to how many more such *mysteria* are to be calculated solved and expounded by *cabbalistic* means as will appear sufficiently *ex veritate Exemplorum*.[27]

More than a century later Schmidt was to warn Lutheran Christians against this use of Cabbala Speculativa:

If anyone wished to do as the cabbalists do, and carve out of them articles of faith and arcana, and assert the same, then he would fall into foolish error and sheerly superstitious or even godless ways.[28]

But then Hörner was no eighteenth-century Lutheran: he was a seventeenth-century Rosicrucian, whose book was probably published with Rosicrucian funds.[29]

[26] Ibid., p. 60.   [27] Ibid., opposite p. 56.
[28] Schmidt, *Biblischer Mathematicus*, p. 10. See p. 15 and p. 48 above.
[29] The great Rosicrucian revivals throughout Europe in the fifteenth century and in Germany in the early seventeenth century are described by H. Spencer Lewis in *Rosicrucian Questions and Answers*, pp. 101–11. The publication of *Fama Fraternitatis* in German between 1610 and 1616 attracted many into the order (see p. 51 above). Hörner himself may have been converted by reading the new publication, but in this case his numerical calculations, which were mostly completed by 1604, could not have been

Typical of Hörner's number-line style is the following, which uses the trigonal alphabet to explain the number 2300:

2300
1. Summen der Zahlen deß Alphabets
2. Die [*sic!*] Element aller Lateinischen Zahlen
3. Numerus, numerus Daniëlis
4. Alphabetum, numerus duplex
5. Centies 23. dies, Literarum numeri
6. Centies 23. dies Daniëlis, numeri 23. Daniëlis
7. Cabala vera, numerus Alphabeti Latini
8. Cabala illa, vocatio Johannis Hörneri medici.[30]

(See Appendix 4 pages 152–5.) Each line adds up to 2300, as do Stiefel's number-lines (see pages 61–2 above), but there is a lack of poetic flow due to the mixing of languages. Stiefel had been most careful in 1553 to present unsuperstitious, unsensational poetical meditations on a few important biblical numbers, which ingeniously allude to the biblical text. In 1619 Hörner believed that he was fulfilling his divine charge (see line 8 in the example above) by revealing *the* true interpretation of these numbers. In trying to take Stiefel's ideas further he succeeded only in pushing the paragram form back towards Stiefel's earlier unacceptable use of Cabbala Speculativa in 1532. By using the German language, the Latin and German natural-order alphabets and the Hebrew and Greek milesian alphabets, Hörner extended the paragram form technically, although it was only the addition of the German natural-order alphabet that proved significant in its later development. *Problema Summum, Mathematicum & Cabalisticum* is not a worthy successor of Stiefel's pioneering work, and it is easy to see how the poetical paragram could have died in infancy. However, not all of Stiefel's readers misunderstood him and the paragram form continued to develop healthily.

Michael Poll and Christoph Schwartzbach

While Hörner was occupied with the paragram in Nürnberg, Michael Poll and Christoph Schwartzbach were developing the form 280 miles away in the Silesian town of Breslau (Wratislavia), modern-day Wrocław.[31]

---

motivated by Rosicrucianism. It seems probable that the Rosicrucians sponsored the publication of *Problema Summum, Mathematicum & Cabalisticum* because of the essay by Johannes Jehovah, a brother in the Rosicrucian Order, reproduced between the two parts.

[30] Hörner, *Problema Summum, Mathematicum & Cabalisticum*, p. 76.

[31] Wratislavia must not be confused with the modern Czechoslovakian city of *Bratislava*, which was never part of Silesia. Wratislavia, the Latin form of *Bratislavia*, or *Breslau*,

Christoph Schwartzbach was born on 24 October 1588 in Lauban, where he studied and became a teacher of mathematics and poetry. In 1625 he was appointed to the Mary Magdalene College in Breslau where he later became Prorector (Vice-Chancellor) and Librarian. He remained there until 1637 and died a year later.[32] Michael Poll (1577– 1631) taught at the other gymnasium in Breslau, St Elisabeth College, where he became Rector in 1621.[33] Five years after Poll's death Schwartzbach wrote:

In our own time, Magister Michael Poll, Rector and Professor at the Gymnasium at Breslau and a man of the greatest ingenuity, amused himself with the following type of intellectual recreation [*ingeniosis*]. His scheme was this: when he wanted to make a commendation of a married person, he turned the name of that person, husband or wife, into numbers using the trigonal alphabet, following the letters of the name in order: next he added the figures together and made a note of the total; he then thought up a short phrase which would be pleasing and suitable and which would relate to the circumstances concerning the personality he was considering, keeping to the rule that the words he found should produce the same total when the letters were added together. He then used these words as the material for an epigram.[34]

Schwartzbach gave an example of Poll's work, which he called a *lusus artificium*. It was written for the noble Berhardo â Neidharten and his wife:[35]

JOANNES BERNHARDUS	= 1362
IHOVA HOC CONJUGIUM	= 1362
MAGDALENA ELISABET	= 797
IS ET BENEDICAT	= 797

(See Appendix 4 pages 155–6.) Unfortunately, Schwartzbach did not include the accompanying congratulatory poem based on these number-lines. Nevertheless, Poll's *lusus artificium* can still be recognised as a major development of Stiefel's number-line technique. This is confirmed by seven further paragrams by Poll, recently discovered in Wrocław. Each one generates the ideas for an epigram or poem without using a

---

lies on the River Oder and is about 200 miles east of Leipzig. In 1630 it was part of Silesia; today it is in Poland and known as Wrocław.

[32] Martin Hanke, *Vratislavienses eruditionis propagatores* (Leipzig, 1701), s.v. 'Schwartz-bach, Christophorus'; and Gotlieb Friedrich Otto, *Lexicon Oberlausizischen Schrift-steller und Künstler* III (Görlitz, 1803), s.v. 'Schwartzbach, Christoph'.

[33] Adelung, *Fortsetzung und Ergänzungen zu Christian Gottlieb Jöchers Allgemeinem Gelehren Lexicon* (Bremen, 1819), s.v. 'Poll, Michael'.

[34] Christoph Schwartzbach, *Lusus Paragrammaticus per numeros figuratos angulares* (Leipzig, Vratislavia, 1636), pp. 3–4.

[35] Ibid., pp. 5–6.

biblical verse, and has no significance other than intellectual recreation.[36]

Christoph Schwartzbach published at least thirty items between the years 1606 and 1637, some of which used number-line techniques showing the influence of Michael Poll.[37] One of the most important is *Wratislavia, Urbs Augusta*, whose full title reads:

Wratislavia, Venerable City, the Imperial Capital, the Mother town of Silesia, Great, Abundant and Distinguished to the highest degree. A Lusus Paragrammatis that comes from Mystic Doctrines drawn from Multangulars;[38] [Wratislavia] described in an elegaic poem and some epigrams and given in dedication to the illustrious Senate and glorious Citizenship of that city by the author as a monument of the gratitude that he owes.

Wratislavia is a curious book which contains a series of number-lines, for which Schwartzbach uses fourteen different number alphabets without giving a key or any other explanation, followed by an extraordinarily long poem covering the next thirty-three pages. It gives an account of the history of the city of Breslau, and has references in the margin both to notable events alluded to in the text, and to the alphabet used in the number-lines from which that portion of the text was generated. For example, the following section of the poem has a marginal reference to 'Pronica' and 'Quadrata':

> Hac viget Eusebies ara, Astrææque tribunal:
> Hac Arete regnat cultior, alma Dea.
> Hac resedit Phoebus, Sais, & Cyllenia proles,
> Et quot ovans Musas mons Heliconis alit.[39]

The associated number-lines read:

In Pronicis

| Exactè: | ABI, HAC ARETE REGNAT ALMA DEA. |
| Exactè: | OH! EUSEBEA, DICE, AC MUSA! |

In Zensicis sive Quadr.

Exactè:	REDI JUSTITIA.
Ad.3:	DIA JUSTITIÆ ARA!
A.3:	THIOLOGIS FIDEI BEATA!

---

[36] The seven paragrams are held in the University Library, Wrocław, in a manuscript dated 17 Mar. – 25 Sept. '98, call mark Ms. Akc. 1949/1180. Besides these programs and his medical treatises published between 1603 and 1605, few of Poll's works have survived. There are more than ten extant poetical publications dedicated to him dating from the 1620s. The undated manuscript in the University Library, Wrocław, call mark IV F 127, I. N. Henelius, *Silesia Togata*, lib. XI item 46, s.v. 'Michael Poll', also hails Poll as the inventor of the poetical paragram.

[37] There are over thirty works by Schwartzbach in the University Library, Wrocław including a paragram dedicated to the memory of Poll, call mark 535067.

[38] There is no entry in Zedler, *Lexicon*, s.v. 'Multangular'.

[39] Christoph Schwartzbach, *Wratislavia, Urbs Augusta* (Vratislavia, 1630), p. B recto.

A.1:   HA! PURA DOCTRINA!
A.1:   VATEM AMAS; NEC DIVA?[40]

(See Appendix 4 pages 156–7.) The poem amplifies the ideas contained in the condensed number-lines. The numerical total of the *Pronica* group is *Exactè*, both lines coming to 2225. The first *Zensica* line comes to 2101 *Exactè*, with the second and third coming to 2101 + 3, and the fourth and fifth 2101 + 1. Later the numerical totals amount to over 12,000 per line! At the end of the poem there are four acrostics on the name Wratislavia, the first of which reads:

> Vere Virent Rura: Asiduè Tumet Inclita SLESIS
> Lectis Aucta Viris, Ingenuis Animis.[41]

(See Appendix 4 page 158.) The acrostics are followed by two good-wishes or prayers for the city, each in the form of a chronogram, i.e. a verse or phrase the sum of whose Roman number-letters gives a year-date. The first reads:

> *Votum pro Urbe Wratislavia*
> SIt bene BresLa tIbI, bene sIt tIbI, DIVa, faVentI;
> HostI perpetVo, sIt MaLè perpetVò.[42]

(See Appendix 4 page 158.) The Roman numerals in order of appearance are ILIIIIIDIVVIIVIMLV, i.e. MDLLVVVVIIIIIIIII or 1630, the year in which the book was published.

The fifty-two poetical number-lines, which possibly represent the number of weeks in the year, combined with the chronograms suggest that *Wratislavia* was written for a special civic celebration in 1630. It is possible that Schwartzbach chose to write an excessively long Latin poem of 1180 lines because 1180 is the numerical sum in the natural-order alphabet of all that appears in capital letters on the title-page, although evidence from the title-page suggests that he arranged the capital letters after writing the poem. (See Appendix 4 pages 158–9.)

Another important work by Schwartzbach, *Lusus Paragrammaticus*, appeared six years later and clarifies several of the puzzles contained in *Wratislavia*. Its thirty-four pages are divided into two parts, the first of which is a seventeen-page history and explanation of the paragram form. Schwartzbach begins by stating that Latin number alphabets are artificial imitations of those used by the Jews, Greeks and cabbalists. He names Michael Stiefel as the inventor (*inventor primus*) of the trigonal alphabet, saying that Stiefel began a tradition in which trigonal was used to interpret the numbers in the biblical books of Daniel and Revelation and in Rabbinical sayings. The tradition, he says, was continued by Abraham

---

[40] Ibid., p. A3 recto.   [41] Ibid., p. F2 verso.   [42] Ibid., p. F4 recto.

Schönvvaldt in 1572,[43] Johann Hörner in 1619 and many others, but was broken by Poll's 'type of intellectual recreation'. It is significant that Schwartzbach thought he and Poll were doing something entirely new. The historical survey is followed by a description of three methods facilitating the composition of a poetical paragram: the use of 'addita' and 'demta' to adjust the total (as in *Wratislavia*); the use of different spellings of the same word, such as Johannes or Joannes, Coelum, Cælum or Celum, and Inclutus, Inclitus or Inclytus; and the use of different number alphabets. Schwartzbach lists in succession eight alphabets (see Appendix 1) and then explains how to form each one.

The second half of *Lusus Paragrammaticus* is an 'arithmetico-theological' meditation on the name of Jesus. Schwartzbach takes the number six, which is the Roman numerical value of the name Jesus (where J is equivalent to I and U to V), and performs various arithmetical operations on it. His meditation focuses on the idea (found in Isaiah 11, Romans 15 and Revelation 5 and 22) that Jesus was the root or stem of Jesse. Schwartzbach lists several different powers of the number six and incorporates them by means of Roman numerals into a verse, much as in a chronogram. His first example reads:

JESUS

Radix Quadrata, sive, Zensica, de 36

NAte veni Soter! nobis re roret ô Æther!

Esai 45:   Juste puer purâ Virgine nate, veni![44]

(See Appendix 4 page 159.) The square root (*Radix Quadrata* or *Zensica*) of 36 is 6, and the Roman numerals that appear in the verse are successively VIIIVVVVIIVI, i.e. 36. There are ten verses in all, nine on the numbers 36 (6^2), 42 ($6^2 + 6$), 216 (6^3), 1296 (6^4), 23,328 (3×6^5), 46,656 (6^6), 279,936 (6^7), 1,679,616 (6^8) and 10,077,696 (6^9) and the tenth on the quality of perfection, because the number six is the first perfect number.[45]

The meditation at the end of *Lusus Pragrammaticus* is entirely different from the number-lines and subsequent poem in *Wratislavia*, because Schwartzbach combines the use of verses containing Roman numerals with biblical ideas. This sounds like the work of a cabbalist, but Schwartzbach pre-empts any such accusation by writing that he finds it detestable to use numbers in conjunction with a name or names to

---

[43] I have not yet traced Abraham Schönwald (or Schönvvaldt)'s book of 1572, nor any other work by him.

[44] Schwartzbach, *Lusus Paragrammaticus*, p. 18.

[45] A perfect number is one which can be expressed as the sum of its factors, thus 6 is a perfect number because it is equal to both $1 \times 2 \times 3$ and $1 + 2 + 3$. See Harsdörffer, *Mathematische und Philosophische Erquickstunden* II (1651), 34.

prophesy or predict the future in any way.[46] The meditation is arithmetic-ally more complex than any paragram seen so far. Had Schwartzbach lived longer he might have invented even more contorted forms and taken the paragram along a different path, but that was not to be. He died two years later, and arithmetico-theological meditations seem to have died with him.

Schwartzbach made an important contribution to the historical development of the poetical paragram. He was the first to use many different alphabets and to use the word 'paragramma' in his description of the form. *Wratislavia* is the first full-length example of the number-line technique devised by Poll, in which non-biblical number-lines create ideas for a poem which is itself unrestricted by numerical devices. Furthermore, Schwartzbach points to a difference of intention behind Poll's work and that of his predecessors: his paragrams had no deeper significance than straightforward 'intellectual recreation'.

In 1707 Müller wrote that the Cabbala could be used in Cabbala Practica and in two forms of Cabbala Speculativa, one to interpret the Scriptures, which he considered unacceptable, and the other to allude to the Scriptures in an ingenious manner.[47] So far in the history of the paragram we have seen three different uses of number-lines: Stiefel (in 1532) and Hörner exemplifying Müller's unacceptable form of Cabbala Speculativa using number-lines to interpret the Scriptures, which, according to Schmidt writing in 1736, would lead to 'foolish error and sheerly superstitious or even godless ways';[48] Stiefel (in 1553) exemplifying Müller's acceptable form of Cabbala Speculativa, using number-lines to allude ingeniously to the Scriptures; and Poll and Schwartzbach, whose poetical use does not fall into any of Müller's cabbalistic categories. There is no similarity between their number-lines and alphabet processes used in the idolatrous or magical forms of Cabbala Practica, and since Poll and Schwartzbach do not use or allude to the Scriptures,[49] their number-lines cannot be a form of Cabbala Speculativa: a sign of the rift between the poetical paragram and its cabbalistic origins.

One hundred years after Stiefel, Georg Philipp Harsdörffer rationalised the different number-word and number-verse techniques he had encountered. His books present a record of the middle period of the paragram's development, before its eventual fruition in the early eighteenth century.

---

[46] Schwartzbach, *Lusus Paragrammaticus*, pp. 7–8.
[47] Müller, *Judaïsmus*, p. 1222. See also pp. 47–8 above.
[48] Schmidt, *Biblischer Mathematicus*, p. 10. See also p. 15 and p. 48 above.
[49] Schwartzbach's arithmetico-theological meditations in the second part of *Lusus Paragrammaticus* are not poetical paragrams.

HARSDÖRFFER AND THE DOCUMENTATION
OF THE PARAGRAM

Georg Philipp Harsdörffer

Georg Philipp Harsdörffer was born in Nürnberg on 1 November 1607. He studied law at the Universities of Altdorf (1623–6) and Straßburg (1626–9) and then travelled for more than five years throughout southern and western Europe. From 1637 he was a legal assessor in Nürnberg and from 1655 until his death on 22 September 1658 served as a member of the Nürnberg city council. He published over fifty volumes of poetry and occasional writings and in 1642 was invited to become a member of the celebrated literary society, the *Fruchtbringende Gesellschaft*. This brought him into contact with the most fashionable noblemen of northern Europe. In 1643 he became a member of another society, the *Deutschgesinnte Genossenschaft*, and in the same year he founded the *Pegnesischer Blumenorden* with his friend Johann Klaj (1616–56).[50]

The *Fruchtbringende Gesellschaft* or *Fruchtbringende Palm-Orden* was the paradigm for all later literary societies. It was founded on 24 August 1617 by the Marshall of the court in Weimar, Caspar von Teutleben,[51] for both political and aesthetic purposes. German scholars were accustomed to write in Latin, but the *Fruchtbringende Gesellschaft* had as one of its chief aims the establishment of the vernacular as a literary medium. At this time, on the eve of the Thirty Years' War (1618–48), Germany had little or no reputation for scholarship or culture. To remedy this situation members pledged themselves to a threefold rule:

1 to be honourable, prudent, decorous, useful and merry, without any regard to their station;
2 to apply themselves to the German language and its purity;
3 to wear a gold badge in honour of the Society, having a palm tree and its

---

50 Zedler, *Lexicon*, s.v. 'Harsdörffer'. In *German Baroque Literature: A Catalogue of the Collection in the Yale University Library*, 2 vols. (New Haven, Conn., 1958 and 1969), I (1958), 135, Curt von Faber du Faur suggests that the *Pegnesischer Blumenorden* was born as a result of the decline in activities of the *Fruchtbringende Gesellschaft* under the presidency of Prince Ludwig of Anhalt. There are several variants of the title of the society formed by Harsdörffer and Klaj (also known as Johannes Clajus), including *Pegnitzische Schäfer-Gesellschaft* (Zedler), *Pegnitzer Hirtengesellschaft* (*The New Encyclopædia Britannica*). The form which I adopt, *Pegnesischer Blumenorden*, is taken from Heinz Zirnbauer's 'Bibliographie der Werke Georg Philipp Harsdörffers', *Philobiblon* (1961), 12. The usual English translation is 'Shepherds of Pegnitz'.
51 Zedler, *Lexicon*, s.v. 'Fruchtbringende Gesellschaft'.

symbol engraved on one side, and on the other the name and portrait of the member, and a green silk ribbon.[52]

On admission to the society each member had to write a book and present it to the society for deposit in the Weimar court archives. When writing on behalf of the society, members had to adopt a pen-name.[53] Membership was drawn largely from the nobility, but occasionally a commoner, such as Harsdörffer, was admitted in recognition of services rendered to the German language. One of its most distinguished founder members, still involved in Harsdörffer's day, was August II of Braunschweig-Lüneburg, otherwise known as Gustavus Selenus.[54] His son Anton Ulrich of Braunschweig-Lüneburg was to become President of the society later in the century.

Although their primary purpose was to reform the German language, the influence of the literary societies was felt in every area of German culture. In 1689 the music theorist Wolfgang Caspar Printz cited the work of the *Fruchtbringende Gesellschaft* as a model for musical reform. He wrote:

¶2   With reference to this, certain societies and academies were established by excellent people who banded together with certain rules, either to ensure the purity of a particular language, or to study various sciences and arts; so that what one man cannot do alone, because of the brevity of this life, can be accomplished by many collectively, and each can thus assist the other and together bring about what would be impossible for one to do alone.

¶3   The German language would never have attained to its present purity and elegance had it not been for the laudable *Fruchtbringende Gesellschaft*, which had that very thing as its purpose, and a single man, even the most learned and most capable of all mankind, could not have accomplished what this entire praiseworthy society has done . . .

¶5   . . . if a musical society of that kind could be established, in which good minds joined together in pursuit of the study of musical sciences, of artistic inventions and of demonstrations of *res musicae* by the application of certain rules, music would attain, in the shortest time, to an especial perfection and great glory.[55]

Half a century later, in 1738, one of Bach's pupils, Lorenz Christoph Mizler, was to take up Printz' challenge and form the *Sozietät der musikalischen Wissenschaften*.

---

52   Ibid. It is not clear whether the green silk ribbon was used to hang the badge around the neck, or whether it was worn in addition to the badge, as a sash.

53   Harsdörffer gained three different pen-names, 'der Spielende' in the *Fruchbringende Gesellschaft*, 'der Kunstspielende' in the *Deutschgesinnte Genossenschaft* and 'Strephon' in his own *Pegnesischer Blumenorden*.

54   Zedler, *Lexicon*, s.v. Augustus, Herzog zu Braunschweig und Lüneburg.

55   Wolfgang Caspar Printz, *Exercitationum Musicarum Theoretico-Practicarum Curiosarum*, 8 vols. (Frankfurt, Leipzig, 1687–9), VIII (1689), 5.

Erquickstunden II *(1651)*

Harsdörffer's earliest discussion of number alphabet devices appears as the thirty-fourth exercise (*Aufgabe*) of his second volume of *Erquick-stunden* under the heading: 'How to find equal Names and Verses through Numbers'. He gives a table with eight different number alphabets (see Appendix 1) and writes:

> To find equal names and verses through numbers is similar to the Jewish practice of *gematria*, a form of Cabbala, and is easily grasped by anyone who understands a harmony [*Zusammenstimmung*] such as Selenus describes in his number game . . .[56]

Selenus' number game is *Rhythmomachia*, a complex game not dissimilar to chess, which involves detailed knowledge of the harmonic series (see pages 108–9 below). Harsdörffer continues:

> This is how Archimedes distinguished and denominated the numbers in his *Arenario*:

a	1	Einer	I
b	10	zehner	X
c	100	hunderte	C
d	1000	tausende	M
e	10000	zehentausende	XM
f	100000	hundert tausende	XMƆ
g	1000000	tausend tausende	CQƆ
h	10000000	zehenhunderttausend	ICQƆI

Everything can be expressed in accordance with these eight orders.

The above table was sent to me as a mark of special friendship by the Noble Lord Abraham von Frankenberg, a Silesian nobleman renowned for his courage and accomplishment; it has a use in regard to the letter-numbers which, though rarely called for, is none the less fundamentally suited to this skill. I say letter-numbers in accordance with right usage in our language, in which the last word in compound words says what a thing is, and the first says what it is like. Thus in Exercise II we discussed those letters which signify a number, and called them number-letters, namely MDCLXVI. From which, without the M, we obtain the number of the Beast, 666. Now let us give a little thought to the letter-numbers, or such letters as may be understood by means of numbers.

A name can have various letter-numbers, according to various methods of calculation. Let us take the name of our Saviour IesVs as an example:

---

[56] Harsdörffer, *Mathematische und Philosophische Erquickstunden* II (1651), 32–6.

IesVs

Summa	70	394	612	1154	390	4020	7428	20518
	M	D	△	□	○	△	⊡	
I	9	9	45	81	48	105	288	729
E	5	5	15	25	24	35	55	125
S	18	90	171	324	102	1140	2109	5832
V	20	200	210	400	114	1540	2870	8000
S	18	90	171	324	102	1140	2109	5832

Note that VI [are] the number-letters in the name IesVs, the first perfect number . . .

He then cites Schwartzbach's *Lusus Paragrammaticus* (discussed on pages 68–70 above) and gives several examples which link a proper name with a short motto or *Spruch*, one of which reads:

Johannes Baptista	165	and	Joannes Dux Saxoniæ	200
Hic Elias secundus	165		Confessio Augustana	200

(See Appendix 4 pages 159–60.) Harsdörffer's next example uses number-lines (*die Gleichen*) as the basis of an occasional poem (*Programma*):

Using the same method, I devised the following Programma in honour of the Noble Lord Cambyses Bianchi, Count di Piano, my gracious lord, who scarcely has an equal in Italian poetic art:

Cambyses Bianchius Comes	217
Sic secundus Petrarcha	217

Convenit, heus lepide niveum Tibi Nomen Oloris
cum celebrat[ur tu]um Castalis unda melos.
Sic numeris secreta latent. Petrarcha secundus
audis; sed Laurum quæ Tibi Laura dabit?
Exemplo jubeas bene nunc sperare Camaenas:
dum Tu Mecænas, ipse Poeta, canis.

(See Appendix 4 page 160.) There is a similarity between this example and Schwartzbach's *Wratislavia*, because the ideas in the number-lines are incorporated into a poem. The obvious difference is the relative brevity of Harsdörffer's poem, which makes redundant any marginal references to the number-lines. The Bianchi example is in fact a foretaste of the eighteenth-century poetical paragram where number-lines are used as a means of invention, and which Harsdörffer was to describe two years later in *Poetischer Trichter*. Exercise XXXIV ends with a warning about the superstitious use of number-lines:

In these exercises it is wise to avoid the superstition which frequently insinuates itself in calculations of this kind. Johann Hornerus, a Rosicrucian, for example,

A dedicatory paragram written by Georg Philipp Harsdörffer for Frederick III of Denmark from the prefatory material to *Erquickstunden* III (1653).

purported to uncover many of the secrets of Scripture on this basis, and wrote a whole book about it, entitled *Problema Summum, Mathematicum & Cabalisticum*, setting out his discovery that large numbers of Latin, Hebrew and Greek words added up to the same totals when reckoned in this way: his own name, Hörner, made 19, the same as the words Cabala and Sophia. There is much in this book that the reader will find strange [*wunderlich*].

Erquickstunden III *(1653)*

In the nineteenth enquiry (*Frage*) of *Erquickstunden* III, 'On the peculiar characteristic of Latin number-letters', Harsdörffer uses the same adjective (*wunderlich*) to refer to Stiefel's prophecy of 1532. After describing the natural-order and trigonal alphabets, he continues by explaining the significance of the numbers:

Although it is now apparent that these numbers, invented by the human mind, cannot reveal any mysteries, yet the little book mentioned above [*Ein Rechen Büchlin vom End Christ* (1532)] teaches that most of the numbers that appear sealed in the prophecy of Daniel and the Revelation of St John can be revealed and resolved by this means. But because these 'Hours of Delight' [*Erquickstunden*] do not concern themselves with sacred matters, we will append only a few general examples.[57]

He gives some of Stiefel's examples, choosing the number-values of the words *primus*, *secundus*, *tertius* and using them to illustrate Stiefel's complex number-transpositions of 1532. At the beginning of the nineteenth enquiry Harsdörffer had stated that the chief languages, Hebrew, Greek and Latin, had all made use of number-letters, and that the German number-letters were an artificial imitation of these. He then refers the reader to the thirty-fourth exercise in *Erquickstunden* II for a fuller explanation of the uses of German number-lines, and proceeds to write about the supposed mysterious properties of Latin number-letters. It is curious that he does not describe these as cabbalistic, and that his criticism of Stiefel is less caustic than his earlier treatment of Hörner.

Poetischer Trichter II *(1648) and* III *(1653)*

Harsdörffer's final mention of number-lines comes in a volume devoted entirely to poetry. In the second volume of *Poetischer Trichter*, published five years earlier in 1648, Harsdörffer had discussed *Zahlreimen* and *Jahrreimen*, otherwise known as chronograms. He formed them from a German rather than the more usual Latin phrase, and one of his examples reads:

Der hoChLobLICHen FrVChtbrIngenDen GeseLLsChaft VrsprVng

('the origin of the laudable *Fruchtbringende Gesellschaft*'). The sum of the Roman numerals is 1617, the year in which the society was founded. Harsdörffer then shows how the chronogram can be used as the basis of a poem:

These dates or numerals do indeed serve the poet in the manner illustrated in the *Teutscher Palmbaum* and in the sixteenth poem of Part V of the *Gesprächspiele*, but they can also be applied in a short verse metre: although it can seldom be done without coercion. For example:

57 Ibid., III (1653), 67.

BeLIebter IVgenD ZVCht	662
Von stehen fLeIßgesVCht	161
trägt VVahrer TVgenD frVCht /	620
TrVtz Langer ZeIten FLVCht	296 [*sic!*]
	———
The sum is this year's date	1648 [*sic!*][58]

(See Appendix 4 page 160.) Harsdörffer next describes a similar procedure, this time using a number alphabet. He takes an altered milesian alphabet, and writes the following hymn:

> Die wir Fried und Freude hoffen
> hat nun Streit und Leid betroffen.
> Höchster gibt doch dieser Zeit
> endlich Sieg und Einigkeit.

Die	3	Höchster	194
Wir	210	gieb [*sic!*]	6
Fried	58	doch	11
und	23	dieser	115
Freude	58	Zeit	170
hoffen	34	endlich	40
hat	67	Sieg	65
nun	40	und	23
Streit	253	Einigkeit	103
und	23		———
Leid	12		
betroffen	140		727
	→		921
			———
makes a total of the year			1648[59]

(See Appendix 4 page 161.) These syncretistic number-line forms are nothing more than intellectual games, and as Harsdörffer said, they often require 'coercion' (*Zwang*) to make them work!

Poetischer Trichter III contains the earliest explicit description of the poetical paragram. It appears in the seventh study (*Betrachtung*) under the title 'On decorative speech':

Words with more than one meaning, from which have been derived inventions concerning time, names, numbers and so on, will not be discussed here, because all that sort of thing was explained with regard to every kind of circumstance in Part I of the *Poetischer Trichter*; we need cite only this almost new source of invention concerning the number-letters set out as follows:

[58] Georg Philipp Harsdörffer, *Poetischer Trichter. Die Teutsche Dicht- und Reimkunst ohne Behuf der Lateinischen Sprache*, 3 vols. (Nürnberg, 1647–53), II (1648), 27.
[59] Ibid., II (1648), 28–9.

a	b	c	d	e	f	g	h	i	k	l	m	n	o	p	q	r	s	t	v	w	x	y	z
1	2	3	4	5	6	7	8	9	10	11	12	13	14	15	16	17	18	19	20	21	22	23	24

When once I have a name, I then invent a phrase which adds up to the same number.

Jesus ist Christus} ⟩ 218

makes

unser Helfter und Heile} ⟩ 218

Names and phrases amounting to the same totals in this way are the source of real invention, and are to be found in the *Philosophische und Mathematische Erquickstunden.*[60]

(See Appendix 4 page 162.) This 'almost new source of invention' corresponds to Harsdörffer's earlier example of Count Cambyses Bianchi's number-lines, and, as a compositional device making use of the natural-order number alphabet, it is particularly significant.

Rôle and influence

Harsdörffer is important not only because of his timely systematisation of the various alphabetic devices, but also because of his strategic place in the literary circles of his day. Through his books, most of which ran to several editions,[61] he influenced a broad spectrum of German culture, and through his contact with the literary societies, he made the personal acquaintance of many authors and was able to influence their thinking. In all probability these alphabetic devices would have died out without the widely known work of Harsdörffer.

One of Harsdörffer's teachers was the brilliant mathematician and linguist Daniel Schwenter (1585–1636). Although not a member of a literary society, Schwenter was to become the chief figure among several influential writers, including Harsdörffer, Johann Hörner and Selenus (August II of Braunschweig-Lüneburg), focused on his home town of Nürnberg. In 1608 Schwenter was made Nürnberg's city Poet and Adviser on the Hebrew language, while continuing to teach at the university in neighbouring Altdorf. From 1624 his advisory duties in Nürnberg were expanded to include the Chaldean and Syrian languages, and in 1628 he was made Professor of Mathematics, and Inspector of the University and College libraries in Altdorf. In 1636 he died of a broken heart within an hour of his wife and new-born twins: a sad ending to the life of one of Nürnberg's most talented citizens.[62]

In 1619 Schwenter wrote a dedicatory poem in Hebrew for Hörner's

---

[60] Ibid., III (1653), 72.
[61] Zirnbauer, 'Bibliographie der Werke Georg Philipp Harsdörffers', 12–49.
[62] Zedler, *Lexicon*, s.v. 'Schwenter'.

Problema Summum, Mathematicum & Cabalisticum.[63] However, it seems that Schwenter was more renowned for mathematical than linguistic ability. The entry in Zedler's *Lexicon* reads:

The fame of his mathematical science was so great that even some princes and other persons of rank received his instruction and good advice in the subject, and for that reason he enjoyed exceptional favour with many of high rank, but especially with the learned Duke August of Braunschweig-Lüneburg.[64]

In the year of his death, Schwenter published his *Erquickstunden* and dedicated the book to August II of Braunschweig-Lüneburg (Selenus). August II was among the most respected noblemen and scholars of his day, and in 1643 founded the Herzog August Bibliothek in Wolfenbüttel. Schwenter's reputation as a respected mathematician was no doubt furthered by his relationship with August II and with the many other noble members of the *Fruchtbringende Gesellschaft*.

Schwenter's pupils included the young Georg Philipp Harsdörffer. He was only twelve years old when Hörner's book was published, but Schwenter probably showed him a copy in later years. Schwenter was dead by the time that Harsdörffer was invited to join the *Fruchtbringende Gesellschaft*,[65] but through the society he too made the acquaintance of August II. In 1651 Harsdörffer republished Schwenter's *Erquickstunden*, which contains several alphabetic devices although no paragrams,[66] and then published his own *Erquickstunden* as parts II and III in 1651 and 1653 respectively.

Harsdörffer's personal influence on other writers is often acknowledged in print. Justus Georg Schottel, for example, included a paragram by Harsdörffer at the beginning of his classic work *Ausführliche Arbeit von der Teutschen Haubt Sprache* (1663). Schottel was Ludwig von Anhalt's court Poet and Assessor, and an illustrious president of the *Fruchtbringende Gesellschaft*. His first major work, *Teutsche Sprachkunst* (1641), earned him much praise. Wolfgang Hecht has recently written:

Teutsche Sprachkunst not only procured him a place in the *Fruchtbringende Gesellschaft* (as 'The Searcher' [*Der Suchende*]) although the Society and Prince Ludwig in particular were never reconciled to his thinking on the philosophy of language – but also proved a successful rival to Johannes Clajus's *Grammatica Germanicæ Linguæ* (1st edition 1578), which was still very popular as a school textbook and had appeared in numerous editions. In 1645 Harsdörffer was able

---

[63] See pp. 63–5 above.
[64] Zedler, *Lexicon*, s.v. 'Schwenter'.
[65] See p. 71 above.
[66] See the example of Simon Jacob's mathematical puzzle cited on p. 52 above.

◄๏(०)๏►   ◄๏(०)๏►   ◄๏(०)๏►

Beati Harsdörferi
Paragramma,
Ex progreſſione literarum & numerorum,
ita ut primus numerus A. 1. & Z. 23.
denotate præſumatur.
Juſtus Georgius Schottelius,   345.
Varro Teutonicus, vindex Lingvæ 345.
Applicatio

T u *vindex Lingvæ,* Tu *Varro Teutonicus ſis.*
(Sic compar numerus, vel Paragramma notat)
Ceu *Varro* quondam peregrinos duxit in Urbe *
Atq; leves Patriæ condidit ante novâ:
Sic *Tu* follicitis Germanis, tramite certo
Pergendum monſtras, quæq; tuenda via.
Magni Varronis numeros implere laboras,
Dum latices Lingvæ ſicce patere jubes.

* Cicero Acad. quæſt. l. 1. Varro nos in urbe noſtrâ peregrinantes,
errantesque hoſpites ſuis libris domum quaſi deduxit, ut poſ-
ſemus aliquando, qui & ubi eſſemus, agnoſcere.

A dedicatory paragram written by Georg Philipp Harsdörffer, from
Justus Georg Schottel's *Ausführliche Arbeit* (1663).

to inform the Prince of Anhalt that *Teutsche Sprachkunst* was very highly thought
of in Ulm and Nürnberg, and had already been introduced into a number of
schools.[67]

Schottel published *Teutsche Sprachkunst* in several enlarged versions
with different titles, the last and most complete of which was *Ausführliche Arbeit*, which Hecht describes as

not only the *summa philologica* of Schottelius personally, but also that of his
entire age. Nowhere are the grammatical tenets and linguistic theories of the
period between Ickelsamer and Leibniz presented more comprehensively than
here.[68]

Harsdörffer's dedicatory 'Paragramma' would therefore have been seen
by many people. It reads:

[67] Wolfgang Hecht (ed.), *Justo-Georg Schottel. Ausführliche Arbeit von der Teutschen
Haubt Sprache. Braunschweig, 1663* (Tübingen, 1967), p. 5. See also Gottlieb Krause,
*Der Fruchtbringende Gesellschaft ältester Ertzschrein. Briefe, Devisen und anderweitige
Schriftstücke* (Leipzig, 1855; reprint edn New York, 1973).
[68] Hecht (ed.), ibid., p. 7.

Beati Harsdörferi[69]
Paragramma,
Ex progressione literarum & numerorum,
ita ut primus numerus A.1. & Z.23.
denotate præsumatur.
Justus Georgius Schottelius. 345.
Varro Teutonicus, vindex Lingua 345.

Applicatio
Tu vindex Linguæ, Tu Varro Teutonicus fis.[70]
(Sic compar numerus, vel Paragramma notat)
Ceu Varro quondam peregrinos duxit in Urbe*
Atq; leves Patriæ condidit ante novâ:
Sic Tu sollicitis Germanis, tramite certo
Pergendum monstras, quæq; tuenda via.
Magni Varronis numeros implere laboras,
Dum latices Linguæ sicce patere jubes.[71]

* Cicero Acad. quæst. I.1. Varro nos in urbe nostra peregrinantes, errantesque hospites suis libris domum quasi deduxit, ut possemus aliquando, qui & ubi essemus, agnoscere.

(See Appendix 4 pages 162–3.) This is a true poetical paragram; its title contains the word 'Paragramma', and it makes use of the natural-order number alphabet in the two number-lines which generate ideas for the following poem.

Although Harsdörffer does not place number-line phenomena in strict categories, his criticism of Stiefel (1532), and Hörner (1619), together with his endorsement of Schwartzbach (1636), suggests that he concurs with the four categories already outlined: the acceptable and unacceptable uses of Cabbala Speculativa, and the two poetic uses. Harsdörffer developed Schwartzbach's poetical number-line technique, simplifying its complexity and using the number-lines to generate ideas for a Latin poem. In view of the aims of the literary societies it is surprising that Harsdörffer did not apply the technique to the creation of German number-lines and poems. His avoidance of the Greek-based word 'paragramma' in favour of the German term 'Gleichen' is perhaps a token gesture of support for the vernacular.

The transformation of number-lines into a means of poetical invention was, in part, a response to the philosophical climate of the time.

[69] Harsdörffer had died in 1649, four years earlier than the publication of Schottel's *Ausführliche Arbeit*.
[70] Harsdörffer reports that Schottel was known as the German Varro (after the Roman author Marcus Terentius Varro, who flourished 127–116 BC). See Erdmann Neumeister, *De Poëtis Germanicis. 1695*, ed. Franz Heiduk and Günther Merwald (Bern, München, 1978), p. 98, p. 239 and p. 549.
[71] Hecht (ed.), *Justo-Georg Schottel. Ausführliche Arbeit* (1967), preface.

Rationalism was the order of the day and interest in superstitious, strange or *wunderlich* phenomena was declining. Practitioners of cabbalism still existed in certain Jewish and Christian circles, but from Harsdörffer's day onwards the paths of cabbalism and the poetical paragram were to be separated once and for all.

THE FRUITION OF THE PARAGRAM

Johann Henning

Johann Henning's *Cabbalologia* contains the clearest proof that in the mind of a late seventeenth-century Lutheran there was a distinction between the poetic 'Cabbala' (i.e. the paragram) and cabbalism. Born in 1645 in Salzwedel, Henning was a well-educated historian and theologian. He studied in Wittenberg, Jena and Helmstedt, became Protector of the gymnasia in Salzwedel and Quedlinburg, and published several books. His last post, which he held until his death in 1695, was as Pastor of St Egidien's Church in Quedlinburg.[72]

Henning divides *Cabbalologia* into two parts. In the first, 'Institutionis Cabbalisticae', he describes three species of Cabbala: *gematria*, *notaricon* and *temura*, and refers to the work of Pico della Mirandola and Johannes Reuchlin. His first two examples of *gematria* are the same as Schmidt's.[73] He writes about two kinds of *notaricon*, one using the first or last letters of each word, as in an acrostic:

In Einem Stehet Unser Seligkeit ('our redemption comes through one man')
Ich Erlöse Sie Von Sünden ('I will redeem you from your sins')[74]

and the other using just the vowels. With this technique relationships can be found between many biblical words or verses. Henning gives three examples of his third species of Cabbala, *temura* or anagram. In Hebrew, מלאכי ('my angel') from Exodus 23:23, when reordered, reads מיכאל ('Michael'); similarly in Greek, 'Ιησοῦς ('Jesus') becomes σὺ ἡ ὄις ('you are he, the lamb'); and in Latin *Jesus* becomes *vis es* or *jus es* ('you are strength' or 'justice').[75] He lists eleven authors whose works contain examples of these three species of Cabbala, including Elchanon Paulus, Theodor Hackspan and Johann Müller.

The second part of *Cabbalologia*, 'De Cabbala Poetarum Paragrammatica', is presented in much the same form as Schwartzbach's

---

72 Zedler, *Lexicon*, s.v. 'Henning, Johann'.
73 Johann Henning, *Cabbalologia, i.e. Brevis Institutio de Cabbala cum Veterum Rabbinorum judaica, tum Poëtarum Paragrammatica, Artis Cabbalistico-Poëticæ* (Leipzig, 1683), pp. 5–6. See pp. 14–15 above.
74 Ibid., p. 7.   75 Ibid., p. 10.

46   SECTIO POSTERIOR

H	M	D	P	P
E	A	E	O	L
M	G	D	L	A
N	N	I	Y	U
E	I	I	M	S
O	F	A	N	U
	I	L	I	M
	C	M	A	
	O	A		Summa

— — — — — — — omnium
138.   155.   174.   610.   601.   1678.

§. XXIV. Huic Cabbalæ generi non adeo diffimilis eſt ea ſupputandi ratio, qva uti à denario, ſic etiam à Centenario numerorum ſaltus per denariū mdo fit, ita ut qvatuor poſteriores Alphabeti literæ ſaltem denario creſcant hoc modo:

1.   2.   3.   4.   5.   6.   7.   8.   9.   10. 20. 30.   40.
A. B. C. D. E. F. G. H. I. K. L. M. N
50.   60. 70. 80. 90.   100. 110. 120. 130.
O.   P. Q. R. S.   T. V. W. X.
140.   150.
Y.   Z.

e.g. *Georgius Seidelius hodie Natalem ſuum accelebrat læte.* Numerorum ſumma qvæ prodit *Annum*, eſt 1664.
Simile Exemplum invenies in *promulſ. noſtrâ Poëticâ p. 78.*

§. XXV. Omnium autem *ſimpliciſſima* eſt *Cabbala,* qvæ juxta ſimplicem numerorum literis impoſitorum ordinem componitur ſeqventi modo:

CHRO-

DE CABBALA PARAGRAMMATICA.   47

1. 2. 3. 4. 5. 6. 7. 8. 9. 10. 11. 12. 13.
A. B. C. D. E. F. G. H. I. K. L. M. N.
14. 15. 16. 17. 18. 19. 20. 21. 22. 23. 24.
O. P. Q. R. S. T. V. W. X. Y. Z.
17.   104.   62.   79.
v.g. *Dn. Statius. Cauffman. Conſul.*   (262.)
κατ᾽ ἀριθμαντείαν.
33.   66.   62.   101.
Pii. poſt. funera. vivunt.   (262.)
CHRONOLOGIA CABBALISTICA.
Dominus Joannes Fridericus Heckelius, *Gera Variſcus, Vates Laureatus Cæſ. felicissimus, Philologus & Criticus eximius, vocatur ſcholæ Reichenbachenſis Rector (Summa eſt Ann. 1682.)*
Aliud Exemplum Cabbalæ Chronologicæ.
Dominus Georgius Andr. Fabricius, *Magdeburgenſis, in Academiâ Wittebergenſi die vigeſimo qvarto Februarii hujus Anni, magno cum Adplauſu doctorum Virorum* de Duello in ſpecie *bene diſputat.* Harum literarum numeros ſi per *Additionem* computes, prodit 1683. qvod tempus *præſentis*, qvo vivimus, qvoqve hæc ſtudioſæ juventutis Bono ſcribimus, *Anni* eſt.

SoLI DEo gLorIa, & eXoptata paX atqVe ſaLVs GerMânIæ.

The final pages of Johann Henning's *Cabbalologia* (1683), showing an adapted milesian and the natural-order number alphabets, and two number-lines.

introduction to *Lusus Paragrammaticus* published fifty years earlier. Henning gives a brief historical overview which is followed by a description of twelve different number alphabets (see Appendix 1), the last of which is the natural-order, and thirty-seven paragrams, some with accompanying poems. Michael Stiefel is once again hailed as the inventor of the paragram. Hörner too is mentioned, but, interestingly, Henning considers that Hörner's work resembles the old Rabbinical cabbalism.[76] According to Henning it is the work of Poll and Schwartzbach which marks the beginning of a totally unsuperstitious use of the paragram for inventing 'ingenious songs and elegant poems'.[77] The work he cites most frequently is Joachim Bussen's *Promulside nostra poëtica*.[78] Henning also includes a section on chronograms, which he terms Cabbala Chronologica.

Cabbalologia thus makes a clear differentiation between the poetical

[76] Ibid., p. 11.   [77] Ibid., p. 12.
[78] Ibid., many times cited between pp. 15 and 42. I have so far been unable to trace this book or its author.

paragram and the old Jewish Cabbala. Henning places Müller's work in
Part One, which is important evidence for the developing hypothesis
that the poetical paragram was not included in the category of Cabbala
Speculativa as defined by the Lutheran theologian Müller and his early
eighteenth-century contemporaries.

Johann Christoph Männling

Johann Christoph Männling's contribution to the poetical paragram
form was to write German poems based on ideas generated by Latin
number-lines. Männling was born in Wabnitz near Oels in Silesia on 14
October 1658. He studied in Breslau and then moved to Wittenberg to
complete his training. In 1688 he returned to his homeland of Silesia, to
a pastorate in Creuzberg, although he was forced to leave twelve years
later as a result of pressure imposed by the Counter-Reformation.[79]
Next he served as Deacon at St John's Church in Stargard, then as Pastor
of St Augustine's and finally as Chaplain to the Stargard garrison. He
died on 4 July 1723.[80] During his important Wittenberg period he was
awarded a Master's degree and the distinguished title *Poeta Laureatus
Cæsareus*, an honour that had been conferred on Christoph Schwartzbach fifty years earlier. There he also published his first major work,
Europäischer Parnassus (1685),[81] which he decided to augment and
republish in 1704 under the title *Der Europæische Helicon*.

   Der Europæische Helicon is divided into three parts devoted
respectively to theory, practice and examples of German poetry. It
contains two references to the poetical paragram. The first appears in
Chapter XII of Part One 'On Invention and Structure', where the sixth
of nine rules for poetical invention describes it under the heading 'the
meaning of names, through the exchange of letters'.[82] The more extensive description of the paragram appears among the examples of
German poetry in Part Three. Chapter II lists many different verse
forms, of which the seventeenth concerns 'Cabbalas, chiefly Cabbala
simplex':

[79] Zedler, *Lexicon*, s.v. 'Mänling, Johann Christoph'.
[80] Gerhard Dünnhaupt, *Bibliographisches Handbuch der Barock Literatur* (Stuttgart,
   1981), p. 1116.
[81] In *Bibliographisches Handbuch der Barock Literatur*, p. 1117, Dünnhaupt states that
   the only extant copy of Männling's *Europäischer Parnassus* (1685) is in the Staatsbibliothek, Preußischer Kulturbesitz, West Berlin. Unfortunately this is not the case. The
   copy with the pre-war call mark Yb 5477 is neither in the Staatsbibliothek, Preußischer
   Kulturbesitz nor in the Deutsche Staatsbibliothek, East Berlin, and was probably lost as
   a result of the Second World War.
[82] Johann Christoph Männling, *Der Europæische Helicon, Oder Musen-Berg* (Alten
   Stettin, 1704), p. 80.

Rule 1. A Cabbala or Programma is a new form of refinement, whereby the A.B.C. is laid out arithmetically, and then a name, a sentence or a saying is worked out accordingly; but there is more than one kind. Firstly there is Cabbala simplex and communis, e.g. A = 1 to Z = 24.[83]

Quoting the third volume of Harsdörffer's *Poetischer Trichter*, Männling reiterates that this is a new use. He writes that the Jews formerly made great mysteries out of the technique and that the Christian Michael Stiefel founded 'our Cabbala' in 1560. Männling then includes a table of ten different number alphabets (see Appendix 1) and gives an example:

I have used my own name as an illustration of this:

12	58	180	131						
M.	Johann	Christophorus	Mænnlingius,						

153	108	15	11	3					= 671
Berostaadiensis	Silesius	P.	L.	C.					

In juxtaposition, the words of Augustine:

63	41	128	52	26	24	76	24	52
Inter	Brachia	Salvatoris	JESU	mei	&	vivere	&	mori

61	39	22	19	44				= 671
cupio,	ut	in	eo	maneam.				

(See Appendix 4 pages 163–4.) The Latin number-lines provide the basis for the following poem, originally written in German:

> Let thunder, hail and lightning come down on many heads,
>> But no distress shall tear me away from JESU's side;
>> My trusty ship of faith shall run for this shore
> And seek peace from the tempest here.
>> As a dove will shelter in a hollow cleft,
>> My shelter shall be in the crimson rock of JESU's innocence;
> With greatest joy I see the mirror open to view,
>> Which reflects only blessedness and the true life:
>> My Saviour, only remain inclined towards your servant,
> Who wishes to touch your heart with his true repentance,
>> Do not cast out this image which was won by your faith
>> When you, Life itself, died for the dead.
> For as long as my spirit pulses in these veins [and]
>> The body's eye can look upon the light of day,
>> You shall be the foundation stone on which I safely build
> The house of my soul's hope, that no storm shall shake;
>> And when my life's wick has no more oil to feed it,
>> Your soul shall bury me in its bosom.[84]

---

[83] Ibid., p. 140. [84] Ibid., pp. 142–3.

This is a perfect illustration of number-lines generating the ideas for a subsequent poem; and because Männling chose a religious text, rather than a verse from the Bible, his poetical paragram, or 'Cabbala' as he terms it, is definitely not an example of Cabbala Speculativa.

The poetical paragram was now developing fast: German number alphabets were being introduced, the use of German for the poem was superseding Latin and the paragram was being recognised as one of many different techniques of poetical invention, entirely distinct from Jewish or Christian cabbalism. The contribution of the next paragrammatist, the anonymous author of *Das ABC*, is not so much in terms of innovation, although he does introduce German into the number-lines, but more in terms of consolidation.

Das ABC cum notis variorum

Das ABC cum notis variorum was published in 1695 by Johann Christoph Mieth and Johann Christoph Zimmermann in Leipzig and Dresden, and republished with a second volume in 1703. The original publication has been described as

> an amusing, robustly humorous, rambling discourse on the alphabet, individual letters, anagrams, letter-games, letter-puzzles etc., with numerous verses in both German and Latin, excerpts from Christian Weise (who is quoted frequently, along with other contemporary writers) and anecdotes.[85]

Towards the end of the first volume there is a section devoted entirely to the poetical paragram. The fourteen paragraphs are immediately preceded by a section on anagrams, and followed by a description of chronograms or *chronodisticha*. The anonymous author, hereafter referred to as ABC, writes:

> ¶332 Another Lusus Poëticus involving letters arose with an interest in the Cabbala or so-called Paragramma. It is said to have originated with the well-known mathematician Michael Stiefel, whom others then followed, notably Abraham Schönwald, Anno 1572, and Johann Hornejus [Hörner], physician of Heilbrunn. If only they had not become convinced that special wonders and skills were concealed in it, they would not have insisted that this skill provided the means of understanding certain difficult passages in Revelation and the Prophet Daniel . . .
>
> ¶333 The practice has become quite common since then on the occasion of weddings and funerals, and many have marvelled not a little at what their own names held concealed, which was brought into the open by profound calculations. For those who did not know how it was done, it seemed a mysteriously holy and arcane thing.

---

85 Adolf Seebaß (ed.), *Deutsche Literatur der Barockzeit*, revised edn (Basel, 1975), p. 1.

¶334 And yet it is child's play, and judicious people take even less time to do it than they do to make an anagramma. I will describe the process briefly.
¶335 It is of prime importance to have the Table, or so-called Paragrammatic alphabet. Until now, there have been 7 of them. But recently a friend in Silesia devised an 8th, and still more could be invented.[86]

His first example, using German for the number-lines, is a logical extension of Männling's innovatory use of German for the poem. ABC recommends that one begin with the numerical total of a name before searching for a motto with approximately the same numerical total:

Johan = 268   Georg = 329   Churfurst = 1150
Summa: 1747

Der = 178   Herr = 357   segne = 310   Dich = 97   und = 310
staerke = 606   Dich = 97   aus = 382   Zion = 541
Summa: 2899

The motto he chooses is a biblical-sounding elaboration of Psalm 128:5. The numerical total of the name does not equal that of the motto, but with the addition of an extra N, three Es (one of them as an umlaut), and the words 'zu Sachsen', the total of the names and motto becomes identical:

Johann George Churfürste zu Sachsen = 2899

(See Appendix 4 pages 164–5.) ABC continues: 'That is the whole skill. I put the two together, turn it into verse, like an anagramma, and leave it to people to try or admire', adding:

¶358 Sometimes, however, it may be that the numbers will not accord exactly. But the paragrammatists have something up their sleeves: the last may fall short by 1, 2 or 3, and that is then called *demta Monade, Dyade, Triade*; if it is added to, then it is called *addita Monade, Dyade, Triade*.

Among the authors I have cited above, Schwartzbach, Männling and Kuhnau (in his mathematical puzzle) all had to resort to using the technique of 'demta' and 'addita' when it was not otherwise possible to make the numbers equal. ABC also explains how to make a table of alphabets, and, in ¶341, adds: 'He who wishes to make these things frequently works the names out at his leisure and writes them down in a notebook where he can find them; thus he has them ready when needed and can complete the task in a trice.'
ABC writes that paragrams were commonly composed by 'Herren Paragrammatisten' for weddings and funerals. His account in every way

---

[86] *Das ABC cum notis variorum* (Leipzig, Dresden, 1695), pp. 181–5. ABC was incorrect: by this time many more than eight 'paragrammatic' alphabets had appeared in print.

confirms the distinctions made by Harsdörffer and Henning between a
poetical use of the paragram and cabbalistic *gematria*, and his simple
explanation of the technique would have allayed the fears of any reader
who still connected the paragram with strange or shady practices.

The identity of ABC

In no dictionary of Anonymi and Pseudonymi is there any mention of
Das ABC cum notis variorum or its author, but there are nevertheless a
few clues to his identity. The first lies in the full title of the book, which
reads: *Das ABC cum notis variorum. Herausgegeben von einem Dessen
Nahmen im ABC stehet*. The final clause, *Written by one whose name is
found in the ABC*, can be understood in one of two ways: either the
author's name is found in the ABC, that is, his initials could be anything
from A to Z, or the author's name is found in the letters ABC, in which
case the author's initials are made up of the letters ABC in some order or
another. Considered alone, this clue does not take us very far since many
authors have used the initials ABC, or various permutations of these
three letters, as a pseudonym.

A second clue can be drawn from stylistic analysis. Adolf Seebaß
writes that 'the whole thing breathes the spirit of the writings of Johann
Prätorius, but since he died in 1680, his authorship is really out of the
question'.[87] Johann Prätorius was the pseudonym of Hans Schultze, who
was born in 1630 and lived in Zetlingen. Prätorius held a Master of
Philosophy degree from Leipzig University and was a *Poeta Laureatus
Cæsareus*, as were Schwartzbach and Männling.

Nowhere in *Das ABC cum notis variorum* does the author refer to his
other writings, and naturally it would be difficult to discover any unless
he had used the same cryptic phrase, i.e. 'written by one whose name is
found in the ABC'. As luck would have it, in the preface to his *Catalogus
derer Eintausend funffzig Paragrammatum Cabbalisticorum Trigonalium*
(1719) Johann Friedrich Riederer writes of 'the oft-mentioned author of
the *ABC* and *Einmahl Eins cum notis variorum*'.[88] *Das Einmahl Eins
cum notis variorum* was also published by Johann Christoph Mieth in
Dresden and Leipzig in the same year (1703) as the revised two-volume
version of *Das ABC cum notis variorum*. There are several copies in
different British and German libraries, but unfortunately the title
contains no clue to its authorship. Riederer's reasons for linking the two
books are unknown and he may have been mistaken. However, it does
seem highly likely that they have the same author on account of their

---

[87] Seebaß, *Deutsche Literatur*, p. 1.
[88] Johann Friedrich Riederer, *Catalogus derer Eintausend funffzig Paragrammatum
Cabbalisticorum Trigonalium* (1719), opposite p. B3 in the preface.

related titles, related subject matter (ABC and 123) and common publisher.

In Seebaß's bibliography of German literature the entry under *Das Einmahl Eins cum notis variorum* directs the reader to a late edition (1783) of August Bohse's *Gründliche Einleitung zu Teutschen Briefen* which was bound together with a copy of the original edition of *Das Einmahl Eins*. Seebaß does not identify the author, but writes:

The unassuming title conceals a complete textbook about numerical knowledge, which also deals with number mysticism, and examines much material of cultural-historical interest, for example, in its long excurses on the numbers three and seven. The text is interspersed with anecdotes, arithmetical exercises, poems, chronologies, etc.[89]

However, Seebaß makes no link between this book and *Das ABC cum notis variorum*. It is not insignificant that August Bohse's initials are AB. Is it possible that August Bohse was the author of all three books? Libraries and collectors bind books together for many reasons and not always because the authors are the same, but it is worth noting that *Das ABC cum notis variorum* has been bound with *Das Einmahl Eins cum notis variorum* on at least one occasion.[90]

August Bohse was born on 2 April 1661, the son of a high-ranking magistrate in Halle and member of the *Schöppenstuhl*. He attended the gymnasium in Halle when Prätorius was Rector and Drechsler the third master, after which he travelled with his father to Vienna and other cities. In 1679 he entered the University of Leipzig to read oratory and law. Outbreaks of the plague disturbed his studies and necessitated his temporary transfer to Jena and Halle. In 1685 he went to Hamburg for three years to teach young noblemen law, oratory and letter-writing. He then spent two years in Dresden, interrupted by a brief spell in Berlin. In 1690 Bohse returned to Halle, and then, after his father's death in 1691, to Leipzig as a lecturer at the University. During his first six months he received great acclaim for his lectures in rhetoric, and was subsequently invited to become court Secretary to Duke Johann Adolf I of Saxe-Weißenfels, an honour he accepted gladly (see page 99 below). His duty was chiefly to prepare libretti for operas performed at the recently opened court theatre, but the duke also gave him permission to continue his academic career at a local university of his choice, and he chose Jena. At some point he married Susanna Helene Reichhelm (1670–1732) from Halle.[91] After the death of Duke Johann Adolf I in 1679, Bohse moved

[89] Seebaß, *Deutsche Literatur*, p. 33.
[90] For example, the copy in The British Library, call mark GB: Lbm – 1331. b. 16 (1 & 2).
[91] For a more detailed discussion of the Bohse and Reichhelm links with Bach see pp. 121–3 below.

to Erfurt, where he first published under his famous pseudonym Talander. In 1700 he moved back to Jena, lecturing at the university once more until 1708, when he became a professor at the Ritterakademie in Liegnitz, Silesia. He retired from this post in 1730, but stayed there as an emeritus professor until his death on 11 August 1742.[92] As far as I know Bohse never wrote about number alphabets, unless it can be proved that he was ABC.

Unfortunately the Johann Prätorius of the gymnasium in Halle who so influenced the young August Bohse is not the same as the Johann Prätorius of Zetlingen whose writing style ABC's apparently resembled! Nevertheless it is interesting that in 1695, as ABC was writing his paragram examples on Johann Georg, the founder of the royal house of Saxe-Weißenfels, August Bohse was court Secretary to the reigning Duke Johann Adolf I.

Another possible candidate for the authorship of *Das ABC cum notis variorum* is Johann Riemer, who by 1695 had used the pseudonym ABC for several publications.[93] Johann Riemer was born in Halle on 11 February 1648 and died there on 10 September 1714. In 1678 he had succeeded the famous poet Christian Weise as Professor of Poetry, Eloquence and Politics at the gymnasium in Weißenfels.[94] In 1690 Riemer moved to Hildesheim and then to Hamburg, where he preceded Erdmann Neumeister as Pastor of St Jacob's Church. Unlike Bohse, Riemer is known to have written about number alphabets on at least one other occasion. In *Über-Reicher Schatz-Meister* (1681) Riemer described the anagram, epigram, chronogram and the paragram or 'Cabbala' in the third article, 'On the number of syllables in verses', of the seventh chapter, 'On tuneful compliments', of Part One, 'The origin and rules of compliments':

Also related to these are the Cabbalas, which produce a certain number: but through the use of Greek or German numerals, not Roman ones. To start with, you need to have the entire Alphabet numbered, as follows:

---

[92] Zedler, *Lexicon*, Supplement (1752), s.v. 'Bose, oder Bohse, August', and Neumeister, *De Poëtis Germanicis. 1695* (1978), s.v. 'Bose' and 'Bohse'. There is a discrepancy over the date of Bohse's death. In Dreyhaupt's *Saal-Creyses* (Halle, 1749, 1751) the date is given as 19 July 1732, two days before the death of his wife Susanna Helene.

[93] Including *Die Politische Colica oder das Reissenin Leibe Der Schulkranken Menschen welche in mancherley zustanden ohne Leibs Schmerzen zu Bette liegen. Niemanden sonst als Hohen und Gelehrten zur belustigung vorgestellet durch A.B.C.* (Leipzig, 1680). Riemer wrote under more than one pseudonym; see Dünnhaupt's *Bibliographisches Handbuch*, s.v. 'Riemer, Johann'.

[94] Founded in 1664, the gymnasium was soon expanded into a university, while retaining its original name. See *Handbuch der historischen Stätten Deutschlands*, vol. XI: *Provinz Sachsen-Anhalt* (Stuttgart, 1975), s.v. 'Weißenfels'.

1 2 3 4 5 6 7 8 9 10 20 30 40 50 60 70 80 90 100 1000 2000
a b c d e f g h i k l m n o p q r s t   u   vv
3000 4000 5000
x   y   z

Secondly I select the numbers, according to the letters of the name, and add them up; if the sum amounts to a year, or such other number as one desires, then the Cabbala is done.[95]

According to Riemer whole poems or songs could be invented on the ideas generated from anagrams,[96] and the context of the section on the paragram or 'Cabbala' quoted above implies that it too could be as a means of invention.

Das Einmahl Eins cum notis variorum

Leaving aside the question of authorship, there is one passage in *Das Einmahl Eins cum notis variorum* which is relevant to the poetical paragram. Towards the end, under the heading 'On the extraction of roots and of Algebra', the author writes:

In this section of mathematics there occur the so-called Paragrammata, as we are reminded by Master Hoffmann in his *Vers- und Ticht-Kunst* page 134, where, for example, from the words 'Pope of Rome', using the *numeris monadicis*, he produces the number of the Beast, namely 666, Rev. 13:18. This is the very thing understood by P. Casp. Knittel in *Via Reg.* page 16, when he divides the *ars combinatoria* into Anagrammata, Algebra, the Elements and the Arts or Sciences.[97]

This is a description of the 'unacceptable' practice of Cabbala Speculativa used to interpret the biblical number 666. The author moves on to describe other cabbalistic practices and then proceeds to the poetical paragram:

There is also the Cabbala simplex, which calls a 1, b 2, c 3, d 4 and so on until it reaches 23 or 24 with the last letter. It is astonishing to find that some Christians make a great skill and mystery out of this, when it is nothing more than a *lusus ingenii* and the opposite can be extracted for exactly the same pains. Those whose opinion of it is more ingenious say that this kind of cabbalistic calculation does at

---

95 Johann Riemer, *Über-Reicher Schatz-Meister Aller hohen Standes und Burgerlichen Freud- und Leid-Complimente* (Leipzig, Frankfurt, 1681), p. 126.
96 Ibid., p. 114.
97 *Das Einmahl Eins cum notis variorum* (Leipzig, Dresden, 1703), p. 347. See also Caspar Knittel, *Via Regia Ad Omnes Scientias et Artes. Hoc est, Ars Universalis* (Prague, Leipzig, 1687), p. 16. I have so far been unable to trace *Vers- und Ticht-kunst* by Hoffmann.

least produce compositional invention; but anyone who knows about invention will easily perceive that the Patrons of this art are deceived.[98]

There is nothing here to contradict the views presented in *Das ABC*. The comment on the limited value of the paragram for invention is complementary to the bald, technical description in *Das ABC*, and nowhere in *Das ABC* does the author discuss either the Jewish cabbalistic techniques of *gematria* or the *wunderlich* use of number-letters.

The next major work in the history of the poetical paragram is *Die Allerneueste Art Zur Reinen und Galanten Poesie zu gelangen* (1707) by Christian Friedrich Hunold, otherwise known by his pseudonym Menantes. His work marks the final stage in the development of the poetical paragram: its incorporation into a system of *loci topici*.

Christian Friedrich Hunold

Christian Friedrich Hunold was born in Wandersleben on 29 September 1681. On the death of his parents in 1691 he was sent to school in the neighbouring town of Arnstadt and showed early promise of musical and poetical talent. In 1697 he moved to the Lateinschule in Arnstadt and then to the gymnasium in Weißenfels, where Weise had taught until 1678 and Riemer until 1690. At the age of eighteen Hunold entered the University of Jena to study law. This involved learning about language, poetry, letter-writing, history and morality as well as public and state law. In 1731, a decade after his death on 6 August 1721, his biographers recorded that during this period he had frequently held discussions with August Bohse.[99] Hunold's extravagant lifestyle curtailed his university studies and he left Jena to travel to Hamburg where he began an illustrious career as a poet, novelist and librettist. In 1706 an unexpected turn (see pages 117–18 below) forced him to return home and settle in Halle.[100]

Hunold's best school-friend, Meister, the son of the Weißenfels court Chef, had a beautiful sister whom Hunold loved, but who married Erdmann Neumeister, the court Chaplain at Weißenfels (see page 99 below). At some point Meister gave Hunold a copy of the notes his brother-in-law Neumeister had written for a series of lectures he had delivered at the University of Leipzig in 1695. By 1707 Neumeister was taken up with pastoral responsibilities and this is perhaps one reason why Hunold quite shamelessly decided to publish *Die Allerneueste Art Zur*

---

[98] *Das Einmahl Eins*, pp. 349–50.
[99] *Geheime Nachrichten und Briefe von Herrn Menantes Leben und Schrifften* (Köln, 1731; reprint edn Leipzig, 1977), p. 4.
[100] *The New Grove Dictionary of Music and Musicians*, s.v. 'Hunold, Christian Friedrich', by George J. Buelow.

Reinen und Galanten Poesie zu gelangen as his own work,[101] albeit under his pseudonym Menantes.

Hunold's comments on the paragram appear in a section devoted to invention, which he describes as 'the most important element in the whole of poetry. Invention is the soul, the character, of the body that is a poem, whereas the verses and rhymes are only as it were a graceful garment.'[102] He goes on to introduce the popular system of *loci topici* which he uses to categorise the different methods of invention. He describes fifteen different *loci*:

Locus (i) *notationis*; (ii) *definitionis*; (iii) *generis & specierum*; (iv) *totius & partium*; (v) *causæ efficientis*; (vi) *causæ materialis*; (vii) *causæ formalis*; (viii) *causæ finalis*; (ix) *effectorum*; (x) *adjunctorum*; (xi) *circumstantiarum*; (xii) *comparatorum*; (xiii) *oppositorum*; (xiv) *exemplorum*; (xv) *testimoniorum*.

He then divides *locus notationis* into five sub-categories: (i) *derivation*; (ii) *æquivocation*; (iii) *synonyma*; (iv) *anagramma*; and (v) *artificium cabbalæ*.[103] This fifth sub-category of *locus notationis* includes the acrostic, for example

Margaretha:
Mein **A**maranth **R**iechet **G**ar **A**nmuthig: **R**iechet **E**twan **T**ugend **H**ier **A**lso[104]

(see Appendix 4 page 165), and the paragram, although nowhere in his explanation does Hunold actually use the word 'paragram'. In his description Hunold mentions five different German alphabets, including the natural-order and the trigonal, and explains:

So I place an alphabet before me, whichever one I choose, take the letters of the main word, write over each letter the number which corresponds to the letter in the alphabet and add them together. Whatever the total comes to I place on one side. And then I think of another or several other words which, using the same alphabet, add up to the same total as the main word. And from there I can proceed with the invention. It is customary to indicate at the beginning which alphabet has been used, and what numerical total the words come to.[105]

Hunold's recommendation to choose a 'main word' as the starting-point is in contrast to the directions given by both ABC and Harsdörffer who recommend beginning with a name and a verse. Hunold's examples, however, show that his main words were often names:

---

101 *Geheime Nachrichten und Briefe*, p. 100. See also *The New Grove Dictionary of Music and Musicians*, s.v. 'Neumeister, Erdmann', by Kerala Johnson Snyder.
102 Hunold, *Die Allerneueste Art Zur Reinen und Galanten Poesie zu gelangen* (Hamburg, 1707), p. 540.
103 Ibid., p. 542.   104 Ibid., p. 543.   105 Ibid., p. 545.

Alphabetum Ordinario
| Margaretha | 88 |
| Meine Seele | 88 |

Alphabetum vulgare
| Margaretha | 295 |
| Ach und mein Leben | 295 |

(See Appendix 4 page 165.) Hunold's five number alphabets or *species* all have the word 'cabbala' or 'cabbalisticum' in the title, and he states that there are many more alphabets, adding disparagingly: 'For there is no limit to the useless notions that idle and foolish heads will dream up!'[106] And this sentiment is echoed in his final comment on the paragram: 'It is somewhat laborious. But a whimsical fellow will find it amusing. At least it gives us cause for the fifth invention in the case of the unique *locus notationis*.'[107]

Although Hunold does not wholeheartedly recommend the paragram as a means of invention, he does nevertheless classify it as a poetical form of *locus notationis*. The *loci* were used originally as oratorical and rhetorical devices to aid in the construction of a speech or sermon. They became popular in Germany around the turn of the eighteenth century, and were adapted for use in other disciplines including musical and poetical composition. Previous authors had thought of the paragram as a means of invention, but Hunold, or maybe Neumeister, was the first to place it in a system of *loci topici*. In many ways this elevated the status of the paragram.

Johann Friedrich Riederer

As the author of over 5000 poetical paragrams, there can be little doubt that Johann Friedrich Riederer was the 'Herr Paragrammatist' *par excellence*. Riederer was born in Nürnberg on 20 February 1678. According to Zedler, it was under the guidance of Samuel Faber at the St Egidien Gymnasium in Nürnberg that poetry first came alive for the boy.[108] Faber was later to become a famous Rector of the gymnasium, and Riederer expressed his gratitude by dedicating to him two paragrams and a book.[109]

In 1692 Riederer was forced into business, but he continued to study poetry and literature in his spare time. For the next ten years or so commercial enterprises took him to many different places, including

---

[106] Ibid.   [107] Ibid., p. 546.
[108] Zedler, *Lexicon*, s.v. 'Riederer, Johann Friedrich'.
[109] The paragrams appear in Riederer's *Catalogus derer Eintausend funffzig Paragrammatum Cabbalisticorum Trigonalium* (1719), numbers 442 and 443, and the book is *Das Portrait eines getreuen Schul-Lehres in der Person Samuelis Fabris. Gymnasii Ægidiani Rectoris* (Leipzig, 1716).

Canterbury, Dover, Calais, Normandy, Picardy and Paris, where he arrived for New Year's Day 1700, Lyons, where he worked for eighteen months, Switzerland and Swabia. He returned to Nürnberg in 1703, but apparently felt that the Bavarian war was too close at hand, and left shortly afterwards. He travelled through Bohemia to Vienna where he worked with the Löschenkohl Company until 1708. Finally he returned to his home town of Nürnberg, where he lived and worked until his death in 1734.[110] In 1710 he was invited by the former president, Christoph Fürer of Haimendorff, to join Harsdörffer's *Pegnesischer Blumenorden*.[111] He took the pen-name IriFloR (I F R standing for Johann Friedrich Riederer), although he did not always publish under this pseudonym.

Of the 5000 paragrams mentioned in his catalogues, it seems that only about one hundred were ever published. His *Catalogus derer Eintausend funffzig Paragrammatum Cabbalisticorum Trigonalium* (1719) is particularly important in the history of the paragram. It is a sales catalogue listing 1050 poetical paragrams on different subjects and people prepared by Riederer. Most of the paragrams are for well-known public names, including past and present monarchs and politicians, for celebrated literary figures, including Hofmann von Hofmanns-Waldau and Johann Caspar Wetzel, and for family and friends, including several Riederers, who would no doubt have sponsored his work. As an experienced salesman, his comprehensive preface, addressed to the 'Unprejudiced Reader', gives the clearest possible explanation of the paragram, discussing its technique, status and reputation. He reveals that he did not know what a paragram was until 1714, when he was asked to write something for the wedding of an eminent professor in Altdorf and came across the section on the paragram in *Das ABC cum notis variorum*. It is interesting that a widely travelled member of Harsdörffer's literary society had not come across a paragram before the age of thirty-six.

Stylistically Riederer's paragrams are fairly consistent. His titles always contain the term 'paragramma' or some close variation of it, and he always uses the trigonal alphabet, a biblical text or verse of a hymn and an elaborate version of the name of the dedicatee. The poem based on the number-lines is invariably set in alexandrines, the popular metre introduced by Opitz von Boberfeld a century earlier.[112] Riederer obviously delighted as much in the arithmetical aspects of the paragram as in the poetical, and, as in Picander's *Paragramma Cabbalisticum trigonale*, the numerical totals for the name and verse are frequently over 10000! A

---

110 Zedler, *Großes vollständiges Universal Lexicon*, s.v. 'Riederer'.

111 Although the entry in Zedler, *Großes vollständiges Universal Lexicon*, s.v. 'Riederer' says that he was a member of the *Pegnesischer Blumenorden*, the archives of the society have no record of his membership.

112 I am grateful to Dr Hans Popper (University College of Swansea) for drawing my attention to the form of Riederer's poems.

third catalogue was projected for completion in 1732 under the title
Paragrammata Cabbalistica trigonalia: . . . über 5000, but it is uncertain
whether it was ever published.[113]

The following paragram is typical of Riederer's style. It was written in
1718 to celebrate the consecration of the newly built church of St Egidien
in Nürnberg. His father was the Pastor and Riederer had known and
loved the church since his childhood.[114] The paragram was published
separately and a copy is preserved in the Stadtbibliothek, Nürnberg:[115]

Paragramma Cabbalisticum trigonale on the new church of St Egidien.
1718

2 Chron. 24:13

Die	70	Und	311
nunmehr	674	die	70
neu =	316	Arbeiter	575
erbaute	587	arbeiten	513
schöne	424	daß	182
Kirche	310	die	70
bey	294	Besserung	857
Sanct	459	im	123
Egidien	249	Wercke	475
in	136	zunahme	731
der	178	durch	415
Keyserlichen	944	ihre	249
freyen	571	Hand /	138
Reichsstadt	988	und	311
und	311	machten	417
Weltberühmten	1293	das	182
Republicq	754	Haus	418
Nüremberg	746	Gottes	699
		ganz	420
		fertig	452
		und	311
		wol	402
		zugericht.	983
Facit	9304	Facit	9304

(See Appendix 4 page 165.)

[113] A catalogue of Riederer's published and projected works appears in the introduction to
Johann Friedrich Riederer, *Gedichte und Historische Erzelhlungen über die bedenck-
liche und Geheimnis-Reiche Zahl Drey* (Frankfurt, Leipzig, 1748). Entry no. 33
describes the projected publication of 5000 paragrams in 1732, just two years before
Riederer died.

[114] Zedler, *Großes vollständiges Universal Lexicon*, s.v. 'Riederer'.

[115] This paragram has been reproduced with the kind permission of Dr Günther Thomann,
Librarian of the Stadtbibliothek, Nürnberg.

An example of an individually published paragram by Johann Friedrich Riederer.

The alphabet is as follows:

a. b. c. d. e. f. g. h. i. k. l. m. n. o. p. q. r.
1. 3. 6. 10. 15. 21. 28. 36. 45. 55. 66. 78. 91. 105. 120. 136. 153.
s. t. u. w. x. y. z.
171. 190. 210. 231. 253. 276. 300.

> Praise God! The church that lay these two and twenty years,
> desolate, in dust and ashes,
> is now restored and rebuilt
> so that we see it more glorious than ever it was before.
> As everyone who reflects on the builder's art says:
> It has been done right seemly, well and gracefully.
> Therefore it remains our wish, the prayer of all the faithful,
> that our lamp shall never be removed from the altar.

Many of Riederer's contemporaries also wrote poetical number-lines and paragrams, the majority of which appeared in journals and anthologies. Among these are several, including one each by Philipp von Bornier and Johann Gottfried Mittag, which have no accompanying poem and which cannot therefore be considered as means of invention.[116]

The Weißenfels court

Since 1650 the poetical paragram had regularly been mentioned as a technique for poetical invention in books published in various parts of Europe. By the beginning of the eighteenth century, however, the form was becoming less popular and might have passed into oblivion had it not been for the literary activity of a handful of men involved directly or indirectly with the Weißenfels court. The Duchy of Saxe-Weißenfels was granted royal status by Johann Georg I of Saxony in 1657, and the dukes were August (1657–80), Johann Adolf I (1680–97), and his three sons, Johann Georg (1697–1712), Christian (1712–36) and Johann Adolf II (1736–46). The court moved to Weißenfels after the death of August in 1680.[117]

Johann Adolf I was the first duke who actively encouraged the arts, especially music, establishing a court chapel in 1680 and a court theatre in 1685. In 1680 Johann Philipp Krieger (1649–1725) was appointed to the newly created post of Kapellmeister. When the court opera was opened

---

[116] *Neue Zeitungen von gelehrten Sachen*, ed. Johann Gottlieb Krause, XVII (27 February 1717), p. 133, where the French nobleman and director of the Erlangen Ritterakademie, Philipp von Bornier, uses number-lines to express the hope that the French Church might be freed from its current governing body; Johann Gottfried Mittag, *Leben und Thaten Friedrich August III* (Leipzig, 1737), p. 322, where the number-lines celebrate the coronation of Friedrich August III as King of Poland.

[117] *The New Grove Dictionary*, s.v. 'Weißenfels', by Horst Seeger.

in the New Augustus Palace in 1685, Krieger's son Johann Gotthilf assumed directorship of the chapel while Krieger the elder became responsible for the opera.[118] In 1705 the post of court Poet was created and first held by Johann Heinrich Lincke.[119] His chief responsibility was to supply cantata texts and opera libretti, a task that had previously fallen to the court Secretary. Other notable musicians and poets connected with Weißenfels and its court include the possible author of *Das ABC cum notis variorum*, August Bohse (1661–1742), the author of the material pirated by Hunold in *Die Allerneueste Art*, Erdmann Neumeister (1671–1756), the musician, novelist and ducal librarian Johann Beer (1655–1700), the novelist and poet Christian Weise (1642–1708), and the novelist, poet, amateur music theorist, and other possible author of *Das ABC*, Johann Riemer (1648–1714).[120]

August Bohse was appointed court Secretary to the reigning Duke Johann Adolf late in 1691, and by 11 December of that year had been commissioned to write an aria on the occasion of the death of Johann Georg III of Saxony.[121] The birthday of Duke Johann Adolf on 2 November 1696 found Krieger and Bohse working together on 'ein unterthänigstes Freuden-Opffer', and again, after the duke's death in the summer of 1697, on a 'Trauer- und Ehren-Denckmahl' for his burial.[122] By 1696 Bohse was a well-known novelist, as the young scholar Neumeister testifies in his Master's thesis, published in 1695 as *De Poëtis Germanicis*:

Bose (August)
    Is very well known under his pseudonym; who, namely, is not acquainted with the fame of Talander? Who does not respond to the elegant style, adorned with rhetorical ornament and full of all refinements? Who, finally, has ever yet withheld applause from his ingratiating style and other gifts? Our Bose is altogether an inspired poet, who has a felicitous poetic vein at his service even when he does not work it; he adorned his *Römische Fabeln*, as he calls them, with numerous verses, like so many lamps, which the reader will find it easy to judge.[123]

It is extremely likely that during Bohse's seven-year period at Weißenfels (1691–8) Neumeister and he became acquainted through Neumeister's academic research and his visits to the Krieger household. By the time Erdmann Neumeister was court Chaplain in Weißenfels (1704–6), his

---

118 Ibid., s.v. 'Krieger, Johann Philipp', by Harold E. Samuel.
119 Ernst Schubert, *August Bohse, genannt Talander* (Breslau, 1911), p. 14.
120 *Handbuch der historischen Stätten Deutschlands* XI, s.v. 'Weißenfels'. See also *The New Grove Dictionary*, s.v. 'Beer, Johann', by George J. Buelow.
121 Schubert, *August Bohse*, p. 13. The text is published in *Die Lebenden Todten* (Leipzig, 1698), pp. 289–90.
122 These two works were to be published in *Geistliche Cantaten statt einer Kirchen-Music* (1704). See *The New Grove Dictionary*, s.v. 'Krieger, Johann Philipp'.
123 Neumeister, *De Poëtis Germanicis. 1695* (1978), p. 147.

reputation as a poet was well established. His cantata texts were set by Krieger as early as 1696 and he gave Krieger copies of several other cantata texts which were not to be published until 1704.[124]

In 1696 Neumeister had married the sister of Hunold's best friend Meister (see page 92 above) and had moved from Leipzig to take up his first pastorate in the neighbouring town of Bad Bibra.[125] Hunold left Weißenfels in 1698 to study in Jena, but his continued friendship with Meister brought him back from time to time, and by 1708, after his period in Hamburg, he was in the area once more, teaching oratory at the University of Halle. Although in 1731 his biographers were at great pains to point out that it was Hunold's industry rather than his teachers or professors that secured him success, they considered it worthwhile mentioning one professor whose work had provided an important model for Hunold, August Bohse:

> It occurs to us that he often spoke very highly of Dr Bose (who is sufficiently well known under the name Talander, and was in Jena in those days, where he gave lectures), and everyone who has read the writings of both must admit that the disciple very nearly surpassed his master.[126]

Bohse was therefore well known to the young Hunold, who was seventeen in 1698 when the duke died and Bohse left Weißenfels. Whether a young man like Hunold would ever have spoken to a respected court Secretary is not clear. It seems that Hunold chose the University of Jena rather than Halle or Leipzig because he knew that Bohse lectured there, although there is some dispute over this. Hermann Vogel claims that Bohse had already left the university when Hunold registered on 8 June 1698,[127] but Ernst Schubert contests this, stating that Bohse and Hunold knew each other personally.[128]

The interaction between Bohse, Neumeister and Hunold, made possible by their common location at the Weißenfels court, may have helped to perpetuate the knowledge of the paragram. None thought highly of the form, but all considered it noteworthy. Bohse and Neumeister were poets whose gifts and interests would naturally have drawn them towards new ideas of invention. In the preface to his novel *Amazoninnen* (1696) Bohse admits that he has 'an exceptional liking for poetry and such like invention'.[129] It is not possible to prove that Bohse told Neumeister or Krieger about the poetical paragram, but it is highly probable that through their meetings and publications an exchange of ideas took place.

[124] Schubert, *August Bohse*, p. 15, footnote 4. The texts are published in *Die Lebenden Todten*, p. 224.
[125] *The New Grove Dictionary*, s.v. 'Neumeister'.
[126] *Geheime Nachrichten und Briefe*, p. 4.
[127] Hermann Vogel, *Christian Friedrich Hunold, Sein Leben und Seine Werke* (Lucka, 1898). Quoted in Schubert's *August Bohse*, p. 51, footnote 1.
[128] Schubert, ibid., pp. 50–1.   [129] Ibid., p. 12.

Although not formally linked with the Weißenfels court, Christian Friedrich Henrici (1700–64), the pseudonymous Picander, was deeply influenced by the works of Hunold and Bohse. In his *Academischer Schlendrian* Picander talks about the contemporary novel:

What Menantes and Talander wrote may be all very well, but what Seladon, Selamintes, Iccander etc. have scribbled is not worth reading.[130]

The pseudonyms Talander and Picander are remarkably similar. This is because both men belonged to the literary society of the *Blumen- und Elbschwanorden* where similarly Greek-sounding names were frequently used.[131] By the time Picander was old enough to be admitted to the society, however, Bohse was far away in Liegnitz. One has to remember that *Das ABC cum notis variorum* may not have been written by August Bohse at all, and that even if it were, Picander may not have known that ABC was August Bohse. Nevertheless it is interesting to see that Picander was at least conversant with the works of both Hunold and Bohse (i.e. Menantes and Talander), and that he may therefore have learnt about the poetical paragram from Hunold's *Die Allerneueste Art*.

The history of the poetical paragram shows that it underwent a formal metamorphosis in five stages. Stiefel's Latin number-lines of 1553, the earliest example of the poetical paragram, were possibly a form of Cabbala Speculativa. They refer to biblical numbers (2300, 666 etc.) and use the trigonal alphabet. Hörner's Latin, Greek, Hebrew and German number-lines of 1619, which exemplify the second stage in the poetical paragram's development, were an 'unacceptable' form of Cabbala Speculativa. They too again refer to biblical numbers, but use the natural-order alphabet. The third stage is represented by Schwartzbach's Latin number-lines of 1630 which, as a means of poetical invention, were definitely not a form of Cabbala Speculativa. They refer to neither biblical numbers nor texts, and use many different number alphabets. Schwartzbach's was the first true poetical paragram. Riederer's paragrams (1715–32) mark the fourth stage, the maturity of the poetical paragram; his German number-lines were, like Schwartzbach's, a means of poetic invention and not a form of Cabbala Speculativa. They invariably use the trigonal alphabet and a biblical text, but never allude to biblical numbers. This was the form of paragram which Hunold had earlier classified as the fifth sub-category of *locus notationis*. A fifth stage, which marks the beginning of the decline of the paragram form, is represented by Mittag and von Bornier, whose German and Latin

---

130 Quoted in Schubert, ibid., p. 54.
131 Ibid., p. 11. Schubert lists several other similar names including Isander, Sarcander and Leander.

number-lines use a biblical text and one of many different number alphabets without becoming the means of invention for a poem. As their number-lines do not use biblical numbers, it is highly improbable that they were a form of Cabbala Speculativa. Although the use of poetical number-lines for 'acceptable' and 'unacceptable' forms of Cabbala Speculativa diminished after Schwartzbach, the word 'Cabbala' lingered in paragram titles, and until the 1720s it continued to be necessary for paragrammatists to reassure their readers that their poetical form had little or nothing to do with cabbalistic practices.

Smend quoted Schmidt's use of the term *lusus ingenii* in connection with the paragram, but Schmidt refers to a cabbalistic practice and not to the poetical paragram. As we have seen, although the term *lusus ingenii* was often used of the paragram, it had a much broader meaning.[132] The word 'Cabbalisticum' in Picander's title also misled Smend, because he did not know what an eighteenth-century poetical paragram was. Unfortunately Smend's misunderstanding has caused the majority of his successors to link the poetical paragram with cabbalism and to assume that Bach did the same.

[132] For further examples, see Mizler's use of the term in his work, *Lusus Ingenii de Praesenti Bello* (Wittenberg, 1735), and Neumeister's in *De Poëtis Germanicis. 1695* (1978), p. 46, s.v. 'Harsdörffer'.

4

A musical paragram?

Musical alphabets and codes

Just as the poetical paragram has been described as a *lusus ingenii*, and more specifically as a *lusus poëticus*,[1] so there are several techniques using musical notation in seventeenth- and eighteenth-century books that could be termed *lusus musicus*.[2] The first of these is the cryptographic use of musical alphabets.

Musical alphabets appear regularly in books on cryptography and secret writing, and the following, which differs only in small details from author to author, is quoted in Giovanni Porta's *De furtivis literarum notis* (1583), Daniel Schwenter's *Steganologia* (1620) and *Erquickstunden* (1636), Athanasius Kircher's *Musurgia Universalis* (1650) and Gaspar Schott's *Schola Steganographica* (1665):[3]

Porta	b a c d e f g h i k l m n o y z r s t u w x	q p
Schwenter	b a c d e f g h i k l m n o y z r s t u w x	q p
Kircher	a b c d e f g h i l m n o p q r s t u x y z	
Schott	a b c d e f g h i k l m n o p q r s t v w x y z	

---

[1] The term *Lusus Poëticus* is used to describe the anagram by several authors, including Christoph Pelargus in *Lusum Poeticum Anagrammatum* (Frankfurt, 1595), and to describe the poetical paragram by ABC on p. 181 of *Das ABC cum notis variorum* (1695) and by Johann Friedrich Riederer on p. 2 of the preface to his *Catalogus derer Eintausend funffzig Paragrammatum Cabbalisticorum Trigonalium* (1719).

[2] As far as I am aware the term *lusus musicus* was not used in the eighteenth century.

[3] Giovanni Porta, *De furtivis literarum notis*, 3rd edn (Naples, 1602), p. 152; Resene Gibronte Runeclus Hanedi (alias Daniel Schwenter), *Steganologia et steganographia nova* (Nürnberg, 1620), p. 302 and Daniel Schwenter, *Erquickstunden* (Nürnberg, 1636), p. 239; Athanasius Kircher, *Musurgia Universalis* (Rome, 1650; reprint edn in 1 vol. Hildesheim, New York, 1970), II, 362; Schott, *Schola Steganographica*, p. 325.

Two methods of musical cryptography, from Daniel Schwenter's
Erquickstunden (1636).

The alphabet is used to hide messages, and Kircher's example reads:

Cedere cogemur, or 'we will be compelled to give way'.

A composer who uses this technique is Johann Christoph Faber in his
Invention wie zwey Concerten of 1729, in which the full title reveals that
the viola part hides the following poem:

> Sehr stark der Argwohn ist bei hitzigen Verliebten,
> Redt man mit andern nur, vermeint man, daß sie Liebe übten.[4]

(See Appendix 4 page 166.) A similar technique widely employed by
cryptographers is Polybius' system of signalling,[5] which was first adapted
for a form of musical cryptography by Selenus (August II of Braunschweig-Lüneburg) in the 1620s. He gives three different examples, the
first of which is a piece of music in four parts hiding in the tenor voice the
words: *Der Spinola ist in die Pfaltz gefallen: Væ illi*[6] (see Appendix 4

---

[4] Johannes Wolf, *Handbuch der Notationskunde*, 2 vols. (Leipzig, 1919; reprint edn
Wiesbaden, 1963), II, 465.
[5] See Kahn, *The Codebreakers*, p. 83.
[6] Selenus, *Cryptomenytices et Cryptographiæ*, p. 324.

pages 166–8). Twenty-five years later Athanasius Kircher used Polybius'
principle for an aural form of musical cryptography, in which the
repetition of notes on different musical instruments was decoded by
means of letters of the alphabet:[7]

	1	2	3	4	
Fistula	A	B	C	D	Ordo 1
	O	O	O	O	
Cymbalum	E	F	G	H	Ordo 2
	O	O	O	O	
Tintinnabulum	I	K	L	M	Ordo 3
	O	O	O	O	
Chorda	N	O	P	Q	Ordo 4
	O	O	O	O	
Crepitaculum	R	S	T	V	Ordo 5
	O	O	O	O	
Vox	W	X	Y	Z	Ordo 6
	O	O	O	O	

Eighty years later Johann Christoph Faber combined repetition and the
Latin milesian alphabet to incorporate the name *Ludovicus* into his *Neu
erfundene Composition*, written for festivities on 25 August 1729 celebrating the name-day of Duke Ludwig Rudolf of Braunschweig-Lüneburg.
Faber hid the message in the solo line of this nine-movement work for
trumpet and strings. In the first movement the trumpet plays twenty
notes, over the first of which is written: 'L = 20', in the second it plays 200
notes, over which is written: 'U = 200', etc.[8]

It is unclear how widespread these techniques were among composers,
but their survival probably depended more upon their repeated inclusion
in cryptographic books than upon contemporary practice. It is nevertheless interesting to see Faber's use of them and to notice that Harsdörffer
reproduced Kircher's table in the third volume of his *Erquickstunden*
(1653).[9]

Another form of musical cryptography is the mnemonic-like device
espoused by Guido d'Arezzo in *Ut Queant Laxis*. Dufay adapted this and
frequently used it to make a rebus: Guillermus du ♮♮ y. In his widely

[7] Athanasius Kircher, *Musurgia Universalis* II, 361. Kircher divides the alphabet into six
  parts, labelling them *Ordo*, 1, 2, etc. to facilitate reference.
[8] Walther Dehnhard, 'Kritik der Zahlensymbolischen Deutung im Werk Johann Sebastian
  Bachs', *Kongreßbericht Stuttgart 1985* (Kassel, Basel, 1985), p. 450.
[9] Harsdörffer, *Erquickstunden* III (1653), 377.

Noftrum deniquè Exemplum, non tantùm nudâ, Notarum Muficalium in TENO RE, fecretum repræfentantium ferie, fed etiam Confonantium trium aliarum Vocum eleganti, prò re natâ, veftitu, à Friderico Hollandto, Lunæburgenfe Cive, *Mufico non inter extremos habendo, ornatum, exhibemus, in modum fequentem:*

'Der Spinola ist in die Pfaltz gefallen: væ illi', from Gustavus Selenus'
Cryptomenytices et Cryptographiæ (1624).

LIBER SEXTUS.   Cap. 19.

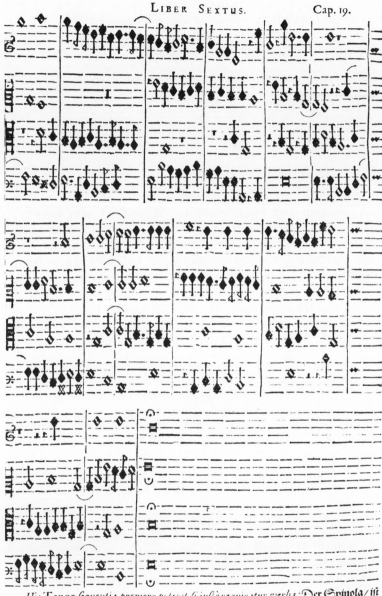

Hic Tenor *sequentia promere poterit si juste requiratur, verba:* Der Spinola/ ist
in die Pfaltz gefallen: *Væ illi.*
                                                    CAPUT

circulated book, *Les Bigarrures du Seigneur des Accords* (1583), Estienne Tabourot documents several similar examples, which are repeated
or adapted by later authors. The following, quoted by Schwenter in 1636
and Kircher in 1650, is a typical example:

A distinguished poet and musician composes a song of this nature:

By that he means this verse: *Fama latere nequit, micat ut Sol inclyta virtus*: A good
name will not be hidden, virtue shines as bright as sunlight.[10]

Johann Sebastian Bach's well-known use of b-a-c-h, first brought to the
attention of the musical public by Walther in his *Musicalisches Lexicon*
(1732), is a more modern adaptation of this form of cryptography.

   These musical codes and alphabets are far too simple to have been of
use to professional encoders, such as diplomats, and would have been
broken by a trained cipher analyst in minutes. At the end of a discussion
of the cryptographic content of Selenus' *Cryptomenytices et Cryptographiæ*, Athanasius Kircher's *Polygraphia Nova et Universalis* and Gaspar
Schott's *Schola Steganographica*, David Kahn concludes:

These books, plus the even less important ones that were also published at this
period, have a certain air of unreality about them. There is good reason for this.
The authors borrowed their knowledge from earlier volumes and puffed it out
with their own hypothesizing, which seems never to have been deflated by
contact with the bruising actuality of solving cryptograms that they themselves
had not made up. The literature of cryptology was all theory and no practice. The
authors did not know the real cryptology that was being practised in locked
rooms here and there throughout Europe, by uncommunicative men working
stealthily to further the grand designs of state.[11]

Selenus' *Rhythmomachia*

A second *lusus musicus* is *Rhythmomachia*, a board game invented by
Pythagoras when he discovered the proportions of the harmonic series.
Selenus, who was also a renowned chess-player, appended to his major
chess treatise, *Das Schach- oder König-Spiel* (1616),[12] his German

---

[10] Schwenter, *Erquickstunden*, pp. 238–9, and Kircher, *Musurgia Universalis* II, 363.
[11] Kahn, *The Codebreakers*, p. 156.
[12] Gustavus Selenus, *Das Schach- oder König-Spiel. von Gustavo Seleno, in vier unterschiedene Bücher mit besonderm fleiß grund und ordentlich abgefasset. Auch mit
dienlichen Kupfer-Stichen gezieret: Desgleichen vorhin nicht außgangen. Diesem ist zu*

translation of Francisco Barozzi's recent Latin version of *Rhythmoma-chia*. The game is played on a chequered board eight squares long by sixteen squares wide. The two players each have twenty-four pieces or 'men', which are circle-, triangle-, square- and castle-shaped. On the surface of each 'man' is a number. The object is to capture the opponent's 'men', which is done when 'men' bearing two equal numbers meet, or in a variety of ways which include the addition, subtraction, multiplication and division of the numbers. A player wins when he has succeeded in making the following numerical relationships between three or four 'men': arithmetical, in which the difference between the two smallest numbers is the same as that between the two greatest numbers; geo-metrical, in which the quotient of the two smallest numbers is the same as that between the two greatest numbers; and harmonic, in which the differ-ence between the two smallest numbers is contained in that between the two greatest numbers as frequently as the smallest number appears in the greatest.[13] There are three kinds of victory, which depend upon the type and number of relationships formed by the 'men': a small victory being when three 'men' form one relationship, a large victory, when four 'men' form two of the different relationships, and an outright victory when four 'men' form all three kinds of relationship. It is because knowledge of the proportions of the harmonic series is required to play *Rhythmomachia* that this complex board game can be classified as a *lusus musicus*.

Mizler's *Lusus Ingenii*

Another *lusus musicus*, Lorenz Christoph Mizler's musical allegory *Lusus Ingenii de Praesenti Bello*, was published in Wittenberg in 1735.[14] It is written in Latin and dedicated to the amateur musician Jacobo de Lucchesini, an Imperial Centurion of the Serian legion and founder member of Mizler's society, whose concerto for solo voice, German flute and bass had impressed Mizler.[15] The tactics of the allies in the recent European war are expressed through a growing harmonic pro-gression, in which each voice represents a nation. Dissonance or conflict is caused when one nation steps out of line with the others:

---

ende angefüget ein sehr altes Spiel genandt Rythmo-machia (Leipzig, 1616; facsimile reprint, ed. Klaus Lindörfer, Zurich, 1978). Selenus' German has been described as 'früh-neuhochdeutsch', and is difficult to understand. See *Das Schach- oder König-Spiel* (1978), p. iii of the introduction.

[13] Ibid., p. iii for comments on the musical content and p. xiii for a precise description of the rules.

[14] Lorenz Christoph Mizler, *Lusus Ingenii de Praesenti Bello Augustissimi atque Invictiss-imi Imperatoris Carolii VI cum Foederatis Hostibus Ope Tonorum Musicorum Illustrato* (Wittenberg, 1735).

[15] *The New Grove Dictionary*, s.v. 'Mizler von Kolof, Lorenz Christoph', by George J. Buelow.

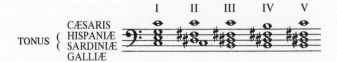

TONUS { CÆSARIS / HISPANIÆ / SARDINIÆ / GALLIÆ

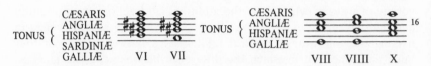

TONUS { CÆSARIS / ANGLIÆ / HISPANIÆ / SARDINIÆ / GALLIÆ   TONUS { CÆSARIS / ANGLIÆ / HISPANIÆ / GALLIÆ

Mizler clearly did not intend his allegory to be a music lesson, as the progression violates the rules of harmony. Two years later Mizler admitted that his *lusus ingenii* no longer pleased him:

The musical war between harmony and composition is still joined, and anyone who has a taste for things of that nature may well gain a lot of pleasure from it, for all kinds of charming ideas are deployed therein. But I have lost my taste for such things, although I myself produced some things of the sort in the previous war.[17]

Other forms

The shorthand musical notation commonly known as figured bass can also be considered a form of *lusus musicus*. I have found no evidence, however, to suggest that figured bass was ever used cryptographically.

More game-like than figured bass is the puzzle- or riddle-canon, which has no formal relationship with any musical alphabet, but whose spirit is similar to that of other cryptographic devices. In 1475 Tinctoris defined canon as 'a rule which shows the intention of the composer in an obscure way',[18] and the element of obscurity seems to have lingered on into the eighteenth-century puzzle-canon. J. S. Bach left some extremely eso-teric and complex puzzle-canons, several of which have never been solved. In 1947 Smend proposed a solution for the canon BWV 1073 using the natural-order number alphabet,[19] but until it has been shown

---

[16] Ibid., p. 15.

[17] Lorenz Christoph Mizler, *Neu eröffnete Musicalische Bibliothek* (Leipzig, 1735–54), I, iii, 65.

[18] *Harvard Dictionary of Music*, s.v. 'Canon III'. For a particularly spectacular example see Wil Dekker, 'Ein Karfreitagsrätselkanon aus Adam Gumpelzhaimers *Compendium Musicæ* (1632)', *Die Musikforschung* 27 (1974), 323–32. A photograph of the original canon appears on p. 324.

[19] Friedrich Smend, *Kirchen-Kantaten* III (1947), 8–9. A similar solution using the natural-order number alphabet has been proposed by Jacques Chailley for a rondeau by Guillaume de Machaut, in which the numbers in the text

> *Dix et sept cinq trese quatorse et quinze*
> *M'a doucement de bien amer espris*

[17, 5, 13, 14, and 15] form the letters RENOP, which he interprets as an anagram of

that the natural-order alphabet was used compositionally his solution must remain hypothetical.

Ars Combinatoria[20] (i.e. *Erfindungskunst* or the art of invention) produced several more *lusi musici*.[21] In his dissertation *De Arte Combinatoria* (1666), the great philosopher and mathematician Leibniz discussed the principle of a universal language.[22] Twelve years later he described a fully developed artificial language, which he believed could be translated into musical and poetical terms to aid invention. The language is based on the principle of his first system of logical calculus,[23] in which numbers are used to symbolise basic concepts. Thus 'animal' could be represented by the number 2, 'rational' by the number 3 and so 'man', who is a rational animal, by the number 6, i.e. 2×3. To transform these 'symbolic' numbers into a spoken or written language, Leibniz adapted a type of variable number alphabet devised by Dalgarno,[24] in which the first nine consonants b, c, d, f, g, h, l, m, and n represent the numbers 1 to 9 and the five vowels a, e, i, o, u represent the decimal units in ascending order (1, 10, 100, 1000, 10,000). To transform a number into words, Leibniz took the consonants corresponding to each successive digit in the number, following each consonant by the vowel indicating its decimal unit: for example, the number 81,374 is written Mubodilefa. Since the decimal value of each syllable is fixed by the vowels, the syllables can be placed in any order; 81,374 can therefore be written in several other ways, including, for example,

Bo	di	fa	le	mu
1000	300	4	70	80000 [25]

Péronne, the name of a friend of the composer. See Herbert Anton Kellner, 'Zum Zahlenalphabet bei Guillaume de Machaut', *Musik und Kirche* 51 (1981), 29, and Jacques Chailley, *4000 ans de musique* (Paris, 1961), p. 137.

[20] See Caspar Knittel's use of the terms *ars combinatoria* and *ars inveniendi* in *Via Regia Ad Omnes Scientias et Artes*. Arnold Schering begins an interesting discussion in 'Geschichtliches zur *ars inveniendi* in der Musik', *Jahrbuch der Musikbibliothek Peters 1925* (Leipzig, 1926), pp. 25–34, which Franz Wöhlke continues in chapter 2 of *Lorenz Christoph Mizler. Ein Beitrag zur musikalischen Gelehrtengeschichte des 18 Jahrhunderts* (Würzburg, 1940), pp. 38–57.

[21] See Athanasius Kircher, *Musurgia Universalis*, 2 vols. (Rome, 1650; reprint edn Hildesheim, New York, 1970), II, 3–26.

[22] Gottfried Wilhelm Leibniz, *Dissertatio de arte combinatoria* (Frankfurt, 1666). See Louis Couturat, *La Logique de Leibniz d'après des documents inédits* (Paris, 1901), p. 61.

[23] Couturat, *La Logique de Leibniz*, p. 62, pp. 277–9 and pp. 323–35.

[24] See George Dalgarno, *Ars Signorum, vulgo Character universalis et lingua philosophica* (London, 1661). In *La Logique de Leibniz* Couturat reproduces Dalgarno's 'number alphabet' on p. 546 as part of a comprehensive discussion of Dalgarno's philosophical language on pp. 544–8.

[25] See *Lingua generalis*, an unpublished fragment written in February 1678 and held in the Königliche Bibliothek, Hannover, call mark: Phil. VII B III, 3, discussed on p. 62 and p. 78 of Couturat's *La Logique de Leibniz*. See also Eric Aiton, *Leibniz. A Biography* (Bristol, Boston, Mass., 1985), p. 93.

Leibniz believed that this artificial language could be translated into music, by using intervals, instead of consonants and vowels, to develop an infallible method of composition in which everything is predetermined.[26] It must be said, though, that Leibniz was not a practical musician, and without a demonstration of good music invented in this way his method has to remain a purely theoretical *lusus musicus*.

The *loci topici*

The final and most important form of *lusus musicus* is the musical adaptation of the rhetorical and poetical *loci topici*. Hunold used the poetical paragram to illustrate a fifth form of *locus notationis* and the possibility that theorists applied Hunold's poetical illustrations to music should be considered.

According to Zedler the *loci topici* or *loci dialectici* were not known to the ancient Greeks.[27] It seems that in the early sixteenth century the Latin words *locus*, meaning simply a 'proof', and *topicus*, referring to the logical procedure which introduces the proof, were combined to describe a system of invention often used for devising philosophical and rhetorical arguments. There was, however, no single system: each philosopher developed his own. Thus books on rhetoric, poetry and, later, music have different divisions or species of *loci topici*. Zedler cites four books to demonstrate this diversity: there are fourteen species in Peter Ramus' *Dialecticæ Institutiones* (1543), fifteen in Weise's *Curieuse Fragen über die Logica* (1696), nineteen in Rudrauff's *Cursus Logicus Recognitus* (1702) and twenty-three in Roetenbeck's *Logica Veteri et Nova* (1703).[28]

JOHANN DAVID HEINICHEN

The year before his death the musician Johann David Heinichen (1683–1729) published at his own expense one of the most significant music treatises of the century, *Der General-Bass in der Composition* (1728), which includes a section on the musical use of the *loci topici*. George J. Buelow writes:

Just as an orator had first to invent an idea (*inventio*) before he could develop his oration, so the Baroque composer had to invent a musical idea that was a suitable basis for construction and development . . . in *Der General-Bass in der*

[26] Couturat, ibid., pp. 62–3. I assume that by 'intervals', Leibniz intends note-names to replace the consonants and the register of the notes to replace the vowels.

[27] Zedler, *Großes vollständiges Universal Lexicon*, s.v. 'Loci Topici'.

[28] Peter Ramus (Pierre de La Ramée), *Dialecticæ Institutiones* (Paris, 1543); Christian Weise, *Curieuse Fragen über die Logica* (Leipzig, 1696), pp. 196–282; Kilianus Rudrauff, *Cursus Logicus Recognitus* (Geissæ-Hassorum, 1702), pp. 87–90; Georg Paul

Composition (1728), Heinichen extended the analogy with rhetoric to include the *loci topici*, the standard rhetorical devices available to help the orator uncover topics – i.e. ideas – for a formal discourse.[29]

Heinichen confines his remarks on the *loci topici* to *locus circumstantiarum*:

It is certain that inventing an idea is only half the labour if the composer can create a good idea from the texts before him (which are sometimes quite barren). But in my opinion there is no better way of guiding our thoughts towards good ideas and encouraging the natural fantasy than by means of the oratorical *locos topicos*. Even with the most barren materials, one has only to examine 3 *fontes principales*, namely *Antecedentia*, *Concomitantia* and *Consequentia Textus* and, occasion the words, to assess the concomitant circumstances of the person, the matter, the quiddity, the origin, the style and manner, the purpose, the time, the place, etc., then the innate, good, natural fantasy (we are not speaking of *ingenia stupida*) will never lack for the expression of well-liked ideas, or, to speak more plainly: of skilful invention.[30]

In a footnote Heinichen admits that on occasions he has had to resort to using the technique, demonstrating its effectiveness on an aria text which contains no word suggestive of mood or musical affect.

Heinichen was born near Weißenfels. In 1696 he attended St Thomas' school in Leipzig and in 1702 proceeded to the university there to read law. His organ teacher was Kuhnau, and while still at St Thomas' he became Kuhnau's assistant. Through correcting and copying Kuhnau's manuscripts he gained valuable first-hand experience of compositional technique. On completing his law studies in the winter of 1705–6 he decided to return to Weißenfels. Buelow considers the reasons for Heinichen's decision:

This city's proximity to Crössuln, Heinichen's home, might have drawn him there. More important perhaps was the attraction of an active music center under the artistically enthusiastic Duke Johann Georg, who imported student musicians from Leipzig to his court, either for guest performances or permanent positions. The court capellmeister was Johann Philipp Krieger (1649–1725), his assistant, Gottfried Grünewald (1675–1739), and the court organist, Christian Schieferdecker (1679–1732). Krieger's presence in Weißenfels had unquestioned

---

Roetenbeck, *Logica Veteri et Nova* (Altdorff, 1703), p. 712. Coincidentally, Roetenbeck's maternal grandfather was Daniel Schwenter.

[29] *The New Grove Dictionary*, s.v. 'Rhetoric and Music', by George J. Buelow. See also George J. Buelow, 'The Loci Topici and Affect in Late Baroque Music: Heinichen's Practical Demonstration', *The Music Review* 27 (1966), 161–76.

[30] Johann David Heinichen, *Der General-Bass in der Composition* (Dresden, 1728), p. 30. It is interesting to note with reference to p. 111 and footnote 20 above Heinichen's frequent use of the term *ars combinatoria* in *Der General-Bass*.

significance for Heinichen's musical growth, although we can only guess at the extent to which the older musician influenced the young lawyer from Leipzig.[31]

Krieger certainly knew some of Heinichen's operas and cantatas, including a cantata which he conducted in Weißenfels on St Michael's Day in 1711.[32]

In 1710 Heinichen was appointed composer to the Zeitz court of Duke Moritz Wilhelm, cousin of Duke Anton Ulrich of Braunschweig-Lüneburg. He was later granted leave of absence to travel to Venice and Rome where several of his operas were well received. His reputation grew to such an extent that the young Prince Leopold of Anhalt-Cöthen, a future patron of Johann Sebastian Bach, studied music under him, and later invited him to be his companion on several Italian journeys.[33] In 1716 Heinichen was appointed Kapellmeister to the Elector Friedrich August of Saxony (August III, King of Poland) whose court was in Dresden, and although he was married in Weißenfels in 1721 and his son was born there in January 1723, Dresden was to remain his professional base until his death from tuberculosis in 1729.[34]

It is interesting that Heinichen, the first to suggest the use of the *loci topici* for generating ideas in musical composition, was connected to the Weißenfels circle of poet-scholars, among whom were Neumeister and Hunold, the first to suggest the *loci topici* for generating ideas in poetical rather than rhetorical composition. Neumeister briefly overlapped with Heinichen in Weißenfels during the latter part of his period as court Chaplain (1704–6). Hunold on the other hand had already left Weißenfels when Heinichen arrived. No doubt *Die Allerneueste Art* was received there with interest and it is extremely likely that Heinichen knew of and read Hunold's work soon after its publication. It may even have been in Weißenfels that Heinichen first came across the idea of using the *loci topici* for invention. Hunold was a gifted musician as well as writer, and it is possible that, on Hunold's return from Hamburg in 1708, Heinichen sought his company to discuss the musical application of the *loci topici*. But whether in Weißenfels, or through his work with Kuhnau, Heinichen somehow thought of using the *loci topici*, and specifically the technique of *locus circumstantiarum*, in musical composition.

[31] George J. Buelow, *Thorough-Bass Accompaniment according to Johann David Heinichen* (Berkeley, Los Angeles, 1966), p. 7.
[32] See *Denkmäler Deutscher Tonkunst*, vol. 53, p. lvi of the preface.
[33] Buelow, *Thorough-Bass*, p. 10.
[34] Ibid., p. 13.

JOHANN MATTHESON

The *locus circumstantiarum* used by Heinichen is the eleventh category of Hunold's fifteen species of *loci topici*, whereas the *locus notationis*, with the paragram as its fifth sub-category, is the first. One can safely assume, therefore, that Heinichen never linked the poetical paragram with musical composition. Ten years later than Heinichen, Johann Mattheson was to write about other musical applications of the *loci topici*, in *Der vollkommene Capellmeister* (1739). In a chapter devoted to melodic invention he explains:

¶14   The first [point], in so far as musical invention is concerned, consists of these three things: *thema, modus, tactus*, i.e. theme, key, meter, which must be especially well chosen and written down before one can consider anything else; regardless of what the purpose is otherwise.[35]

A little later he continues:

¶20   All of this concerns the invention of a good theme, which we call a main theme, and requires the greatest art or skill; whereas the key and the beat, though they must likewise be selected well, do not have such a broad impact. Thus we will impart further below some instruction on these last; yet now we will note a few more things about the main theme: since the familiar *loci topici* (though I for my part make no great thing out of them) occasionally can provide *quite pleasing* expedients for invention in the art of composing melody as well as in poetry and oration.[36]

Two paragraphs on the contemporary reputation of the *loci topici* are followed by a list of fifteen species of *loci*:

¶23   They are called: *locus notationis; descriptionis; generis & speciei; totius & partium; causæ efficientis, materialis, formalis, finalis; effectorum; adjunctorum; circumstantiarum; comparatorum; oppositorum; exemplorum; testimoniorum:* which we want to explain.

¶24   Now though many might think that it would require a great deal of coercion to extend all these to the art of musical composition; the following will convince everyone that such not only could occur in a completely natural way but that in fact it must be so in the theory of invention: this is notwithstanding the fact that no one has attempted to do this in an orderly manner nor even that each dialectic *locus* is equally as appropriate and important for this, since, on the contrary, the first and the second are preferred before all others.

---

[35] Johann Mattheson, *Der vollkommene Capellmeister: Das ist Gründliche Anzeige aller derjenigen Sachen, die einer wissen, können, und vollkommen inne haben muß, der einer Capelle mit Ehren und Nutzen vorstehen will* (Hamburg, 1739), and Ernest C. Harriss, *Johann Mattheson's 'Der vollkommene Capellmeister': A Revised Translation with Critical Commentary* (Ann Arbor, Mich., 1981), p. 283. I shall be using Harriss' translation throughout.

[36] Ibid., p. 285.

¶25 The first place (*locus*), namely *notationis*, furnishes perhaps the richest source. Since *notare* means *to denote*, we understand through *notationem* the external form and design of notes: as in oratory the letters of a name or thing are understood as that which can give cause to many ideas. Just thus, indeed, in even a better way, the form and disposition of the notes, as musical letters, lead us to innumerable variations of which especially these four ways are to be considered: 1) through the value of the notes; 2) through inversion or permutation; 3) through repetition or reiteration; and 4) through canonic passages.

He considers the second species, *locus descriptionis*, to be the next most fruitful source of invention after *locus notationis*:

¶46 The renowned Neidhart wrote very well on this in the foreword of his *Temperatur* as follows: 'the purpose of music is to stimulate all affections solely through tones and through their *rhythmum*, the best orator notwithstanding'. And that is a part of the description-*locus* of invention.[37]

Mattheson gives a brief account of the other thirteen species, pausing at the tenth, *locus adjunctorum*, to give examples of musicians whose compositions and performances illustrate it. When writing about *locus circumstantiarum* he comments on Heinichen's work:

¶78 Heinichen alone appears to have derived his whole theory of invention and perspective from this circumstance-*locus* when he expounds purely on the *antecedentia, concomitantia & consequentia*; which are just a part of a single *locus* out of fifteen.[38]

  Johann Mattheson was born on 28 September 1681 in Hamburg and was a child prodigy as both organist and singer. He gained much of his early musical experience in the theatre and, between 1690 and 1705, performed in at least sixty-five new operas. In 1704 he became tutor to the son of Sir John Wich, the English ambassador in Hamburg. Two years later he was appointed the ambassador's secretary, a post he retained when Wich's son became ambassador in 1715. At the same time he was also Kapellmeister at the Cathedral in Hamburg from 1715 to 1728 and at the court of the Duke of Holstein from 1719. He died at the age of eighty-two on 17 April 1764. Although he composed operas, more than two dozen oratorios, and a variety of cantatas and instrumental works, his most lasting contribution to music is as an author: he published over thirty works.[39]

  When considering the origin of Mattheson's idea of adapting the *loci topici* to music, one immediately thinks of the influence of Heinichen,

---

[37] Ibid., pp. 285–6 and p. 290. Neidhart here refers to Johann Georg Neidhart, author of *Die beste und leichteste Temperatur* (Jena, 1706), and not to the noble Bernhardo â Neidharten referred to on p. 66 above.
[38] Ibid., p. 297.
[39] *The New Grove Dictionary*, s.v. 'Mattheson, Johann', by George J. Buelow.

but, as mentioned above, Heinichen uses only one of the many possible
loci. Furthermore Mattheson criticises Weissenborn, the one rhetoric-
ian he quotes in connection with the *loci*, for using only eleven of the
most common *loci*.[40] A clue to the main influence on Mattheson lies in
the name and order of the *loci* he selects. Mattheson lists exactly the
same fifteen species of *loci topici* as Hunold in *Die Allerneueste Art*
(1707), in the same order and with the same names. They, in turn, are
identical to those given by the former Weißenfels professor, Christian
Weise, in his *Curieuse Fragen über die Logica*, a year after Neumeister
presented his lectures in Leipzig.[41] Given the variety of possible species it
is highly likely that Mattheson was stimulated by either Hunold's or
Weise's work and decided to apply all fifteen species to music.

When Hunold left his home region of Weißenfels and Jena in 1700, he
moved to Hamburg, where he began to establish himself as a writer and
critic. His first novel, *Die verliebte und galante Welt* (1700), brought him
considerable success,[42] and his popularity secured him commissions for
writing opera and oratorio libretti, several of which were to be set by the
composer Reinhard Keiser.[43] In 1706, however, Hunold overstepped the
unwritten bounds of social civility by publishing his *Satyrischer Roman*,
which

recounted the scandalous affairs of singers and others connected with the
Hamburg opera, not the least of whom was the famous soprano Mme Conradine.
The resulting uproar, as members of Hamburg society recognized themselves in
the novel, grew so large, and Hunold was threatened with so many legal
processes and even assassination, that he fled the city and returned home to
Wandersleben.[44]

There can be no doubt that Mattheson would have known Hunold by
repute through this notorious novel, whether or not he had already
known Hunold personally in Hamburg. Mattheson would doubtless have
been eager to read the *Satyrischer Roman*, and he of all people would
have been able to recognise prominent Hamburg citizens and his former

---

[40] Harriss, *Mattheson*, p. 285, ¶21. See also Christoph Weissenborn, *Gründliche Einleitung zur Teutschen und Lateinischen Oratorie* (Frankfurt, 1713), p. 223.

[41] Christian Weise, *Curieuse Fragen über die Logica* (Leipzig, 1696), pp. 196–282. Weise
(1642–1708) attended the University of Leipzig and was a Professor of Poetry,
Eloquence and Politics at the gymnasium in Weißenfels from 1670 to 1678, before
moving to Zittau near Dresden as Rector of the gymnasium there. Since Neumeister
gave his lectures in 1695 and Weise published his oratorical treatise in 1696, it would
seem that Weise and Neumeister came up with the same scheme of *loci topici* independently, unless Hunold read Weise, and amended the Neumeister notes to comply with
Weise's scheme, before publishing *Die Allerneueste Art* in 1707.

[42] *The New Grove Dictionary*, s.v. 'Hunold, Christian Friedrich', by George J. Buelow.

[43] George J. Buelow, 'Music, Rhetoric, and the Concept of the Affections: A Selective
Bibliography', *Notes* 30 (1973–4), 250–9.

[44] *The New Grove Dictionary*, s.v. 'Hunold'.

opera colleagues. As a result of this scandal the whole city would surely have been interested in Hunold's next publication: it happened to be *Die Allerneueste Art.*

Mattheson may also have come to know about Hunold's fifteen species of the *loci topici* through their originator, Erdmann Neumeister. In 1715, the year Mattheson became Kapellmeister at the Cathedral in Hamburg, Neumeister became Senior Pastor of St Jacob's Church. Over the next decade or so Mattheson and Neumeister must have met on many occasions, and perhaps it was Neumeister who encouraged Mattheson to incorporate a section on the *loci* in a future music treatise.

By 1739, when *Der vollkommene Capellmeister* was published, use of the *loci topici* was going out of fashion. Even so Mattheson comments dismissively on Heinichen's limited application of them to music and was pleased to claim that he himself was the first to publish a fully developed musical account of the *loci*.[45] It is interesting that Mattheson considers the first species, *locus notationis*, to be the most important for musical invention. While he admits that his examples of 'the form and disposition of the notes, as musical letters', are only four of 'innumerable variations',[46] they do not resemble Hunold's fifth sub-category of the species, the poetical paragram.

Mattheson understood notes in music to be the equivalent of letters in language. But this is a limited interpretation of the phrase 'musical letters'.[47] Faber's musical letters and Bach's inventive use of b-a-c-h, for example, are a far more literal equivalent of the oratorical 'letters of a name or thing'.[48] The poetical paragram was both a form of *lusus poëticus* and one of at least five forms of *locus notationis* used for poetical invention. Although the paragram is not among the suggested techniques for a musical application of *locus notationis*, and there is no currently known seventeenth- or eighteenth-century musical treatise which recommends the use of musical alphabets as a means of invention, it is nevertheless worth considering how an eighteenth-century musician might have adapted Hunold's fifth sub-category to music.

Hunold recommends taking the letters of the main word, which is usually a name, and finding its numerical total by means of a number alphabet.[49] One or several other words applying to the person and adding up to the same total are then chosen, and the resulting number-lines used to help generate ideas for the poem. In his *Neu erfundene Composition* Faber followed the first part of Hunold's advice, by taking

---

45 Harriss, *Mattheson*, p. 286, ¶24 'that is notwithstanding the fact that no one has attempted to do this in an orderly manner nor even that each dialectic *locus* is equally as appropriate and important . . .' quoted on p. 115 above.
46 Ibid., p. 286, ¶25.   47 Ibid.   48 Ibid., see p. 105 above.
49 Hunold, *Die Allerneueste Art*, p. 545.

the numerical value of the word 'Ludovicus'. Instead of finding other words with the same numerical total, however, Faber was content to use the values of this word alone to generate ideas for his composition.[50] As the only extant eighteenth-century example of the inventive use of a number alphabet in music, Faber's *Neu erfundene Composition* is of paramount significance, but there is no reason why other composers should have chosen to use his particular technique. Faber chose the Latin milesian, whereas other composers might have chosen different alphabets. Faber incorporated his numbers into a melodic line; other composers could equally well have incorporated them into the ground-plan of a piece of music, consisting of its division into movements, metres and bars.

Many paragrammatists obviously revelled in the arithmetic of their number-lines, whose totals frequently exceed 10,000, and it is debatable whether many of their poems would have survived had not the number-lines been published too. It would be impossible to detect whether a poet had used number-lines to help him compose a poem unless either the two were published together, or marginal references were given. Use of the hypothetical musical paragram, on the other hand, although extremely difficult, would not be impossible to detect, as the numbers could be found embedded in the composition. The probability of an erroneous interpretation of the numbers, however, would still be great, even if there happened to be marginal references to the number-lines, numerical totals and the choice of number alphabet. Yet, with virtually no evidence of this kind, Friedrich Smend proposed in 1947 that Bach regularly used the natural-order alphabet in his compositions: and his evidence convinced many people.

---

[50] Walther Dehnhard, 'Kritik der Zahlensymbolischen Deutung im Werk Johann Sebastian Bachs', *Kongreßbericht Stuttgart 1985*, p. 450, and p. 105 above.

5

Links to Bach

BACH AND HIS POETS

The earliest documentary evidence we have to link Bach with the Weißenfels area is of the occasion in 1702 when he competed for an organist's position in Sangerhausen. He was offered the post on merit, but at the last minute the Duke of Saxe-Weißenfels, Johann Georg, intervened on behalf of an older and more experienced organist, Johann August Kobelius.[1] Although it is unlikely that the duke heard Bach playing the organ he would at least have realised that Bach was a gifted musician. Eleven years later Bach lodged in the castle at Weißenfels on 21 and 22 February 1713, probably to perform the newly commissioned cantata 'Was mir behagt, ist nur die muntre Jagd', BWV 208 (with text by Salomo Franck) for Duke Christian's birthday on 23 February.[2] Bach's second wife, Anna Magdalena Wilcke, whom he married in 1721, came from Weißenfels. Her parents continued to live there until their deaths in 1731 and 1746, and no doubt Bach made several unrecorded visits to their home both before and after 1721. Also, at some point before 1729 Bach was given the honorary title of *Hochfürstlicher Sachsen-Weißenfelsischer Capell-Meister*, with the qualification, *von Haus aus*,[3] which was an official acknowledgement of his connection with the court.

Although Bach sometimes had to select published libretti for his cantatas, he naturally preferred to work directly with the poet. Picander was among those with whom he collaborated regularly: their partnership began soon after Bach's arrival in Leipzig in 1723. Picander, Christian Friedrich Henrici (1700–64), studied at the University of Wittenberg and moved to Leipzig in 1720, where he worked in the post office and later

[1] David and Mendel, *The Bach Reader*, p. 428.
[2] Ibid. See also Werner Neumann and Hans-Joachim Schultze, *Bach-Dokumente*, 4 vols. (Kassel, Basel, 1963), II, 45. Document 55. Bach wrote another birthday cantata (BWV 249a) for Duke Christian with a text by Picander in 1725.
[3] *The New Grove Dictionary of Music and Musicians*, s.v. 'Weißenfels', by Horst Seeger.

became the Assessment and Liquor Tax Collector, Wine Inspector and Vizier, writing poetry in his spare time.[4] In 1732 he published the third volume of his *Ernst-, Schertzhaffte und Satyrische Gedichte*, which contains both the poetical paragram cited on pages 6–7 above and the text Bach had recently used for his *St Matthew Passion*.[5] The fact that the Bachs invited Picander and his wife Johanna Elisabeth to be godparents to their penultimate daughter, Johanna Carolina Bach, in 1737, is an indication of the personal respect and friendship that had grown up between Bach and Picander over the years.[6]

A certain Sophia Carolina Bose (1713–45), daughter of the late Georg Heinrich Bose (1682–1731), was also Johanna Carolina's godparent. The Bose and Bach families lived next door to each other in Leipzig, and were good friends from at least 1731.[7] Unfortunately the Bose family tree in Dreyhaupt's *Saal-Creyses* gives no evidence to suggest that the Leipzig Boses were any relation of the Halle Boses (or Bohses), that is, to the family of August Bohse, the possible author of *Das ABC*.[8] The name seems to have been fairly common: a Dr Caspar Bose (1704–33) was the school doctor at St Thomas'.[9] A definite link between August Bohse and Bach can be made, however, through Bohse's wife's family and through another of Bach's librettists, Salomo Franck.

August Bohse married Susanna Helene Reichhelm (1670–1732), the daughter of Paul Christian Reichhelm (1642–82), city treasurer of Halle.[10] The Reichhelms, many of whom were educated at the University of Leipzig,[11] were a distinguished Halle family. Paul Christian's cousin, August Theodor Reichhelm (1664–1732), doctor, assessor and since 1693 a member of the board of the Church of Our Lady, had been an outstanding pupil at the gymnasium where, according to Dreyhaupt, Rector Prätorius had paid particular attention both to him and to the young August Bohse.[12] As there were just three years between these two gifted pupils, it is highly likely that they knew each other. And it is

---

[4] *The New Grove Dictionary of Music and Musicians*, s.v. 'Henrici, Christian Friedrich (Picander)', by Joshua Rifkin.
[5] Neumann and Schultze, *Bach-Dokumente* I, 238. Document 170.
[6] Ibid., II, 291. Document 405.
[7] Ibid., II, 208. Document 286. See also Werner Neumann, 'Eine Leipziger Bach-Gedenkstätte. Über die Beziehungen der Familien Bach und Bose', *Bach-Jahrbuch* 56 (1970), 19–31.
[8] Johann Christian Dreyhaupt, *Pagus Neletici et Nudzici, oder ausführliche diplomatisch historische Beschreibung des zum Herzogthum Magdeburg gehörigen Saal-Creyses*, 2 vols. (Halle, 1749, 1751). Part of the Bohse family tree appears as number XIV in the genealogy section of volume II.
[9] Neumann and Schultze, *Bach-Dokumente* I, 65. Document 22.
[10] Schubert, *August Bohse*, p. 18.
[11] Dreyhaupt, *Saal-Creyses* II, 694–5.
[12] Ibid., II, 593, s.v. 'August Bohse'; and II, 694, s.v. 'August Theodor Reichhelm'.

quite probable that they remained in contact owing to the subsequent marriage of August Bohse to Susanna Helene.

In 1713 the eight-member board of the Church of Our Lady, which also included August Theodor's brother Friedrich Arnold Reichhelm (?1668–1722), graduate in law, Halle's treasurer, and since 1701 also a member of the board of the Church of Our Lady,[13] invited Bach to become their organist.[14] There was a lengthy correspondence in which the board considered Bach's conditions of acceptance, but in the end he decided not to take up the appointment. The members of the board thought none the worse of him, however, as in 1716 they invited him, together with Kuhnau from Leipzig and Rolle from Quedlinburg, to test their new organ. On 22 April 1716 Bach accepted the invitation,[15] and the joint report was written on 1 May 1716.[16] On Sunday 3 May a banquet was given to celebrate the dedication of the new organ.[17] In all, Bach seems to have spent at least the first half of December 1713 and a week in late April 1716 in Halle, during which time he must have become acquainted with the members of the board.

Bach's collaboration with Salomo Franck began as early as 1713, and over the subsequent years Franck was to write the libretti for most of Bach's Weimar cantatas.[18] Franck (1659–1725) was the chief consistorial secretary in Weimar, a post similar to that held by August Bohse twenty years earlier in Weißenfels. Franck and Bohse had known each other since their days in Jena, and Franck acknowledged their friendship publicly by writing laudatory verses in two of Bohse's books.[19] In the preface to *Letzte Liebes- und Heldengedichte* (1706) Franck wrote:

> Praiseworthy August!
> Now hast thou, upon the learnèd stage,
> played many scenes
> in sundry right galant and learnèd writings,
> wherein thy goal was use and pleasure:
> What? Is Envy yet so bold

[13] Neumann and Schultze, *Bach-Dokumente* II, 49. Document 62. See also David and Mendel, *The Bach Reader*, p. 65, and the Reichhelm family tree in Dreyhaupt, *Saal-Creyses* II, genealogy section, number CXXIII. Susanna Helene's father, Paul Christian, had been Halle's treasurer before his first cousin Friedrich Arnold.

[14] Neumann and Schultze, *Bach-Dokumente* II, 50–2. See also David and Mendel, *The Bach Reader*, pp. 65–6.

[15] Neumann and Schultze, *Bach-Dokumente* I, 25–6. Document 5.

[16] Ibid., I, 157–9. Document 85. See also David and Mendel, *The Bach Reader*, pp. 72–4.

[17] David and Mendel, *The Bach Reader*, p. 74.

[18] *The New Grove Dictionary of Music and Musicians*, s.v. 'Franck, Salomo', by Joshua Rifkin.

[19] In *Die Lebenden Todten* (Leipzig, 1698) there is a three-page poem in praise of Bohse, as well as the shorter verse from the preface of *Letzte Liebes- und Heldengedichte* (Leipzig, 1706), quoted in the text. See Elizabeth Brewer, 'Addenda to the Bibliography of Works of August Bohse', *Wolfenbütteler Barock-Nachrichten* 8 (1981), 274–86.

to wave above foreigners [the French]
the banner of supposèd victory?
Oh no! Thou art still the Muses' delight,
For Pallas honours thee with this praise:
that thou dost increase her realm like an Augustus![20]

In his biography of Bohse, Ernst Schubert gives extensive details of the links between the two men.[21] It is conceivable that Franck even asked Bach to greet Bohse's parents-in-law while he was in Halle.

Also in Halle at this time was Christian Friedrich Hunold, who spent the years from 1708 until his death in 1721 teaching at the university there. Hunold may have been present at the festivities at the Church of Our Lady in early May 1716, and renewed his acquaintance with Bach on that occasion. As Hunold was much the same age as Bach it is probable that they had met many years earlier in Arnstadt or Weißenfels, but in any case Bach would certainly have known of Hunold by 1713. And in 1718 Bach was to use Hunold's libretti for a series of cantatas, the first of which was performed on 10 December in honour of the birthday of Prince Leopold of Anhalt-Cöthen.[22] It is not unlikely that Bach read Hunold's famous *Die Allerneueste Art*.

On 21 November 1721 Bach was one of the applicants for the post of organist at St Jacob's Church in Hamburg. He was unsuccessful, and it was later discovered that the winning candidate had bribed his way into the job, which displeased Erdmann Neumeister, as Johann Mattheson records:

This took place just at Christmas time, and the eloquent chief preacher [Erdmann Neumeister], who had not concurred in the Simoniacal deliberations, expounded in the most splendid fashion the gospel of the music of the angels at the birth of Christ, in which connection the recent incident of the rejected artist [Bach] gave him quite naturally the opportunity to reveal his thoughts, and to close his sermon with something like the following pronouncement: he was firmly convinced that even if one of the angels of Bethlehem should come down from Heaven, one who played divinely and wished to become organist of St Jacobi, but had no money, he might just as well fly away again.[23]

Neumeister was clearly impressed by Bach's playing. He may have met Bach earlier in Weißenfels, and would in any case have been warmly predisposed towards Bach as a fellow Thuringian. However, this incident took place four months after Hunold's death and a long while after

---

[20] Schubert, *August Bohse*, p. 23.   [21] Ibid., pp. 73–87.

[22] *Lobet den Herren, alle seine Heerscharen* (BWV Anh. 5). See *The New Grove Dictionary of Music and Musicians*, s.v. 'Hunold, Christian Friedrich', by George J. Buelow.

[23] David and Mendel, *The Bach Reader*, pp. 81–2. See also Neumann and Schultze, *Bach-Dokumente* II, 187. Document 253.

Neumeister's heady days in Weißenfels, and his lectures mentioning the fifth sub-category of *locus notationis*.

The paragrammatist Riederer included a paragram written by his friend Johann Caspar Wetzel at the end of *Catalogus derer siebenhundert Paragrammatum Cabbalisticorum Trigonalium* (1719). Wetzel (1691–1755) studied at the Universities of Jena and Halle from 1711 to 1718, where he would have become acquainted with Hunold. It was during this time that he was gathering information for his major work *Hymnopædia* (1719), which is still consulted today for biographical details of early hymn writers. It is highly likely that Bach knew this useful and popular book written by yet another man familiar with the poetical paragram. Riederer himself wrote paragrams for several well-known people with whom Bach came into contact, such as Erdmann Neumeister and Friedrich August II, although the few he wrote for musicians were for local Nürnberg instrumentalists, such as the trumpeter Herr Wacker.[24]

Johann Riemer, the possible author of *Das ABC cum notis variorum*, knew Christian Weise, the Weißenfels professor who first listed the fifteen *loci* later used by Hunold and Mattheson. The Weißenfels musician and novelist Beer knew both Riemer and Weise, and even wrote a satire on their courtly novels.[25] Beer died in 1700 and is unlikely to have met the young Bach, but the Weißenfels court Kapellmeister J. P. Krieger definitely knew Beer, and Bach subsequently came to know Krieger.

It can therefore be shown that Bach had contact with people conversant with the poetical paragram from early in his career, although the most direct link with a paragrammatist cannot be made until the early 1720s, when he met Picander. Since it is uncertain at what point Picander discovered the poetical paragram, Bach's knowledge of the poetical paragram form does not necessarily predate Picander's publication of 1732.

BACH AND INVENTION

In April 1729 Bach became the sales representative in Leipzig for Heinichen's *General-Bass*, as did Mattheson in Hamburg, Graupner in Hessen-Darmstadt, and others in Wolfenbüttel, Berlin and Freiburg

---

[24] Johann Friedrich Riederer, *Catalogus derer Eintausend funffzig Paragrammatum Cabbalisticorum Trigonalium* (1719), number 627, 'Auf Hn. Wacker, Trompetern in Nürnberg'.

[25] *Allgemeine Deutsche Biographie*, 56 vols. (Berlin, 1875–1912), s.v. 'Beer, Johann'. Beer's political novels *Der Politische Feuermäuer-Kehrer* (Leipzig, 1682) and *Der Politische Bratenwender* (Leipzig, 1682) are satirical imitations of Weise's and Riemer's courtly novels.

(Heinichen himself looked after sales in Dresden),[26] which proves that Bach as well as Mattheson knew Heinichen's book. Interesting as the Bach–Heinichen–Mattheson links are, however, they are limited in value, because any possible influence of their treatises on Bach is restricted to his later compositions. The question of how Bach may have come across the idea of *locus notationis* in music when he was younger, therefore, remains to be explored.

The first possibility is that Bach was stimulated to apply the poetical *locus notationis* to music by Hunold's book. If Heinichen and Mattheson found their inspiration from Hunold, why not Bach? It is known that Bach was an 'amateur' poet and it has been suggested that he occasionally wrote his own libretti.[27] It would be no surprise, therefore, to discover that he was familiar with a book on poetical invention written by a famous novelist.

Another possibility is that Bach may have been stimulated to apply the *locus notationis*, and specifically the poetical paragram, to music by other composers interested in invention, such as Telemann. Georg Philipp Telemann was born in Magdeburg in 1681. His long and illustrious career as composer and Kapellmeister took him to various courts in Germany. He was in Eisenach from 1707 to 1711 concurrently with Bach's cousin, Johann Bernard Bach, who was both city organist and involved in the musical life at court; Martin Ruhnke states that Bach and Telemann must have met during this period.[28] In a letter to the biographer Forkel, Carl Philipp Emanuel Bach wrote that in their younger days, Bach and Telemann frequently spent time together, an assertion confirmed by the Bachs' invitation to Telemann to act as Carl Philipp Emanuel's godfather in 1714.[29] While at school Telemann was interested in German poetry and encouraged by his supervisor Caspar Calvoer to think through the relationship between music and mathematics.[30] In a letter to Mattheson in 1717 Telemann stated that he intended to write a treatise on musical invention. It seems that the book was never written, but it is tantalising to speculate on the forms of invention he might have included, whether he would have applied the *loci topici* to music and whether he would have discussed his ideas with Bach. Telemann also knew Neumeister, who had stood godfather to Telemann's first daughter in 1711. Their friendship dates from 1706, when Neumeister moved from Weißenfels to be Chaplain at the court of

---

26 Neumann and Schultze, *Bach-Dokumente* II, 191. Document 260.

27 Examples of poems written by Bach can be found in David and Mendel, *The Bach Reader*, pp. 97–8 and pp. 108–9.

28 *The New Grove Dictionary of Music and Musicians*, s.v. 'Telemann, Georg Philipp', by Martin Ruhnke.

29 Neumann and Schultze, *Bach-Dokumente* II, 54. Document 67.

30 *The New Grove Dictionary of Music and Musicians*, s.v. 'Telemann'.

Sorau, where Telemann was already Kapellmeister.[31] It seems that during this period Telemann set several of Neumeister's cantata texts.[32] Telemann was a key musical figure in the Leipzig–Eisenach–Weißenfels area, where the proximity of the courts allowed a regular exchange of musicians. Among the many he knew were Kuhnau, with whom from 1702 he had an ongoing misunderstanding,[33] and Mizler, whose society he joined at an unknown date between 1739 and 1742.[34]

Johann Gottfried Walther (1684–1748), Bach's first cousin, and, indirectly, Andreas Werckmeister (1645–1706) may also have discussed musical invention with Bach. Werckmeister wrote about the use of symbolic numbers for compositional invention in several of his publications (see page 5 above). There can be little doubt that Walther passed on to his younger cousin interesting ideas he received from the respected older composer and theorist.[35]

BACH AND THE NUMBER ALPHABET

Although it is not possible to prove which *lusus musici* Bach knew, one can say at the very least that he consciously used the notes b-a-c-h to express his name (see page 108 above), that he would have known of Mizler's *lusus ingenii* (Mizler was his pupil from 1731 to 1734), and that he composed puzzle-canons, as did many other eighteenth-century musicians. Bach was familiar with at least two *lusus poëtici*. He indisputably knew Picander's *Paragramma Cabbalisticum trigonale*, the example given by Smend, and the acrostic, as is shown by his puzzle canon 'F A B E Repetatur' (BWV 1078). A Latin poem of five lines is written beneath the staff, line two of which is an acrostic on the name Faber: Fidelis Amici Beatum Esse Recordari.[36]

It is extremely likely that Bach came across many different number alphabets. Techniques of *gematria* were well known in his day and the

---

[31] Ibid.

[32] Werner Menke, *Thematisches Verzeichnis der Vokalwerke von Georg Philipp Telemann*, Vol. I: *Cantaten zum Gottesdienstlischen Gebrauch*, 2nd edn (Frankfurt, 1988), pp. xi–xii, and p. 264.

[33] *The New Grove Dictionary of Music and Musicians*, s.v. 'Kuhnau, Johann', by George J. Buelow, and s.v. 'Telemann'.

[34] Ibid., s.v. 'Mizler von Kolof, Lorenz Christoph', by George J. Buelow.

[35] *The New Grove Dictionary of Music and Musicians*, s.v. 'Werckmeister, Andreas', by George J. Buelow.

[36] Quoted by Smend in *Kirchen-Kantaten* III (1947), 11. See also pp. 26–7 and pp. 35–6 of the critical commentary by Christoph Wolff to the *Neue Bach Ausgabe* VIII/1, 'Kanons, Musikalisches Opfer'. Several people have been suggested as the dedicatee for this canon, including Johann Michael Schmidt, Johann Christian Jakob Schmidt, Johann Balthasar Schmid and Benjamin Gottlieb Faber. Although Riederer's teacher happened to be called Samuel Faber, there is nothing to suggest that Bach knew him or had any reason to dedicate a puzzle-canon to him.

milesian alphabet is used in at least two books he owned: Olearius' *Biblische Erklärung* and Heunisch's *Haupt-Schlüssel über die hohe Offenbahrung*.[37] It is not known whether he owned a copy of Kuhnau's *Musicalische Vorstellung einiger Biblischer Historien* with its prefatory puzzle, but there is little doubt that Bach saw a copy and was familiar with its contents. Popular knowledge of cryptographical techniques, mathematical puzzles and practical cabbalism suggest, but cannot prove, that Bach came across alphabets used in all these forms.

There is no certainty, however, that Bach used any eighteenth-century number-alphabet forms, even assuming that he knew about them. Seventeenth- and eighteenth-century cabbalistic *gematria* was an exegetical technique which employed the Hebrew or Greek milesian alphabet to gain a deeper insight into a word or verse from the Scriptures, and which was particularly useful in persuading Jews that Jesus was the Messiah. A cabbalistic use of the milesian alphabet in music would therefore have had a very specific theological purpose. The possibility of Bach's use of magical number alphabets must be ruled out on the grounds of his reputation and character. Any active involvement in magic would have led to dismissal from his Leipzig post, and rumours of bizarre happenings in the Bach household would hardly have escaped the criticial attention of the Leipzig Council, even less the attention of students and later biographers. Nevertheless it must be admitted that had he incorporated a magic spell into a piece of music by means of one of the infinite number of variable alphabets, it would be impossible to detect! The aim of mathematical puzzles was quite different. Invariably using the natural-order alphabet, the puzzler allowed the inquisitive reader to discover a desirable piece of information, which in Kuhnau's case was the name of an influential musician. It would not only be difficult to hide a name in music as part of a complex mathematical puzzle, but well-nigh impossible to find, unless the puzzler left a written code indicating its presence. To my knowledge Bach left no such codes. Cryptographic uses of the number alphabet, on the other hand, overlap in some ways with Smend's hypothesis, particularly where the natural-order alphabet is

---

[37] Caspar Heunisch, *Haupt-Schlüssel über die hohe Offenbahrung S. Johannis* (Schleusingen, 1684; facsimile reprint edn Basel, 1981), p. 96. Heunisch cites three examples of the number 666: LUDoVICUs and sILVester seCUnDUs using Roman numerals, and the 'well-known' [*bekannt*] example of Martin Luther, which uses the Latin milesian alphabet. He neither cites his source, nor shows how the name Martin Luther comes to 666, and it is unclear whether he had in mind the interpretation by the Roman Catholic Petrus Bongus, who uses the Latin milesian alphabet $A = 1$ to $Z = 500$ (see Appendix 1) and the words *Martin Lutera* in his *De mystica numerorum significatione* (Bergamo, 1583), p. 625, which is cited in Fritz Feldman, 'Numerorum mysteria', *Archiv für Musikwissenschaft* 14 (1957), 114, or the interpretation by the German mathematician Jean Ostulfius (Jofrancus Offusius), who also uses the Latin milesian alphabet and the words *Martin Lauter*, which is cited with misprints in Tabourot, *Les Bigarrures*, I, 136; see also critical comment, ibid., II, 109.

used as part of a simple sign language, as in Schott's example.[38] It is quite plausible that Bach hid messages or names in his compositions with cryptographic intent.

The most important number-alphabet form, however, is the poetical paragram, which makes use of a wide variety of alphabets, and is also related to composition and invention. There is little doubt that Bach's most likely use of a number-alphabet form is in a self-developed musical application of the poetical paragram. Moreover Telemann, Kuhnau, Walther, J. P. Krieger and other composers influenced by the ideas of Neumeister and Hunold within the Weißenfels–Leipzig area are just as likely as Bach to have known about and applied the poetical paragram to music.

Some musicologists, including Smend, would claim that Bach used the natural-order number alphabet in his music to expand upon the theological meaning of his texts. This sounds remarkably like a form of Cabbala Speculativa, and yet, even though Bach's music may be a meditative framework within which the listener is enabled to grasp a biblical idea more fully, there is no evidence to suggest that Bach used a number alphabet as part of a cabbalistic technique. If he had made use of Cabbala Speculativa he would have done so before composing the music, to help him understand a verse or word from the Bible. And, notwithstanding the hugeness of the numerical totals resulting from the milesian alphabet used for *gematria*, he could have incorporated the numbers into the composition. Even if Bach had used the natural-order alphabet as an 'acceptable' form of Cabbala Speculativa, as Smend implies, it would seem strange that his own name appears so frequently in the number-words. The most common names in Cabbala Speculativa are those referring to God, rather than to any human being. Hörner was unusual in enciphering his own name, which he did to show that he was predestined to unlock the mystery of certain biblical prophecies, but his was an 'unacceptable' form of Cabbala Speculativa. Had Bach done likewise, then the current view of him as a pietist or orthodox Lutheran composer would have to be radically altered.

Smend's number-alphabet theory has not been totally disproved, although the historical and interpretative flaws it contains undermine its value. No longer should analysts of Bach's music quote Smend's work as a reliable source: it has to be regarded as a conjectural hypothesis. A reformulated number-alphabet theory, building on Smend's, could perhaps be proposed, but not without systematic study of the pre-compositional ground-plans and the numerical content of many scores by Bach, Telemann, Kuhnau, and others from the Weißenfels area.

---

[38] Schott, *Schola Steganographica*, p. 333. See p. 54 above.

Meanwhile the use of the natural-order alphabet in the analysis of Bach's music should be applied with caution. Three points should be kept in mind. Had Bach used a number alphabet to embed theological meaning into his music through acceptable Cabbala Speculativa, he would almost certainly have used the cabbalistic milesian number alphabet. The natural-order number alphabet, apart from its function in mathematical puzzles as a code, was used in the poetical paragram as a means of invention and had no pious or theological purpose. And, since many composers local to Weißenfels and familiar with the work of Neumeister and Hunold could have applied the poetical paragram to music, the inventive use of number alphabets should no longer be studied in the context of Bach alone.

Appendix 1

The original titles of the alphabets are in German or Latin (including Latin forms of Greek words).

† indicates that an alphabet is used or briefly described by the author, but not written out in full.

Dates after an author's name refer to works cited in 'A chronological list of sources containing a number alphabet' (see pages 169–73 below), except for those published later than 1748 which appear in the subsequent selected bibliography (see pages 173–8 below).

MILESIAN ALPHABETS

Hebrew milesian

Alep (א) = 1 Bet (ב) = 2 Gimel (ג) = 3 Dalet (ד) = 4 He (ה) = 5 Waw (ו) = 6 Zayin (ז) = 7 Het (ח) = 8 Tet (ט) = 9 Yod (י) = 10 Kap (כ) = 20 Lamed (ל) = 30 Mem (מ) = 40 Nun (נ) = 50 Samek (ס) = 60 'Ayin (ע) = 70 Pe (פ) = 80 Sade (צ) = 90 Qop (ק) = 100 Res (ר) = 200 Shin (ש) = 300 Taw (ת) = 400

Paulus (1582); Schickhard (1614), where according to the cabbalists and Masoretes ך = 500, ם = 600, ן = 700, ף = 800 and ץ = 900, although commonly תק = 500, תר = 600, תש = 700, תת = 800 and תתק = 900; Hörner (1619); †Olearius (1681); Henning (1683); †Eisenmenger (1700); †*Einmahl Eins* (1703); †Hocker (1712); †Schudt (1714); †Schmidt (1736).

Greek milesian

Alpha $(A - \alpha) = 1$ Beta $(B - \beta) = 2$ Gamma $(\Gamma - \gamma) = 3$
Delta $(\Delta - \delta) = 4$ Epsilon $(E - \varepsilon) = 5$ Zeta $(Z - \zeta) = 7$
Eta $(H - \eta) = 8$ Theta $(\Theta - \theta) = 9$ Iota $(I - \iota) = 10$
Kappa $(K - \kappa) = 20$ Lambda $(\Lambda - \lambda) = 30$ Mu $(M - \mu) = 40$
Nu $(N - \nu) = 50$ Xi $(\Xi - \xi) = 60$ Omicron $(O - o) = 70$
Pi $(\Pi - \pi) = 80$ Rho $(P - \varrho) = 100$ Sigma $(\Sigma - \sigma) = 200$
Tau $(T - \tau) = 300$ Upsilon $(Y - \upsilon) = 400$ Phi $(\Phi - \varphi) = 500$
Chi $(X - \chi) = 600$ Psi $(X - \psi) = 700$ Omega $(\Omega - \omega) = 800$

Tabourot (1583); Hörner (1619); Schwenter (1636); †Puteanus (1643); †Kircher (1665); †Olearius (1681); Henning (1683), where G = 90, and Ɔ = 900; †*Einmahl Eins* (1703); †Schmidt (1736); Friesenhahn (1935), where G = 90, and Ɔ = 900.

Latin milesian

A = 1 B = 2 C = 3 D = 4 E = 5 F = 6 G = 7 H = 8 I = 9 K = 10
L = 20 M = 30 N = 40 O = 50 P = 60 Q = 70 R = 80 S = 90
T = 100 U = 200 X = 300 Y = 400 Z = 500

Tabourot (1583); †Bongus (1583); Harsdörffer (1649), where P = 60, R = 70, S = 80, T = 90, U = 100 and Z = 1000; Kircher (1665); †Paschasius (1668); †Heunisch (1684); †*Einmahl Eins* (1703); †Faber (1729).

Latin milesian: variant 1

A = 1 B = 2 C = 3 D = 4 E = 5 F = 6 G = 7 H = 8 I = 9 K = 10
L = 20 M = 30 N = 40 O = 50 P = 60 Q = 70 R = 80 S = 90
T = 100 U = 200 W = 300 X = 400 Y = 500 Z = 600

Harsdörffer (1651), where Z = 600, Æ = 700, Œ = 800 and V = 900; Henning (1683); Männling (1704); Hunold (1707), where it is entitled 'Alphabetum Cabbalisticum naturale'; †Mittag (1737).

Latin milesian: variant 2

A = 1 B = 2 C = 3 D = 4 E = 5 F = 6 G = 7 H = 8 I = 9 K = 10
L = 20 M = 30 N = 40 O = 50 P = 60 Q = 70 R = 80 S = 90
T = 100 U = 110 W = 120 X = 130 Y = 140 Z = 150

Henning (1683).

Latin milesian: variant 3

A = 1   B = 2   C = 3   D = 4   E = 5   F = 6   G = 7   H = 8   I = 9   K = 10
L = 20   M = 30   N = 40   O = 50   P = 60   Q = 70   R = 80   S = 90
T = 100   U = 110   V = 120   W = 130   X = 140   Y = 150   Z = 160

Tolstoy (1865–9).

Latin milesian: variant 4

A = 1   B = 2   C = 3   D = 4   E = 5   F = 6   G = 7   H = 8   I = 9   K = 10
L = 11   M = 12   N = 40   O = 50   P = 60   Q = 70   R = 80   S = 90
T = 100   U = 110   W = 120   X = 130   Y = 140   Z = 150

Hunold (1707), where it is entitled 'Alphabetum Cabbalisticum vulgare'.

Latin milesian: variant 5

A = 1   B = 2   C = 3   D = 4   E = 5   F = 6   G = 7   H = 8   I = 9   K = 10
L = 20   M = 30   N = 40   O = 50   P = 60   Q = 70   R = 80   S = 90
T = 100   U = 1000   V = 2000   X = 3000   Y = 4000   Z = 5000

Riemer (1681).

Latin milesian: variant 6

B = 1   C = 2   D = 3   F = 4   G = 5   H = 6   J = 7   K = 8   L = 9   M = 10
N = 20   P = 30   Q = 40   R = 50   S = 60   T = 70   V = 80   X = 90
Z = 100   W = 160   (2 × 80)

Harsdörffer (1648).

THE NATURAL-ORDER ALPHABETS

Latin natural-order

A = 1   B = 2   C = 3   D = 4   E = 5   F = 6   G = 7   H = 8   I = 9   K = 10
L = 11   M = 12   N = 13   O = 14   P = 15   Q = 16   R = 17   S = 18
T = 19   U = 20   X = 21   Y = 22   Z = 23

Stiefel (1532); Schultz (1600); Hörner (1619), with the addition of J = 24 and ß = 25; †von Frankenberg (1639); Harsdörffer in Schottel (1663); *Einmahl Eins* (1703).

Latin natural-order: variant 1

A = 1 B = 2 C = 3 D = 4 E = 5 F = 6 G = 7 H = 8 I = 9 K = 10
L = 11 M = 12 N = 13 O = 14 P = 15 Q = 16 R = 17 S = 18
T = 19 U = 20 W = 21 X = 22 Y = 23 Z = 24

Rudolff (1525); Jacob (1565); Schwenter (1636); Harsdörffer (1651), where Z = 24, Æ = 25, Œ = 26 and V = 27; Harsdörffer (*Poetischer Trichter*, 1653); Schott (1665); Schott (1667), where V = 20, X = 21, Y = 22, Z = 23 and W = 24; Henning (1683); *ABC* (1695); †Kuhnau (1700); †*Einmahl Eins* (1703); Männling (1704); Hunold (1707), where it is entitled 'Cabbala naturalissima'; †*Unschuldige Nachrichten* (1717); †Colonius (1748); †Durning-Lawrence (1910); Smend (*Luther und Bach*, 1947; *Kirchen-Kantaten* III, 1947).

Latin natural-order: variant 2

A = 1 B = 2 C = 3 D = 4 E = 5 F = 6 G = 7 H = 8 I = 9 K = 10
L = 11 M = 12 N = 13 P = 14 Q = 15 R = 16 S = 17 T = 18
U = 19 W = 20 X = 21 Y = 22 Z = 23 O = 0

Schultz (1600); Reimmann (1710).

Latin natural-order: variant 3

A = 1 B = 2 C = 3 D = 4 E = 5 F = 6 G = 7 H = 8 I = 9 L = 10
M = 11 N = 12 O = 13 P = 14 Q = 15 R = 16 S = 17 T = 18
U = 19 X = 20 Y = 21 Z = 22

Selenus (1624).

Greek natural-order

Alpha (A – α) = 1 Beta (B – β) = 2 Gamma (Γ – γ) = 3
Delta (Δ – δ) = 4 Epsilon (E – ε) = 5 Zeta (Z – ζ) = 6
Eta (H – η) = 7 Theta (Θ – θ) = 8 Iota (I – ι) = 9
Kappa (K – κ) = 10 Lambda (Λ – λ) = 11 Mu (M – μ) = 12
Nu (N – ν) = 13 Xi (Ξ – ξ) = 14 Omicron (O – o) = 15
Pi (Π – π) = 16 Rho (P – ϱ) = 17 Sigma (Σ – σ) = 18
Tau (T – τ) = 19 Upsilon (Y – υ) = 20 Phi (Φ – φ) = 21
Chi (X – χ) = 22 Psi (X – ψ) = 23 Omega (Ω – ω) = 24

Friesenhahn (1935); Friesenhahn (1938).

ALPHABETS RELATED TO THE TRIGONAL

Trigonal

A = 1 B = 3 C = 6 D = 10 E = 15 F = 21 G = 28 H = 36 I = 45
K = 55 L = 66 M = 78 N = 91 O = 105 P = 120 Q = 136 R = 153
S = 171 T = 190 U = 210 X = 231 Y = 253 Z = 276

Stiefel (1532); Stiefel (1553); Hörner (1619), where J = 300 and ß = 325; †Poll, quoted in Schwartzbach (1636); Schwartzbach (1636).

Trigonal: variant 1

A = 1 B = 3 C = 6 D = 10 E = 15 F = 21 G = 28 H = 36 I = 45
K = 55 L = 66 M = 78 N = 91 O = 105 P = 120 Q = 136 R = 153
S = 171 T = 190 U = 210 W = 231 X = 253 Y = 276 Z = 300

†Schwartzbach (1630); Schwartzbach (1636); Harsdörffer (1651), where Z = 300, Æ = 325, Œ = 351 and V = 378; Henning (1683); *ABC* (1695); Männling (1704); Hunold (1707); Riederer (1715, 1719, etc.); †*Neue Zeitungen von gelehrten Sachen* (1717); Picander (1732).

Pyramidical (three-sided)

A = 1 B = 4 C = 10 D = 20 E = 35 F = 56 G = 84 H = 120
I = 165 K = 220 L = 286 M = 364 N = 455 O = 560 P = 680
Q = 816 R = 969 S = 1140 T = 1330 U = 1540 W = 1771 X = 2024
Y = 2300 Z = 2600 Æ = 2915 Œ = 3276 V = 3654

Harsdörffer (1651).

Quadrangular or zensica

A = 1 B = 4 C = 9 D = 16 E = 25 F = 36 G = 49 H = 64 I = 81
K = 100 L = 121 M = 144 N = 169 O = 196 P = 225 Q = 256
R = 289 S = 324 T = 361 U = 400 W = 441 X = 484 Y = 529
Z = 576

†Schwartzbach (1630); Schwartzbach (1636); Harsdörffer (1651), where Z = 576, Æ = 625, Œ = 676 and V = 729; Henning (1683); *ABC* (1695); Männling (1704); Hunold (1707).

Pyramidical (four-sided)

A = 1 B = 5 C = 14 D = 30 E = 55 F = 91 G = 140 H = 204
I = 285 K = 385 L = 506 M = 650 N = 819 O = 1015 P = 1240
Q = 1496 R = 1785 S = 2109 T = 2470 U = 2870 W = 3311
X = 3795 Y = 4324 Z = 4900 Æ = 5525 Œ = 6201 V = 6930

Harsdörffer (1651).

Quinquangular or pentagonal

A = 1 B = 5 C = 12 D = 22 E = 35 F = 51 G = 70 H = 9 I = 117
K = 145 L = 176 M = 210 N = 247 O = 287 P = 330 Q = 376
R = 425 S = 477 T = 532 U = 590 W = 651 X = 715 Y = 782
Z = 852

†Schwartzbach (1630); Schwartzbach (1636); Henning (1683); *ABC*
(1695); Männling (1704), where it is entitled 'pentangular'.

Sexangular or hexagonal

A = 1 B = 6 C = 15 D = 28 E = 45 F = 66 G = 91 H = 120
I = 153 K = 190 L = 231 M = 276 N = 325 O = 378 P = 435
Q = 496 R = 561 S = 630 T = 703 U = 780 W = 861 X = 946
Y = 1035 Z = 1128

†Schwartzbach (1630); Schwartzbach (1636); Henning (1683); *ABC*
(1695); Männling (1704), where it is entitled 'hexangular'.

Septangular or heptagonal

A = 1 B = 7 C = 18 D = 34 E = 55 F = 81 G = 112 H = 148
I = 189 K = 235 L = 286 M = 342 N = 403 O = 469 P = 540
Q = 616 R = 697 S = 783 T = 874 U = 970 W = 1071 X = 1177
Y = 1288 Z = 1404

†Schwartzbach (1630); Schwartzbach (1636); Henning (1683); ABC
(1695); Männling (1704), where it is entitled 'heptangular'.

Octangular or octagonal

A = 1 B = 8 C = 21 D = 40 E = 65 F = 96 G = 133 H = 176
I = 225 K = 280 L = 341 M = 408 N = 481 O = 560 P = 645
Q = 736 R = 833 S = 936 T = 1045 U = 1160 W = 1281 X = 1408
Y = 1541 Z = 1680
†Schwartzbach (1630); Schwartzbach (1636); Henning (1683); *ABC*
(1695); Männling (1704).

Nonangular 1 or enneagonal

A = 1 B = 9 C = 24 D = 46 E = 75 F = 111 G = 154 H = 204
I = 261 K = 325 L = 396 M = 474 N = 559 O = 651 P = 750
Q = 856 R = 969 S = 1089 T = 1216 U = 1350 W = 1491 X = 1639
Y = 1794 Z = 1956

†Schwartzbach (1630); Schwartzbach (1636); Henning (1683); *ABC*
(1695); Männling (1704).

Decagonal

A = 1 B = 10 C = 27 D = 52 E = 85 F = 126 G = 175 H = 232
I = 297 K = 370 L = 451 M = 540 N = 637 O = 742 P = 855
Q = 976 R = 1105 S = 1242 T = 1387 U = 1540 W = 1701
X = 1870 Y = 2047 Z = 2232

Henning (1683); *ABC* (1695); Männling (1704).

Undecangular

A = 1 B = 11 C = 30 D = 58 E = 95 F = 141 G = 196 H = 260
I = 333 K = 415 L = 506 M = 606 N = 715 O = 833 P = 960
Q = 1096 R = 1241 S = 1395 T = 1558 U = 1736 W = 1911
X = 2101 Y = 2300 Z = 2508

†Schwartzbach (1630).

Duodecangular

A = 1 B = 12 C = 33 D = 64 E = 105 F = 156 G = 217 H = 288
I = 369 K = 460 L = 561 M = 672 N = 793 O = 924 P = 1065
Q = 1216 R = 1377 S = 1548 T = 1729 U = 1920 W = 2121
X = 2332 Y = 2553 Z = 2784

†Schwartzbach (1630).

Tredecangular

A = 1   B = 13   C = 36   D = 70   E = 115   F = 171   G = 238   H = 316
I = 405   K = 505   L = 616   M = 738   N = 871   O = 1015   P = 1170
Q = 1336   R = 1513   S = 1701   T = 1900   U = 2110   W = 2331
X = 2563   Y = 2806   Z = 3060

†Schwartzbach (1630).

Quatuordecangular

A = 1   B = 14   C = 39   D = 76   E = 125   F = 186   G = 259   H = 344
I = 441   K = 550   L = 671   M = 804   N = 949   O = 1106   P = 1275
Q = 1456   R = 1649   S = 1854   T = 2071   U = 2300   W = 2541
X = 2794   Y = 3059   Z = 3336

†Schwartzbach (1630).

Quindecangular

A = 1   B = 15   C = 42   D = 82   E = 135   F = 201   G = 280   H = 372
I = 477   K = 595   L = 726   M = 870   N = 1027   O = 1197   P = 1380
Q = 1576   R = 1785   S = 2007   T = 2242   U = 2490   W = 2751
X = 3025   Y = 3312   Z = 3612

†Schwartzbach (1630).

ALPHABETS BUILT ON OTHER ARITHMETICAL PROGRESSIONS

Pronica

A = 1   B = 6   C = 12   D = 20   E = 30   F = 42   G = 56   H = 72   I = 90
K = 110   L = 132   M = 156   N = 182   O = 210   P = 240   Q = 272
R = 306   S = 342   T = 380   U = 420   W = 462   X = 506   Y = 552
Z = 600

Theoretically A should equal 2 and not 1. †Schwartzbach (1630).

Circular

A = 1 B = 6 C = 12 D = 18 E = 24 F = 30 G = 36 H = 42 I = 48
K = 54 L = 60 M = 66 N = 72 O = 78 P = 84 Q = 90 R = 96
S = 102 T = 108 U = 114 W = 120 X = 126 Y = 132 Z = 138
Æ = 144 Œ = 150 V = 156

Harsdörffer (1651).

Cubica

A = 1 B = 8 C = 27 D = 64 E = 125 F = 216 G = 343 H = 512
I = 729 K = 1000 L = 1331 M = 1728 N = 2197 O = 2744 P = 3375
Q = 4096 R = 4913 S = 5832 T = 6859 U = 8000 W = 8631
X = 10648 Y = 12187 Z = 13824

†Schwartzbach (1630); Harsdörffer (1651), where Z = 13824, Æ = 15625,
Œ = 17576 and V = 20683.

The transliterations of Hebrew and Greek alphabets have been taken
from John J. Davis, *Biblical Numerology* (Grand Rapids, Mich., 1968),
p. 39 and p. 43 respectively.

Appendix 2

FRIEDRICH SMEND'S NUMBER-SYMBOLISM FILE

Smend's books and papers appear at irregular intervals in the catalogue of the Music Department of the Staatsbibliothek, Preußischer Kultur-besitz, West Berlin, under the general call mark: N. Mus. Nachl. 60. Much of the collection is still uncatalogued, and it was only with the kind permission of Dr Rudolf Elvers and Dr Günther Klein that I was allowed to read the as yet uncatalogued number-symbolism file in November 1985.

The brown envelope file is in its original form. Smend had added nothing since the 1950s. Inside is a series of envelopes, card folders and loose notes dividing the contents into general subject areas, mostly concerned with number symbolism.

The contents fall into twelve distinct sections:

(1) the Smend–Jansen correspondence 1940–3, which is detailed in Appendix 3;

(2) an orange card folder entitled 'Zahlensymbolik bei Bach. (Henk Dieben.) Speziell für die Choralkanons über Vom Himmel hoch', and signed Smend, 1943. This includes:
   (a) a handwritten copy of Picander's *Paragramma Cabbalisticum trigonale*;
   (b) a solution of the trigonal alphabet;
   (c) a sheet headed 'Henk Dieben';
   (d) many figures for the chorale canons;

(3) a set of miscellaneous unbound and undated notes on number symbolism, several pages of which are written on the back of old maps (Smend was working in the map department of the Deutsche Staatsbibliothek during the war):
   (a) 8 sides of handwritten notes (paginated) entitled 'Die Zahlen-symbolik bei Joh. Seb. Bach';

(b) 6 sides of handwritten notes (unpaginated) with several headings, the first of which is 'Gesamt Disposition';

(c) 5 sides of handwritten notes (unpaginated) on a Bach violin sonata;

(d) several sheets of handwritten numbers referring to the *St Matthew Passion*;

(e) a copy of Jansen's article 'Bach und das Jahr', *Allgemeine Musikzeitung* 70 (1943), 1;

(4) an envelope addressed to the Maps department of the Deutsche Staatsbibliothek, dated 18 January 1940, containing working notes on:

(a) 'Choral mit Zahlensymbolik';

(b) the 1931 and 1932 *Bach-Jahrbuch* articles by Hermann Sirp: 'Die Thematik der Kirchenkantaten J. S. Bach in ihren Beziehungen zum protestantischen Kirchenlied';

(c) 'Aufbau-Formen';

(d) 'Instrumental-Formen, die in kirchliche Vokal-Musik eindringen';

(5) an envelope containing:

(a) *Kirchen-Kantaten* III and

(b) *Kirchen-Kantaten* IV, both in the original 1947 booklet form;

(c) some handwritten notes for a lecture delivered in Hamburg on 28 June 1950 and in Erlangen on 14 December 1950;

(d) a typed top- and carbon-copy of Rudolf Steglich's remarks on a number-symbolic interpretation of a theme with twenty notes, from *Wege zu Bach* (Regensburg, 1950), pp. 84–6;

(6) several letters of 1940 and 1941:

(a) to an unnamed professor, dated Berlin, 9 February 1940;

(b) correspondence with Walter Blankenburg dated:
    Vaake, 13 February 1941   (Blankenburg to Smend)
    Berlin, 24 August 1941   (Smend to Blankenburg)
    Berlin, 24 October 1941   (Blankenburg to Smend)
    Berlin, 26 October 1941   (Smend to Blankenburg);

(c) to Dr Elisabeth Hesse, dated Berlin, 24 October 1941;

(7) a set of three paper-bound files:

(a) *Lese-Früchte*;

(b) *Chorale-Kantaten* – (Große Eingangschoräle);

(c) *Gesetz und Evangelium* – (Chorale-Zitate (Wortlos) in die Werke-Mitte);

(8) a brown card folder entitled 'Zu Bachs Weihnachts Oratorium: Smend 1942, 43';

(9) copies of seven lectures and papers given by other people, only one of which is dated:

'Von rechter Kirchenordnung: Eine Denkschrift'. Fehrbellin, den 4. Juli 1945. Lic. Dr Harder;

'Ikone, Wort und Sakrament';

'Handreichung für die Besprechung der dreizehn Sätze über Auftrag und Dienst in der Kirche';

'Engel, Götter, Geist und Geister';

three other unnamed and undated lectures;

(10) miscellaneous documents:

    (a) a programme for a concert on Saturday 18 April 1942;

    (b) some notes on Psalm 90 copied from an unnamed publication;

    (c) a slip of manuscript paper with rough workings of a three-part canon;

(11) two copies of the Kirchliche Hochschule, Berlin lecture timetable for the winter semester 1947–8;

(12) miscellaneous personal correspondence.

Appendix 3

THE SMEND–JANSEN CORRESPONDENCE

The extant letters between Friedrich Smend and Martin Jansen are held in two separate collections: those in Smend's possession on his death in 1980 were deposited in the Music Department of the Staatsbibliothek, Preußischer Kulturbesitz (West Berlin) as part of his Nachlaß (call mark: N. Mus. Nachl. 60); those in Jansen's possession passed to his daughter, who then donated them early in 1988 to the Music Department of the Deutsche Staatsbibliothek (East Berlin) (call mark: Schriftwechsel Smend-Jansen 1931, 1943).

The letters in Smend's Nachlaß are in his number-symbolism file together with many other documents (see Appendix 2). The first nine letters were bound together by a piece of cream-coloured paper, on the cover of which Smend had written the words *Gesetz und Evangelium – Verschiedene* (Korrespondenz). There seems to be no obvious reason why these first nine letters were separated from the remaining correspondence. It is unlikely that the contents of the file had been touched since Smend last closed it: the documents were in no particular order and had not been catalogued.

The letters in Jansen's Nachlaß had been hole-punched some years previously, possibly by Jansen himself, and recently put into a new folder in chronological order. Although the call mark refers to a letter of 1931, the document of 1931 is not in fact a letter, but a carbon copy of a short typewritten review by Smend, dated 24 November 1931, of a performance by the Magdeburg Madrigal Choir under Martin Jansen of Bach's *St Matthew Passion*.

The following index is ordered chronologically according to the date on the letter. I have indicated the nature of the script (whether hand- or typewritten), the letter (whether carbon copy or original), the paper size (whether A4, A5 or a postcard), and the letter length. Where there is documentary evidence of a missing letter, this is indicated. The seventeen letters held in the Jansen Nachlaß in East Berlin are marked E, and the thirty-one held in West Berlin are marked W. The letters of 11 February 1943 and 20 June 1943 are common to both collections.

[At least one letter from Jansen to Smend (dated 1 May 1939) is missing: see Smend's letter of 17 February 1940.]

W	Berlin	17 February 1940	Smend to Jansen
	Carbon copy	A4 Typescript	2 sides.
W	Magdeburg	20 February 1940	Jansen to Smend
	Original	Postcard	1 side.

[At least one letter from Smend to Jansen is missing: see Jansen's letter of 5 March 1940.]

W	Magdeburg	5 March 1940	Jansen to Smend
	Original	A4 Typescript	5 sides.
W	Berlin	8 March 1940	Smend to Jansen
	Carbon copy	A4 Typescript	4 sides.
W	Magdeburg	21 March 1940	Jansen to Smend
	Original	A4 Typescript	2 sides.
W	Berlin	22 March 1940	Smend to Jansen
	Carbon copy	A4 Typescript	5 sides.

[The letters of 21 and 22 crossed in the post: see Smend's letter of 25 March 1940.]

W	Berlin	25 March 1940	Smend to Jansen
	Carbon copy	A4 Typescript	2 sides.
W	Magdeburg	7 April 1940	Jansen to Smend
	Original	A4 Typescript	4 sides.
W	Berlin	14 April 1940	Smend to Jansen
	Carbon copy	A4 Typescript	5 sides.

[At least one letter between April 1940 and October 1941 is missing: see Jansen's letter of 30 October 1941.]

W	Magdeburg	30 October 1941	Jansen to Smend
	Original	A4 Typescript	2 sides.
W	Berlin	3 November 1941	Smend to Jansen
	Carbon copy	A4 Typescript	4 sides.

[At least one letter is missing from Jansen to Smend: see Jansen's letter of 5 January.]

W	Magdeburg	5 January 1942	Jansen to Smend
	Original	A4 Typescript	2 sides.

(This is a list of important figures in the *St Matthew Passion*, and was sent with the handwritten letter of 6 January.)

W	Magdeburg	6 January 1942	Jansen to Smend
	Original	A5 Handwritten	2 sides.

W	[Berlin]	13 January 1942	Smend to Jansen
	Original	A5 Handwritten	6 sides.

(This contains a list of important figures and a systematisation of Bach's use of symbolic numbers in the *B minor Mass*, prepared by Smend during his 1939 summer holiday.)

W	Magdeburg	18 January 1942	Jansen to Smend
	Original	A4 Typescript	2 sides.
W	Berlin	21 January 1942	Smend to Jansen
	Carbon copy	A4 Typescript	10 sides.
W	Magdeburg	1 February 1942	Jansen to Smend
	Original	A4 Typescript	3 sides.
W	Berlin	7 February 1942	Smend to Jansen
	Carbon copy	A4 Typescript	6 sides.
W	Magdeburg	22 March 1942	Jansen to Smend
	Original	A5 Handwritten postcard	2 sides.
W	Magdeburg	29 March 1942	Jansen to Smend
	Original	A5 Handwritten	2 sides.

[At least one letter from Smend to Jansen is missing: see Jansen's letter of 10 May 1942.]

W	Magdeburg	10 May 1942	Jansen to Smend
	Original	A4 and A5 Typescript	4 sides.
W	Berlin	14 May 1942	Smend to Jansen
	Carbon copy	A4 Typescript	1 side.
W	Magdeburg	23 May 1942	Jansen to Smend
	Original	A5 card Handwritten	2 sides.
W	Berlin	30 May 1942	Smend to Jansen
	Carbon copy	A4 Typescript	2 sides.
W	Magdeburg	6 June 1942	Jansen to Smend
	Original	A4 Typescript	4 sides.

[At least one letter from Smend to Jansen (dated 1 May 1939) is missing, in which 'Der große Fragenkomplex "Die Religion J. S. Bachs"' and the *Christmas Oratorio* were discussed: see Jansen's letters of 23 December 1942 and 28 January 1943.]

W	Magdeburg	23 December 1942	Jansen to Smend
	Original	A4 Typescript	1 side.

[At least one letter from Smend to Jansen is missing: see Jansen's letter of 28 January.]

W	Magdeburg	28 January 1943	Jansen to Smend
	Original	A4 Typescript	2 sides.
E	[Berlin]	1 February 1943	Smend to Jansen
	Original	A4 Typescript	3 sides.
W	Magdeburg	11 February 1943	Jansen to Smend
	Original	A4 Typescript	2 sides.

E	Carbon copy of 11 February 1943		
E	[Berlin]	22 & 23 March 1943	Smend to Jansen
	Original	A5 Handwritten	3 sides.
W	Magdeburg	25 March 1943	Jansen to Smend
	Original	A5 Handwritten	4 sides.
E	[Berlin]	21 April 1943	Smend to Jansen
	Original	A5 Handwritten	2 sides.
E	[Magdeburg]	23 April 1943	Jansen to Smend
	Carbon copy	A4 Typescript	2 sides.
E	Berlin	25 April 1943	Smend to Jansen
	Original	A4 Typescript	3 sides.
E	[Magdeburg]	17 May 1943	Jansen to Smend
	Carbon copy	A4 Typescript	2 sides.
E	Berlin	22 May 1943	Smend to Jansen
	Original	A4 Typescript	4 sides.
E	[Magdeburg]	29 May 1943	Jansen to Smend
	Carbon copy	A4 Typescript	1 side.
E	Berlin	5 June 1943	Smend to Jansen
	Original	A4 Typescript	3 sides.
W	[Magdeburg]	8 June 1943	Jansen to Smend
	Original	A5 Handwritten postcard	1 side.
W	Magdeburg	20 June 1943	Jansen to Smend
	Original	A4 Typescript	2 sides.
E	Carbon copy of 20 June 1943		
E	Ratzenburg	20 August 1943	Smend to Jansen
	Original	A4 Handwritten	2 sides.
E	Berlin	1 November 1943	Smend to Jansen
	Original	A4 Typescript	2 sides.

[At least one letter from Jansen to Smend (dated 1 December 1943) is missing: see Smend's postcard of 3 December.]

E	[Berlin]	3 December 1943	Smend to Jansen
	Original	A5 Handwritten postcard	1 side.
E	[Berlin]	3 December 1943	Smend to Jansen
	Original	A4 Handwritten	4 sides.
E	Magdeburg	9 December 1943	Jansen to Smend
	Carbon copy	A4 Typescript	2 sides.
E	[Berlin]	13 December 1943	Smend to Jansen
	Original	A4 Handwritten	4 sides.

[There is no extant correspondence between the two men after December 1943. Jansen died in September 1944.]

Appendix 4

SOLUTIONS AND TRANSLATIONS

Note. The paragrammatists often used unusual and inconsistent spelling in their paragrams as well as making occasional mistakes in their arithmetic. Printers, perhaps trying to correct what they saw as errors, sometimes introduced further mistakes.

Picander's *Paragramma Cabbalisticum trigonale* (pages 6–7)

Translation:
Column 1:
On the occasion of the Daum and Thym wedding, an Old German and close friend desired to convey his sincere wishes to the bridegroom and bride for true love, true constancy, true fidelity, abundant fortune and all pleasurable good, besides the following from Holy Scripture:

Column 2 (Sir. 26:13–15):
A kindly wife delights her husband and her good sense refreshes his heart. A wife who can be silent is a gift of God. A well-disciplined wife is beyond price. There is nothing so lovely on earth as a modest wife and nothing so precious as a chaste wife.

Stiefel's *Væ tibi Papa, væ tibi* (page 61)

Solution:

V	a	e	t	i	b	i	P	a	p	a,
210	+1	+15	190	+45	+3	+45	120	+1	+120	+1
	226	+		283	+			242		

v	a	e	t	i	b	i
210	+1	+15	190	+45	+3	+45
+	226	+		283		

$$= 1260$$

Translation:
Alas for you, Father, alas for you.

Stiefel's *2300* (pp. 61–2)

Stiefel's poem on the number 2300 from Daniel 8:14 has twenty-two lines each of which adds up to 2300. 2300 is also the sum of all twenty-three letters of Stiefel's trigonal alphabet (see p. 134):

$$1 + 3 + 6 + 10 + 15 + 21 + 28 + 36 + 45 + 55 + 66 + 78 + 91 + 105 + 120 + 136 + 153 + 171 + 190 + 210 + 231 + 253 + 276$$

Solution:

I	s	t	a	e	s	t	s	u	m	m	a

$$45 + 171 + 190 + 1 \qquad 15 + 171 + 190 \qquad 171 + 210 + 78 + 78 + 1$$
$$407 \qquad + \qquad 376 \qquad + \qquad 538$$

s	u	m	m	a	r	u	m

$$171 + 210 + 78 + 78 + 1 + 153 + 210 + 78$$
$$+ \qquad\qquad 979 \qquad\qquad\qquad\qquad = 2300$$

S	u	m	m	a	s	u	m	m	a	r	u	m

$$171 + 210 + 78 + 78 + 1 \qquad 171 + 210 + 78 + 78 + 1 + 153 + 210 + 78$$
$$538 \qquad + \qquad\qquad 979$$

e	x	A	l	h	p	a	b	e	t	o	[sic!]

$$15 + 231 \qquad 1 + 66 + 36 + 120 + 1 + 3 + 15 + 190 + 105$$
$$+ \; 246 \; + \qquad\qquad 537 \qquad\qquad\qquad = 2300$$

E	x	A	l	p	h	a	b	e	t	o

$$15 + 231 \qquad 1 + 66 + 120 + 36 + 1 + 3 + 15 + 190 + 105$$
$$246 \qquad + \qquad\qquad 537$$

l	a	t	i	n	o	f	i	t

$$66 + 1 + 190 + 45 + 91 + 105 \qquad 21 + 45 + 190$$
$$+ \qquad\qquad 498 \qquad + \qquad 256$$

N	u	m	e	r	i	s

$$91 + 210 + 78 + 15 + 153 + 45 + 171$$
$$+ \qquad\qquad 763 \qquad\qquad\qquad = 2300$$

A	t	q	u	e	e	s	t

$$1 + 190 + 136 + 210 + 15 \qquad 15 + 171 + 190$$
$$552 \qquad + \qquad 376$$

N	u	m	e	r	u	s

$$91 + 210 + 78 + 15 + 153 + 210 + 171$$
$$+ \qquad\qquad 928$$

D   a   n   i   e   l   i   s
10 + 1 + 91 + 45 + 15 + 66 + 45 + 171
+   444   = 2300

E   c   c   e   **S**   u   m   m   a   s   a   c   r   a
15 + 6 + 6 + 15   171 + 210 + 78 + 78 + 1   171 + 1 + 6 + 153 + 1
   42   +   538   +   332

t   o   t   i   u   s
190 + 105 + 190 + 45 + 210 + 171
+   911

A   l   p   h   a   b   e   t   i
1 + 66 + 120 + 36 + 1 + 3 + 15 + 190 + 45
+   477   = 2300

S   u   m   m   a   a   u   d   i   t   a   a
171 + 210 + 78 + 78 + 1   1 + 210 + 10 + 45 + 190 + 1   1
    538   +   457   + 1

D   a   n   i   e   l   e   **D**   a   n   i   e   l   i   s
10 + 1 + 91 + 45 + 15 + 66 + 15   10 + 1 + 91 + 45 + 15 + 66 + 45 + 171
+   243   +   444

o   c   t   a   u   o
105 + 6 + 190 + 1 + 210 + 105
+   617   = 2300

E t   e   s   t   s   u   m   m   a
15 + 190   15 + 171 + 190   171 + 210 + 78 + 78 + 1
  205   +   376   +   538

s   a   c   r   a   d   e   c   o   e   l   o
171 + 1 + 6 + 153 + 1   10 + 15   6 + 105 + 15 + 66 + 105
+   332   + 25   +   297

s   i   g   n   a   t   a
171 + 45 + 28 + 91 + 1 + 190 + 1
+   527   = 2300

E   c   c   e   **N**   u   m   e   r   u   s
15 + 6 + 6 + 15   91 + 210 + 78 + 15 + 153 + 210 + 171
  42   +   928

T   r   i   a   n   g   u   l   o   r   u   m
190 + 153 + 45 + 1 + 91 + 28 + 210 + 66 + 105 + 153 + 210 + 78
+   1330   = 2300

T   r   i   a   n   g   u   l   i   s
190 + 153 + 45 + 1 + 91 + 28 + 210 + 66 + 45 + 171
                    1000

c   o   m   p   l   e   t
6 + 105 + 78 + 120 + 66 + 15 + 190
+   580

A   l   p   h   a   b   e   t   u   m
1 + 66 + 120 + 36 + 1 + 3 + 15 + 190 + 210 + 78
+   720   = 2300

E   t   e   c   c   f   i   t
15 + 190   15 + 6 + 6 + 15   21 + 45 + 190
  205   +   42   +   256

p   y   r   a   m   i   s
120 + 253 + 153 + 1 + 78 + 45 + 171
+   821

t   r   i   a   n   g   u   l   a   t   a
190 + 153 + 45 + 1 + 91 + 28 + 210 + 66 + 1 + 190 + 1
+   976   = 2300

E   c   c   e   h   i   c   N   u   m   e   r   u   s
15 + 6 + 6 + 15   36 + 45 + 6   91 + 210 + 78 + 15 + 153 + 210 + 17
     42   +   87   +   928

e   s   t   h   o   c
15 + 171 + 190   36 + 105 + 6
+   376   +   147

A   l   p   h   a   b   e   t   u   m
1 + 66 + 120 + 36 + 1 + 3 + 15 + 190 + 210 + 78
+   720   = 2300

E   c   c   e   h   o   c   u   i   g   i   n   t   i
15 + 6 + 6 + 15   36 + 105 + 6   210 + 45 + 28 + 45 + 91 + 190 + 45
     42   +   147   +   654

t   r   i   b   u   s   l   i   t   e   r   i   s
190 + 153 + 45 + 3 + 210 + 171   66 + 45 + 190 + 15 + 153 + 45 + 171
+   772   +   685   = 2300

E   t   e   x   h   o   c   n   u   m   e   r   o
15 + 190   15 + 231   36 + 105 + 6   91 + 210 + 78 + 15 + 153 + 105
  205   +   246   +   147   +   652

c　　o　　m　　p　　u　　t　　a　　t　　i　　o
6 + 105 + 78 + 120 + 210 + 190 + 1 + 190 + 45 + 105
+ 　　　　　　　　1050　　　　　　　　　　　　　　　= 2300

A　c　　c　　o　　m　　p　　u　　t　　a　　t　　i　　o
1 + 6　　6 + 105 + 78 + 120 + 210 + 190 + 1 + 190 + 45 + 105
　7　+　　　　　　　　　1050

l　　i　　t　　e　　r　　i　　s　　　　s　　o　　l　　i　　s
66 + 45 + 190 + 15 + 153 + 45 + 171　　　171 + 105 + 66 + 45 + 171
+ 　　　　　685　　　　　　+　　　　　558　　　　= 2300

S　　o　　l　　i　　s　　　　n　　u　　m　　e　　r　　i　　s
171 + 105 + 66 + 45 + 171　　　91 + 210 + 78 + 15 + 153 + 45 + 171
　　　558　　　　+　　　　　　　763

e　　i　　s　　d　　e　　m　　　　a　　n　　n　　e　　x　　i　　s
15 + 45 + 171 + 10 + 15 + 78　　　1 + 91 + 91 + 15 + 231 + 45 + 171
+ 　　　　334　　　　+　　　　　　645　　　　　= 2300

E　　c　　c　　e　　　　a　　l　　p　　h　　a　　b　　e　　t　　u　　m
15 + 6 + 6 + 15　　　1 + 66 + 120 + 36 + 1 + 3 + 15 + 190 + 210 + 78
　　42　　　+　　　　　　720

l　　a　　t　　i　　n　　u　　m　　　& [et]
66 + 1 + 190 + 45 + 91 + 210 + 78　　　15 + 190
+ 　　　　681　　　　　　+　　205

c　　e　　r　　t　　u　　m
6 + 15 + 153 + 190 + 210 + 78
+ 　　　　652　　　　　　　　　　　　　　　　　= 2300

A　l　　p　　h　　a　　b　　e　　t　　u　　m
1 + 66 + 120 + 36 + 1 + 3 + 15 + 190 + 210 + 78
　　　　720

l　　a　　t　　i　　n　　u　　m　　i　　n
66 + 1 + 190 + 45 + 91 + 210 + 78　　　45 + 91
+ 　　　　681　　　　　　+　　136

n　　u　　m　　e　　r　　i　　s
91 + 210 + 78 + 15 + 153 + 45 + 171
+ 　　　　763　　　　　　　　　　　　　　　　= 2300

H　　a　　e　　c　　　i　　p　　s　　a　　　p　　u　　n　　c　　t　　a
36 + 1 + 15 + 6　　　45 + 120 + 171 + 1　　　120 + 210 + 91 + 6 + 190 + 1
　　58　　　+　　　　337　　　　+　　　　618

d   u   o   m   i   l   l   i   a
10 + 210 + 105   78 + 45 + 66 + 66 + 45 + 1
\+   325   +   301

t   r   e   c   e   n   t   a
190 + 153 + 15 + 6 + 15 + 91 + 190 + 1
\+   661   = 2300

P   e   r   f   i   c   i   u   n   t   d   i   e   s
120 + 15 + 153 + 21 + 45 + 6 + 45 + 210 + 91 + 190   10 + 45 + 15 + 171
           896   +   241

A   n   t   i   o   c   h   i
1 + 91 + 190 + 45 + 105 + 6 + 36 + 45
\+   519

E   p   i   p   h   a   n   i   s
15 + 120 + 45 + 120 + 36 + 1 + 91 + 45 + 171
\+   644   = 2300

D   i   e   s   A   n   t   i   o   c   h   i   a   c
10 + 45 + 15 + 171   1 + 91 + 190 + 45 + 105 + 6 + 36 + 45   1 + 6
   241   +   519   +   7

p   u   n   c   t   a   A   l   p   h   a   b   e   t   i
120 + 210 + 91 + 6 + 190 + 1   1 + 66 + 120 + 36 + 1 + 3 + 15 + 190 + 45
\+   618   +   477

l   a   t   i   n   i
66 + 1 + 190 + 45 + 91 + 45
\+   438   = 2300

E   a   i   n   d   i   c   a   n   t   i   s   t   a   m
15 + 1   45 + 91 + 10 + 45 + 6 + 1 + 91 + 190   45 + 171 + 190 + 1 + 78
  16   +   479   +   485

p   r   o   g   r   e   s   s   i   o   n   e   m
120 + 153 + 105 + 28 + 153 + 15 + 171 + 171 + 45 + 105 + 91 + 15 + 78
\+   1250

d   e   i
10 + 15 + 45
   + 70   = 2300

P   r   o   g   r   e   s   s   i   o
120 + 153 + 105 + 28 + 153 + 15 + 171 + 171 + 45 + 105
            1066

C   o   m   p   u   t   a   t   i   o   n   e   m
6 + 105 + 78 + 120 + 210 + 190 + 1 + 190 + 45 + 105 + 91 + 15 + 78
\+   1234   = 2300

Translation:

This is the Sum of the Sums,
The Sum of the Sums from the Alphabet.
It comes from the Latin Alphabet, from Numbers,
And it is the Number of Daniel.
Behold the sacred Sum of the whole Alphabet.
The Sum heard by Daniel, in the eighth [chapter] of Daniel,
And the sacred Sum is revealed from Heaven.

Behold the Number of the Triangles,
It fills out the Alphabet with Triangles.
And behold there is a Pyramid with three corners.
Behold, this is the Number, this is the Alphabet.
Behold this [Alphabet] [made up] from twenty-three letters.
And from this Number [comes] the calculation,
And the calculation is from single letters,
the single numbers that are the same [as those] being joined [to them]

Behold the Alphabet: Latin, and fixed,
the Latin Alphabet [expressed] in numbers.
These same points, two thousand three hundred [in number],
make up the days of Antiochus [son of] Epiphanes,
The days of Antiochus and the points of the Latin Alphabet.
These things reveal the progress of God,
[and] the progress [reveals] the calculation.

Hörner's *Calendarium Gregorianum* (page 63)

C　a　l　　e　　n　　d　　a　　r　　　i　　u　　m
$6 + 1 + 66 + 15 + 91 + 10 + 1 + 153 + 45 + 210 + 78$
676

G　r　　e　　g　　o　　　r　　　i　　a　　n　　u　　m
$28 + 153 + 15 + 28 + 105 + 153 + 45 + 1 + 91 + 210 + 78$
$+$　　　　　　　　907　　　　　　　　　　　　　　　　　　$= 1583$

Hörner's *2300* (page 65)

1. S　　u　　m　　m　　e　　n　　　　d　　e　　r
$171 + 210 + 78 + 78 + 15 + 91$　　　$10 + 15 + 153$
　　　　643　　　　　　　　　　$+$　　　178

Z　　a　　h　　l　　e　　n　　　d　　e　　ß
$300 + 1 + 36 + 66 + 15 + 91$　　　$10 + 15 + 171 + 171$
$+$　　　　509　　　　　　$+$　　　　367

A l p h a b e t s
1 + 66 + 120 + 36 + 1 + 3 + 15 + 190 + 171
\+   603   = 2300

taking ß as ss (171 + 171) and not ß = 325 as in Hörner's table;

2. **D i e   E l e m e n t**
10 + 45 + 15   15 + 66 + 15 + 78 + 15 + 91 + 190
      70   +   470

   a l l e r
   1 + 66 + 66 + 15 + 153
   \+   301

   L a t e i n i s c h e n
   66 + 1 + 190 + 15 + 45 + 91 + 45 + 171 + 6 + 36 + 15 +91
   \+   772

   Z a h l e n
   300 + 1 + 36 + 66 + 15 + 91
   \+   509   = 2122

Element is in fact neuter (*Das Element*), making 182 instead of 70 for the first word, and a total of 2234. This is 66 short of 2300, the equivalent of an extra letter 'l'. Either Hörner miscalculated, or the printer miscopied Hörner's script, which may have read '*Das Ellement aller Lateinischen Zahlen*' (i.e. 182 + 536 + 301 + 772 + 509 = 2300).

3. **N u m e r u s,**
   91 + 210 + 78 + 15 + 153 + 210 + 171
            928

   n u m e r u s
   91 + 210 + 78 + 15 + 153 + 210 +171
   \+   928

   D a n i ë l i s
   10 + 1 + 91 + 45 + 15 + 66 + 45 + 171
   \+   444   = 2300

4. **A l p h a b e t u m,**
   1 + 66 + 120 + 36 + 1 + 3 + 15 + 190 + 210 + 78
            720

   n u m e r u s
   91 + 210 + 78 + 15 + 153 + 210 + 171
   \+   928

d　　u　　p　　l　　e　　x
10 + 210 + 120 + 66 + 15 + 253
+　　　　　　674　　　　　　　　　　　　　　　　　　　= 2322

Hörner calculated 231 instead of 253 for the final letter 'x', which brought the total to 2300. In Hörner's tables, 'x' (21) in the natural-order alphabet appears immediately alongside the number 231 in the trigonal alphabet (although standing for the letter 'w' and not 'x'), which perhaps explains the error.

5. **C　　e　　n　　t　　i　　e　　s　　　23.　　d　　i　　e　　s,**
　6 + 15 + 91 + 190 + 45 + 15 + 171　　23.　　10 + 45 + 15 + 171
　　　　　　533　　　　　　　　+ 23 +　　　　241

　L　　i　　t　　e　　r　　a　　r　　u　　m
　66 + 45 + 190 + 15 + 153 + 1 + 153 + 210 + 78
　+　　　　　　　911

　n　　u　　m　　e　　r　　i
　91 + 210 + 78 + 15 + 153 + 45
　+　　　　592　　　　　　　　　　　　　　　　　　= 2300

6. **C　　e　　n　　t　　i　　e　　s　　　23.　　d　　i　　e　　s**
　6 + 15 + 91 + 190 + 45 + 15 + 171　　23.　　10 + 45 + 15 + 171
　　　　　　533　　　　　　　　+ 23 +　　　　241

　D　　a　　n　　i　　ë　　l　　i　　s,　　n　　u　　m　　e　　r　　i
　10 + 1 + 91 + 45 + 15 + 66 + 45 + 171　　91 + 210 + 78 + 15 + 153 + 45
　+　　　　　444　　　　　　　+　　　　　　592

　　23.　　D　　a　　n　　i　　ë　　l　　i　　s
　　23　　10 + 1 + 91 + 45 + 15 + 66 + 45 + 171
　+　23　+　　　　　　444　　　　　　　　　= 2300

7. **C　　a　　b　　a　　l　　a　　v　　e　　r　　a,**
　6 + 1 + 3 + 1 + 66 + 1　　210 + 15 + 153 + 1
　　　78　　　　　+　　　　379

　n　　u　　m　　e　　r　　u　　s
　91 + 210 + 78 + 15 + 153 + 210 + 171
　+　　　　　928

　A　　l　　p　　h　　a　　b　　e　　t　　i
　1 + 66 + 120 + 36 + 1 + 3 + 15 + 190 + 45
　+　　　　　477

　L　　a　　t　　i　　n　　i
　66 + 1 + 190 + 45 + 91 + 45
　+　　　438　　　　　　　　　　　　　　　　　　= 2300

8. C a b a l a   i l l   a,
 6+1+3+1+66+1   45+66+66+1
       78   +   178

 v   o   c a t   i   o   J   o   h a n   n   i   s
210+105+6+1+190+45+105   45+105+36+1+91+91+45+171
 +   662   +   585

 H   ö   r   n   e   r   i   m   e   d   i   c   i
36+105+153+91+15+153+45   78+15+10+45+6+45
 +   598   +   199   = 2300

Hörner disregarded the umlaut in his surname.

Translation:

1. Sums of the Numbers of the Alphabet.
2. The Element of all Latin numbers.
3. The Number, the number of [the Book of] Daniel.
4. The Alphabet, a twofold number.
5. A hundred times twenty-three days, the numbers of the Letters.
6. A hundred times twenty-three days of [the Book of] Daniel, the twenty-three numbers of [the Book of] Daniel.
7. The true Cabbala, the number of the Latin Alphabet.
8. That Cabbala [which is] the calling of the physician Johannes Hörner.

Poll's *lusus artificium* (page 66)

J   O   A N   N   E   S
45 + 105 + 1 + 91 + 91 + 15 + 171
         519

B   E   R   N   H   A   R   D   U   S
3 + 15 + 153 + 91 + 36 + 1 + 153 + 10 + 210 + 171
 +   843   = 1362

I   H   O   V   A   H   O   C
45 + 36 + 105 + 210 + 1   36 + 105 + 6
    397   +   147

C   O   N   J   U   G   I   U   M
6 + 105 + 91 + 45 + 210 + 28 + 45 + 210 + 78
 +   818   = 1362

M   A   G   D   A   L   E   N   A
78 + 1 + 28 + 10 + 1 + 66 + 15 + 91 + 1
         291

E   L   I   S   A   B   E   T
$15 + 66 + 45 + 171 + 1 + 3 + 15 + 190$
$+$ 506 $= 797$

I   S   E   T   B   E   N   E   D   I   C   A   T
$45 + 171$ $15 + 190$ $3 + 15 + 91 + 15 + 10 + 45 + 6 + 1 + 190$
216 $+$ 205 $+$ 376 $= 797$

Translation:

Johann Bernard: Magdalene Elisabeth – May God bless this marriage.

Schwartzbach's *Hac viget Eusebies ara* (pages 67–8)

Translation:

Here flourishes the Altar of Reverence and the Seat of Astræa:
Here Virtue reigns, more cherished [than elsewhere], the blessed
Goddess.
Here lives Phoebus and the youth [Mercury], offspring of Cyllene,
And as many of the Muses as the joyfully-crying Mount Helicon
nourishes.

In Pronicis

A   B   I,   H   A   C   A   R   E   T   E
$1 + 6 + 90$ $72 + 1 + 12$ $1 + 306 + 30 + 380 + 30$
97 $+$ 85 $+$ 747

R   E   G   N   A   T   A   L   M   A   D   E   A
$306 + 30 + 56 + 182 + 1 + 380$ $1 + 132 + 156 + 1$ $20 + 30 + 1$
$+$ 955 $+$ 290 $+$ 51
                                          $= 2225$ exactly

O   H!   E   U   S   E   B   E   A,   D   I   C   E,
$210 + 72$ $30 + 420 + 342 + 30 + 6 + 30 + 1$ $20 + 90 + 12 + 30$
282 $+$ 859 $+$ 152

A   C   M   U   S   A!
$1 + 12$ $156 + 420 + 342 + 1$
$+ 13 +$ 919 $= 2225$ exactly[1]

Translation:

In Pronica

Depart: here Virtue reigns, the Blessed Goddess.
Oh! Reverence, Justice and the Muse.

---

[1] The alphabet used in the above solution is different from my proposal in 'J. S. Bach and
the Baroque Paragram: A Reappraisal of Friedrich Smend's Number Alphabet Theory',
Music and Letters 70 (1989), 201.

In Zensicis sive Quadr.

R **E** **D** **I** **J** **U** **S** **T** **I** **T** **I** **A**
$289 + 25 + 16 + 81$ $81 + 400 + 324 + 361 + 81 + 361 + 81 + 1$
411 $+$ 1690 $= 2101$ exactly

D **I** **A** **J** **U** **S** **T** **I** **T** **I** **A** **E**
$16 + 81 + 1$ $81 + 400 + 324 + 361 + 81 + 361 + 81 + 1 + 25$
98 $+$ 1715

A **R** **A!**
$1 + 289 + 1$
$+ 291$ $= 2104$; 3 more than the exact total

T **H** **I** **O** **L** **O** **G** **I** **S** **F** **I** **D** **E** **I**
$361 + 64 + 81 + 196 + 121 + 196 + 49 + 81 + 234$ $36 + 81 + 16 + 25 + 81$
1473 $+$ 239

B **E** **A** **T** **A!**
$4 + 25 + 1 + 361 + 1$
$+$ 392 $= 2104$; 3 more than the exact total

H **A!** **P** **U** **R** **A**
$64 + 1$ $225 + 400 + 289 + 1$
65 $+$ 915

D **O** **C** **T** **R** **I** **N** **A!**
$16 + 196 + 9 + 361 + 289 + 81 + 169 + 1$
$+$ 1122 $= 2102$; 1 more than the exact total

V **A** **T** **E** **M** **A** **M** **A** **S;** **N** **E** **C**
$400 + 1 + 361 + 25 + 144$ $1 + 144 + 1 + 324$ $169 + 25 + 9$
931 $+$ 470 $+$ 203

D **I** **V** **A?**
$16 + 81 + 400 + 1$
$+$ 498 $= 2102$; 1 more than the exact total

Translation:

In Zensica or Quadrangular

Return Justice,
The Divine altar of Justice!
Blessed to the Theologians of Faith!
Ah! Immaculate Learning!
You love the Priest: Are you not Divine?

Schwartzbach's acrostic (page 68)

Translation:
The Countryside flourishes green in the Spring: Famous Slesis is in abundance all the year round, given increase by chosen men and noble minds.

A Prayer for the City of Breslau

May Breslau be well-disposed towards you, may the Divine Goddess be
well-disposed towards you if you favour her;
[But] To your enemies let her always be ill-disposed, always.

Schwartzbach's title-page to *Wratislavia* (page 68)

W R A T I S L A V I A,   U R B S
$20+17+1+19+9+18+11+1+20+9+1$ $20+17+2+18$
                    126   +   57

A U G U S T A,   C A E S A R I A
$1+20+7+20+18+19+1$ $3+1+5+18+1+17+9+1$
+   86   +   55

R E G I A,   M E T R O P O L I S
$17+5+7+9+1$ $12+5+19+17+14+15+14+11+9+18$
+   39   +   134

S I L E S I A E
$18+9+11+5+18+9+1+5$
+   76

A M P L I S S I M A
$1+12+15+11+9+18+18+9+12+1$
+   106

F L O R E N T I S
$6+11+14+17+5+13+19+9+18$ '
+   112

E L E G A N T I S...
$5+11+5+7+1+13+19+9+18$
+   88

C H R I S T O P H O R O
$3+8+17+9+18+19+14+15+8+14+17+14$
+   156

S   C H W A R   T   Z   B A C H I   O
18 + 3 + 8 + 20 + 1 + 17 + 18 + 23 + 2 + 1 + 3 + 8 + 9 + 14
+   145   = 1180

The unusual, although easy-to follow, abbreviations for *florentissima*
and *elegantissima* (*florentis* and *elegantis*) indicate the point at which
Schwartzbach probably adjusted the numerical total of the title to
coincide with the number of lines in the poem.

Translation:
Wratislavia, Venerable City, the Imperial Capital, the Mother town of
Silesia, Great, Abundant and Distinguished to the highest degree . . . by
Christoph Schwartzbach.

Schwartzbach's *Nate veni Soter* (page 69)

Translation:
            Son [of God] [our] Saviour, Come! Oh! Let the heavens
                    truly rain dew upon us!
Isaiah 45:   Just Child, born of the Virgin pure, Come!

Harsdörffer's *Johannes Baptista* and *Joannes Dux* (page 74)

Both examples use the Latin natural-order alphabet and A = 1 to Z = 23.

J   o   h   a   n   n   e   s   B   a   p   t   i   s   t   a
9 + 14 + 8 + 1 + 13 + 13 + 5 + 18   2 + 1 + 15 + 19 + 9 + 18 + 19 + 1
            81   +   84   = 165

H   i   c   E   l   i   a   s   s   e   c   u   n   d   u   s
8 + 9 + 3   5 + 11 + 9 + 1 + 18   18 + 5 + 3 + 20 + 13 + 4 + 20 + 18
    20   +   44   +   101   = 165

Translation:
            John the Baptist. Here is the second Elias.

J   o   a   n   n   e   s   D   u   x
9 + 14 + 1 + 13 + 13 + 5 + 18   4 + 20 + 21
            73   +   45

S   a   x   o   n   i   a   e
18 + 1 + 21 + 14 + 13 + 9 + 1 + 5
+   82   = 200

C   o   n   f   e   s   s   i   o
3 + 14 + 13 + 6 + 5 + 18 + 18 + 9 + 14
            100

A u g u s t a n a
$1 + 20 + 7 + 20 + 18 + 19 + 1 + 13 + 1$
$+ \qquad\qquad 100$ = 200

Translation:
John Duke of Saxony. The Imperial Confession.

Harsdörffer's *Cambyses Bianchius Comes* (page 74)

Harsdörffer uses the natural-order alphabet A = 1 to Z = 24.

C a m b y s e s   B i a n c h i u s
$3 + 1 + 12 + 2 + 23 + 18 + 5 + 18 \qquad 2 + 9 + 1 + 13 + 3 + 8 + 9 + 20 + 18$
$\qquad\quad 82 \qquad\qquad + \qquad\qquad 83$

C o m e s
$3 + 14 + 12 + 5 + 18$
$+ \qquad 52$ = 217

S i c   s e c u n d u s
$18 + 9 + 3 \qquad 18 + 5 + 3 + 20 + 13 + 4 + 20 + 18$
$\quad 30 \quad + \qquad\qquad 101$

P e t r a r c h a
$15 + 5 + 19 + 17 + 1 + 17 + 3 + 8 + 1$
$+ \qquad\qquad 86$ = 217

Translation:
Count Cambyses Biancus
A second Petrarch, as follows:

It fits you, yes! cunningly well, the snow-coloured name of the Swan,
when the Fountain of Castalia resounds famously with your song.
So do secrets lie concealed in [your] measures. You are called a second
    Petrarch;
but what Laura will give you your laurels?
By your example you may order the Muses to hope for good things now
while you sing, Maecenus and poet in the same person.

Harsdörffer's chronogram (pages 76–7)

Translation:

Beloved, stock of youth,
of steadfast diligence,
bears true Virtue's fruit
through the flight of long ages.

Harsdörffer's hymn (page 77)

Harsdörffer uses the Latin milesian alphabet: variant 6, B = 1 to Z = 100.

D i e   W i r   F r i e d   u n d
$3 + 0 + 0$ $160 + 0 + 50$ $4 + 50 + 0 + 0 + 3$ $0 + 20 + 3$
   3   +   210   +   57   +   23

F r   e u d e   h o f f e n,   h a t   n u n
$4 + 50 + 0 + 0 + 3 + 0$ $6 + 0 + 4 + 4 + 0 + 20$ $6 + 0 + 70$ $20 + 0 + 20$
   +   57   +   34   +   76   +   40

S t r e i t   u n d   L e i d
$60 + 70 + 50 + 0 + 0 + 70$ $0 + 20 + 3$ $9 + 0 + 0 + 3$
   +   250   +   23   +   12

b e t r o f f e n   H ö c h s t e r
$1 + 0 + 70 + 50 + 0 + 4 + 4 + 0 + 20$ $6 + 0 + 2 + 6 + 60 + 70 + 0 + 50$
   +   149   +   194

g i e b   d o c h   d i e s e r   Z e i t
$5 + 0 + 0 + 1$ $3 + 0 + 2 + 6$ $3 + 0 + 0 + 60 + 0 + 50$ $100 + 0 + 0 + 70$
   +   6   +   11   +   113   +   170

e n d l i c h   S i e g   u n d
$0 + 20 + 3 + 9 + 0 + 2 + 6$ $60 + 0 + 0 + 5$ $0 + 20 + 3$
   +   40   +   65   +   23

E i n i g k e i t
$0 + 0 + 20 + 0 + 5 + 8 + 0 + 0 + 70$
   +   103 $= 1659$; and not 1648 as given by Harsdörffer.

Translation:

> On us who hope for peace and joy,
> War and sorrow has fallen.
> Almighty, give this age
> victory and unity at last.

Harsdörffer calculated 58 for *Fried*, 58 for *Freude*, 67 for *hat*, 253 for *Streit*, 140 for *betroffen* and 115 for *dieser*. There seems no obvious reason for these mistakes.

Harsdörffer's *Jesus ist Christus* (page 78)

The natural-order alphabet: variant 1 A = 1 to Z = 24 is used.

J e s u s   i s t
9 + 5 + 18 + 20 + 18   9 + 18 + 19
    70   +   46

C h r i s t u s
3 + 8 + 17 + 9 + 18 + 19 + 20 + 18
+   112   = 228

U n s e r   H e l f t e r   u n d
20 + 13 + 18 + 5 + 17   8 + 5 + 11 + 6 + 19 + 5 + 17   20 + 13 + 4
   73   +   71   +   37

H e i l e
8 + 5 + 9 + 11 + 5
+   38   = 219

Again, there seems no obvious reason for the discrepancies between 228, 219 and Harsdörffer's total of 218.

Harsdörffer's paragram on Schottel (pages 80–1)

J u s t u s   G e o r g i u s
9 + 20 + 18 + 19 + 20 + 18   7 + 5 + 14 + 17 + 7 + 9 + 20 + 18
   104   +   97

S c h o t t e l i u s
18 + 3 + 8 + 14 + 19 + 19 + 5 + 11 + 9 + 20 + 18
+   144   = 345

V a r r o T e u t o n i c u s,
20 + 1 + 17 + 17 + 14   19 + 5 + 20 + 19 + 14 + 13 + 9 + 3 + 20 + 18
   69   +   140

v i n d e x L i n g u a e
20 + 9 + 13 + 4 + 5 + 21   11 + 9 + 13 + 7 + 20 + 1 + 5
+   72   +   66   = 347

There is no obvious reason for the error in the second line which, according to Schottel, should also add up to 345.

Translation:
The Paragram of Blessed Harsdörffer [derived] from a progression of letters and numbers such that the number at each end of the series may be taken to be represented as A = 1 and Z = 23.

Justus Georg Schottel:
The German Varro, the Defender of the Language.

You are the Defender of the Language, you have become the German Varro.
(Thus does an equal number even indicate the Paragram.)
As Varro once gave guidance to the strangers in the city* [of Rome],
And when they barely knew where their Country was,
set them firmly in position before their new City,
So do you show the Germans in their anxiety
the way forwards, with a fixed path, and what road they must watch.
You struggle to fill the place of the great Varro
while you command the waters of the language to be clear and precise.

*When we were wandering in our City like strangers, Varro with his books brought us
home like guests, so that we could know at last who we were and where.

Männling's poetical paragram (page 85)

M.   **J   o   h   a   n   n**
12   9 + 14 + 8 + 1 + 13 + 13
12 +   58

C   h   r   i   s   t   o   p   h   o   r   u   s
3 + 8 + 17 + 9 + 18 + 19 + 14 + 15 + 8 + 14 + 17 + 20 + 18
+   180

M   a   e   n   n   l   i   n   g   i   u   s,
12 + 1 + 5 + 13 + 13 + 11 + 9 + 13 + 7 + 9 + 20 + 18
+   131

B   e   r   o   s   t   a   a   d   i   e   n   s   i   s
2 + 5 + 17 + 14 + 18 + 19 + 1 + 1 + 4 + 9 + 5 + 13 + 18 + 9 + 18
+   153

S   i   l   e   s   i   u   s   **P.   L.   C.**
18 + 9 + 11 + 5 + 18 + 9 + 20 + 18   15   11   3
+   108   + 15 + 11 + 3   = 671

I   n   t   e   r   **B   r   a   c   h   i   a**
9 + 13 + 19 + 5 + 17   2 + 17 + 1 + 3 + 8 + 9 + 1
        63   +   41

S   a   l   v   a   t   o   r   i   s   **J   E   S   U**
18 + 1 + 11 + 20 + 1 + 19 + 14 + 17 + 9 + 18   9 + 5 + 18 + 20
+   128   +   52

m   e   i   **& [et]**   **v   i   v   e   r   e**   **& [et]**
12 + 5 + 9   5 + 19   20 + 9 + 20 + 5 + 17 + 5   5 + 19
+ 26   + 24   +   76   + 24

m   o   r   i   **c   u   p   i   o,**   **u   t**   **i   n**
12 + 14 + 17 + 9   3 + 20 + 15 + 9 + 14   20 + 19   9 + 13
+   52   +   61   +   39   +   22

e o   m a n e a m.
5 + 14   12 + 1 + 13 + 5 + 1 + 12
+ 19 +   44   = 671

Translation:
Master Johann Christoph Männling of Berostad.
I desire both to live and to die within the arms of my saviour Jesus so that
I may remain in him.

ABC's *Johan Georg* (page 87)

The trigonal alphabet is used.

J   o   h   a   n   G   e   o   r   g
45 + 105 + 36 + 1 + 91   28 + 15 + 105 + 153 + 28
         278   +   329

C · h   u   r   f   u   r   s   t
6 + 36 + 210 + 153 + 21 + 210 + 153 + 171 + 190
+   1150   = 1757

ABC calculated 268 for *Johan*, and hence arrived at his total of 1747.

D   e   r   H   e   r   r   s   e   g   n   e
10 + 15 + 153   36 + 15 + 153 + 153   171 + 15 + 28 + 91 + 15
     178   +   357   +   320

D   i   c   h   u   n   d   s   t   a   e   r   k   e
10 + 45 + 6 + 36   210 + 91 + 10   171 + 190 + 1 + 15 + 153 + 55 + 15
+   97   +   311   +   600

D   i   c   h   a   u   s   Z   i   o   n
10 + 45 + 6 + 36   1 + 210 + 171   300 + 45 + 105 + 91
+   97   +   382   +   541   = 2883

and not 2899 as stated by ABC. ABC calculated 310 for *segne*, 310 for
und, and 606 for *staerke*. Once again, there seems no obvious reason for
these discrepancies.

J   o   h   a   n   n   G   e   o   r   g   e
45 + 105 + 36 + 1 + 91 + 91   28 + 15 + 105 + 153 + 28 + 15
         369   +   344

C   h   u   r   f   ü [u e]   r   s   t   e   z   u
6 + 36 + 210 + 153 + 21 + 210 + 15 + 153 + 171 + 190 + 15   300 + 210
+   1180   +   510

S   a   c   h   s   e   n
171 + 1 + 6 + 36 + 171 + 15 + 91
+   491   = 2894; and not 2899 as stated by ABC.

Hunold's anagram *Margaretha* (page 93)

Translation:
My Amaranth smells most sweetly: Virtue probably smells thus here.

(The image is that the sweet smell of amaranth is probably the scent of its virtue.)

Hunold's number-lines *Margaretha* (page 94)

This example uses the natural-order alphabet A = 1 to Z = 24.

M   a   r   g   a   r   e   t   h   a
12 + 1 + 17 + 7 + 1 + 17 + 5 + 19 + 8 + 1   = 88

M   e   i   n   e   S   e   e   l   e
12 + 5 + 9 + 13 + 5   18 + 5 + 5 + 11 + 5
     44   +   44   = 88

Translation: Margareta; my soul.

This example uses the Latin milesian alphabet: variant 4.

M   a   r   g   a   r   e   t   h   a
12 + 1 + 80 + 7 + 1 + 80 + 5 + 100 + 8 + 1   = 295

A   c   h   u   n   d   m   e   i   n   L   e   b   e   n!
1 + 3 + 8   110 + 40 + 4   12 + 5 + 9 + 40   11 + 5 + 2 + 5 + 40
   12   +   154   +   66   +   63   = 295

Translation: Margareta; Ah, my life!

Riederer's *Paragramma Cabbalisticum trigonale* (pages 96–7)

Translation:
The now newly rebuilt beautiful church of St Egidien in the imperial free imperial-city and world famous republic Nürnberg.
2 Chron. 24:13: And the labourers labour[ed] so that the work of repair prospered in their hand, and they made the house of God fully ready and completely restored.

Faber's cryptographic invention (page 104)

Key:

a b c d e f g h i k l m n o p q r s t u w x y z

Viola part :

Translation:

Suspicion soars in every ardent lover.
If she but speaks with others, he thinks they're making love.

Selenus' *Spinola* (page 104)

Key:

	Ut	Fa	Sol	Mi	Re
Fa	A	B	C ·	D	E
Re	F	G	H	I	K
Mi	L	M	N	O	P
Ut	Q	R	S	T	U
Sol	W	X	Y	Z	

Tenor voice :

D   e   r   S   p   i   n   o   l   a
FaMi FaRe UtFa   UtSol MiRe ReMi MiSol MiMi MiUt FaUt

i   s   t   i   n   d   i   e
ReMi UtSol UtMi   ReMi MiSol   FaMi ReMi FaRe

P   f   a   l   t   z
MiRe ReUt FaUt MiUt UtMi SolMi

g   e   f   a   l   l   e   n:
ReFa FaRe ReUt FaUt MiUt MiUt FaRe MiSol

V   a   e   i   l   l   i
UtRe FaUt FaRe   ReMi MiUt MiUt ReMi

Translation:
Spinola has fallen into the Palatinate: alas for him.

Bibliography

ENCYCLOPÆDIAS AND GENERAL REFERENCE WORKS

Allgemeine Deutsche Biographie. 56 vols. Berlin, 1875–1912.

Bestermann, Theodore. *A World Bibliography of Bibliographies and of Bibliographical Catalogues, Calendars, Abstracts, Digests, Indices and the like*. 4th edn, revised and greatly enlarged. Lausanne, 1965–6.

Die Musik in Geschichte und Gegenwart. Kassel, Basel, 1949–86.

Die Religion in Geschichte und Gegenwart. 3rd edn. Tübingen, 1957–62.

Dünnhaupt, Gerhard. *Bibliographisches Handbuch der Barock Literatur*. Stuttgart, 1981.

Encyclopædia Judaica. Jerusalem, 1971.

Faber du Faur, Curt von. *German Baroque Literature: A Catalogue of the Collection in the Yale University Library*. 2 vols. New Haven, Conn., 1958 and 1969.

German Baroque Literature: A Descriptive Catalogue of the Collection of Harold Jantz, and a Guide to the Collection on Microfilm. 2 vols. New Haven, Conn., 1974.

Gesamt Verzeichnis des deutschsprachigen Schrifttums (GV) 1700–1910. Edited by Peter Geils and Willi Gorzny. München, New York, 1979.

Goedeke, Carl. *Grundriss zur Geschichte der deutschen Dichtung*. 1862–81.

Neumann, Werner and Schulze, Hans-Joachim. *Bach-Dokumente: Supplement zu 'Johann Sebastian Bach Neue Ausgabe Sämtlicher Werke'*. 4 vols. Kassel, Basel, 1963, 1969, 1972 and 1979.

The New Encyclopædia Britannica. 15th edn. Chicago, London, 1974.

The New Grove Dictionary of Music and Musicians. London, 1980.

Zedler, Johann Heinrich. *Großes vollständiges Universal Lexicon aller Wissenschafften und Künste*. Leipzig, Halle, 1732–52.

A CHRONOLOGICAL LIST OF SOURCES CONTAINING A NUMBER ALPHABET
(1525–1748)

As many of these books are rare, the library sigla and call marks are given to facilitate reference. Abbreviations for the library sigla are taken from *The New Grove Dictionary of Music and Musicians*, which itself draws on the abbreviations devised for R.I.S.M. Books are given in short-title form except where the full title is of particular interest.

Rudolff, Christoff. *Behend unnd Hubsch Rechnung durch die kunstreichen regeln Algebre so gemeincklich die Coss geneñt werden.* Argentorati, Vulfius Cephaleus Ioanni lung, **1525**. GB: Lbm – 08533.df.24.

Stiefel, Michael. *Ein Rechen Büchlin Vom End Christ. APOCALYPSIS IN APOCALYPSIN . . . Vom End der Welt.* Wittenberg. G. Rhaw, **1532**. GB: Lbm – C. 175.i.41.

Stiefel, Michael. *Ein sehr Wunderbarliche Wortrechnung Sampt einer merck-lichen erklerung Zalen Danielis und der Offenbarung Sanct Johannis.* Nürnberg?, **1553**. GB: Lbm – 1003.c.30.

Jacob, Simon. *Ein New und Wolgegründt Rechenbuch.* Frankfurt am Main, **1565**. A: Wn – 72.H.32.

Paulus, Elchanon (Paul, von Prag). *Mysterium novum, ein new . . . beweiss nach der Hebreer Cabala, dass aigentlich der Name und Tittel des Herrn Jesus Christi, Gottes Sohn, in dem fürnembsten Propheceyungen von Messia, verdeckt inn den Hebräischen Buchstaben bedeutet ist.* Wien, **1582**. GB: Lbm – 4033.bb.43(1).

Bongus, Petrus. *De mystica numerorum significatione.* Bergamo, **1583**. 1591 edition, GB: Lbm – 529.c.8.

Tabourot, Estienne. *Les Bigarrures du Seigneur des Accords.* Paris, **1583**. GB: Lbm – 245.b.34. Facsimile reprint of 1588 edn Genève, 1986, edited by Francis Goyet.

Schultz, Anton. *Arithmetica oder Rechenbuch.* Liegnitz, **1600**. A: Wn – 72.H.39.

Schickhard, Wilhelm. *Horologium Hebraeum.* Tübingen, **1614**. Later edition: London, 1639. GB: Lbm – 1568/3094. 14th edition, edited by Balthasar Raith. Tübingen, 1670. D-brd: W – KD3; Pl: WRu – 467506. Also pub-lished as *Institutiones Linguae Ebraeae.* Edited by Joh. Ernest Gerhard. Leipzig, 1689. S: Sk – 163 I 7g.

Hörner, Johann. *PROBLEMA Summum, Mathematicum & Cabalisticum. Das ist: Ein hohe versigelte Mathematische und Cabalistische Auffgab und Figur an alle Gelehrten unnd Kunstliebende Europae. Item Ein Introduction, oder Wegweiser zurgeheymen Theosophischen Cabalae und Mathematic, dieselbe was sie sey erklärende. In zween Theil verfasset dergleichen zuvor nie gesehen worden.* Nürnberg, **1619**. D-brd: Mbs – 4.Math.P.158.

Selenus, Gustavus (August II of Braunschweig-Lüneburg). *Cryptomenytices et Cryptographiæ Libri IX. In quibus et planißima Steganographiæ à Johanne Trithemio. Abbate Spanheynmensi et Herbipolensi, admirandi ingenij Viro, magice et ænigmatice olim conscriptæ, enodatio traditur.* Lüneburg, **1624**. GB: Lbm – 616.l.9.

Schwartzbach, Christoph. *WRATISLAVIA, URBS AVGVSTA, CÆSARIA-REGIA, METROPOLIS SILESIAE AMPLISSIMA, FLORENTIS. ELEGANTIS. L. Paragrammatis Mysticis ex Doctrinis Multangularium erutis. Carmine elegaico, nec non epigrammatis aliquot descripta; EJVS-DEMQUE; INCLITO SENATVI, ET SPECTABILI CIVITATI, In debitæ gratitudinis monumentum, dedicando consecrata.* Wratislavia, **1630**. GB: Lbm – 11409.gg.53 (3).

Schwartzbach, Christoph. *Lusus Paragrammaticus per numeros figuratos angulares. Nec non in SS. Nomen Jesus meletemata aliquot Arithmetico-Theologica.* Leipzig, Vratislavia, **1636**. Pl: WRu – 324907.

Schwenter, Daniel. *Deliciae Physico-Mathematicae. Oder Mathematische und Philosophische Erquickstunden.* Nürnberg, **1636**. D-brd: Tu – Ba 85 R.

Frankenberg, Abraham von. *Raphael oder Artzt Engel. Auff ehmaliges Ersuchen eines Gottliebenden Medici.* **1639**. Amsterdam, 1676. GB: Lbm – 853.l.b.

Puteanus, Erycius. *De anagrammatismo quae Cabalae pars est.* Bruxellae, **1643**. D-brd: Mbs – App. Mil. 1053.

Harsdörffer, Georg Philipp. *Frauenzimmer Gesprechspiele so bey Ehr- und Tugendliebenden Gesellschaft mit nutzlicher Ergetzlichkeit beliebet und geübt werden mögen.* 8 vols. Nürnberg, **1644–9**, VIII (1649). D-brd: Tu – DK XI 35c R 8°.

Harsdörffer, Georg Philipp. *Delitiae Mathematicae et Physicae. Der Mathematischen und Philosophischen Erquickstunden.* 3 vols. Nürnberg, **1651–3**. II (1651). D-brd: Tu – Ba.36R 4°. III (1653). GB: Lbm – 716.f.3.

Harsdörffer, Georg Philipp. *Poetischer Trichter. Die Teutsche Dicht- und Reimkunst ohne Behuf der Lateinischen Sprache.* 3 vols. Nürnberg, **1647–53**. II (1648). D-brd: Tu – Dh.46R.8°. III (1653), *Prob und Lob der Teutschen Wohlredenheit. Das ist: deß Poetischen Trichters Dritter Theil.* D-brd: Tu – Dh.46.8°.

Schottel, Justus Georg. *Ausführliche Arbeit Von der Teutschen Haupt Sprache.* Wolffenbüttel, **1663**. Facsimile reprint edn Tübingen, 1967.

Schott, Gaspar. *Schola Steganographica.* Nürnberg, **1665**. GB: Lbm – 556.b.3.

Kircher, Athanasius. *Arithmologia sive De abditis Numerorum mysteriis. Qua Origo, Antiquitas et fabrica Numerorum exponitur; Abditæ eorundem proprietates aperiuntur; Fontes superstitionum in Amuletorum fabrica aperiuntur; Denique post Cabalistarum, Arabum, Gnosticorum, aliorumque magicas impietates detectas, vera et licita numerorum mystica significatio ostenditur.* Roma, **1665**. GB: Lbm – 50.c.23.

Schott, Gaspar. *Joco-seriorum naturæ et artis, sive Magiæ naturalis centuriæ tres . . .* Frankfurt am Main, **1667**. GB: Lbm – 7945.gg.32.

Paschasius, R. P. F. *Poësis artificiosa, cum sibi præfixa perfacili.* Herbipoli, **1668**. GB: Lbm – 1477.cc.3.

Olearius, Johann. *Biblische Erklärung. Darinnen nechst dem allgemeinen Haupt-Schlüssel Der gantzen heiligen Schrifft.* 5 vols. Leipzig, **1678–81**. V (1681). D-brd: Gs – 4 Theol. Bibl. 602: 70; A: Wn – 5.E.8.

Riemer, Johann. *Über-Reicher Schatz-Meister Aller hohen Standes und Burgerlichen Freud- und Leid-Complimente.* Leipzig, Frankfurt, **1681**. GB: Lbm – 11824.d.40(1).

Henning, Johann. *Cabbalologia, i.e. Brevis Institutio de Cabbala cum Veterum Rabbinorum judaica, tum Poëtarum Paragrammatica, Artis Cabbalistico-Poëticæ.* Leipzig, **1683**. D-brd: W – GV 667.

Heunisch, Caspar. *Haupt-Schlüssel über die hohe Offenbahrung S. Johannis.* Schleusingen, **1684**. Facsimile reprint edn Basel, 1981.

Knittel, Caspar. *Via Regia Ad Omnes Scientias et Artes. Hoc est, Ars Universalis.* Prague, Leipzig, **1687**. GB: Lbm – 535.b.39.

Das ABC cum notis variorum. Herausgegeben von einem dessen Nahmen im

ABC stehet. Leipzig, Dresden, **1695**. GB: Lbm – 1568/2831; 1331 a.54; 011900.de.9 and 1331 b.16(1).

Eisenmenger, Johann Andreas. *Entdecktes Judenthum.* Frankfurt, **1700**. GB: Lbm – 4033.e.36.

Kuhnau, Johann. *Sechs Biblischer Sonaten. Musicalische Vorstellung einiger Biblischer Historien. In 6. Sonaten auff dem Claviere zu spielen.* Leipzig, **1700**. Facsimile reprint edn Leipzig, 1973.

Das Einmahl Eins cum notis variorum. Leipzig, Dresden, **1703**. GB: Lbm – 1331 b.16(2).

Männling, Johann Christoph. *Der Europæische Helicon, Oder Musen-Berg. Das ist Kurtze und deutliche Anweisung zu der Deutschen Dicht-Kunst.* Alten Stettin, **1704**. D-ddr: Bds – Yb 5600ᵃ.

Menantes (Hunold, Christian Friedrich). *Die Allerneueste Art Zur Reinen und Galanten Poesie zu gelangen.* Hamburg, **1707**. Reprint edn 1722. GB: Lbm – 11525.dd.12.

Reimmann, Jacob Friderich. *Versuch einer Einleitung in die HISTORIAM derer Teutschen, und zwar des dritten und letzten Theils Anderes Hauptstück.* Hall in Magdeburgischen, **1710**. GB: Lbm – 275.i.26.

Hocker, Johann Ludwig. *Mathematische Seelen-lust, das ist geistlicher Benutzung derer Mathematische Wissenschaften.* 2 vols. Crailsheim, Frankfurt, **1712–15**. D-brd: Gs – 8° Theol. Bibl. 35020.

Schudt, Johann Jacob. *Jüdische Merckwürdigkeiten.* Frankfurt, Leipzig, **1714**. GB: Lbm – 4033.c.51 (1–2).

Riederer, Johann Friedrich. *Cabbalistischer TRIGONAL- PARAGRAMMA-TUM Erstes Dutzent Auff Hohe gekrönte Häupter mit Darunter gesetzter Poësie, und Biblischen Texten égalisiret Der Curieusen Welt zu fernen Nachsinnen vorgelegt von Einem Teutsch-gesinnten redlichen Patrioten.* Altona, **1715**. D-brd: B – Yk 1756.

Paragramma Cabbalisticum Trigonale auf die S.T.Herren Gesandten in Regenspurg. Regensburg, **1716**. D-ddr: Dlb – Hist German D 36, 36 *V*.

Paragramma Cabbalisticum Trigonale auff die neue Egidier-Kirche. Nürnberg, **1718**. D-brd: Nst – Will II, 1373.

CATALOGUS derer siebenhundert Paragrammatum Cabbalisticorum Trigo-nalium, welche auf die Gottheit, himmlische Cörper, gekrönte Häupter, Cardinäle, Generalen, Grafen, Standes-Personen, Gelehrte, Kauffleute, Handwercks- und Privat- auch auf verschiedene sonderbar-berufene und sonst honnête Leute beederley Geschlechtes etc. etc. durch égalisierung Biblischer Texte oder Strophen aus geistlichen Gesängen, die sich auf Ihre Personen, Conduite, Eigenschafften, Vorhaben, Profession, Kunst, und Gewerbe schicken, ersonnen, und nach ohngefehrer Ordnung hiermit, nur dem Nahmen und dem Stande nach publiciret werden. Nürnberg, **1719**. D-brd: Nst – Philos 1943 8°; D-ddr: B – Yk 1761.

CATALOGUS derer Eintausend funffzig PARAGRAMMATUM CABBA-LISTICORUM TRIGONALIUM. Nürnberg, **1719**. GB: Lbm – 11517.aa.7(2); D-brd: B – Yk 1761.

Ein Wort des Trostes, Vor die arme Salzburgische Emigranten, Deren Eine grosse Anzahl 1732. durch die liebe Stadt Nürnberg passiret, Vermittelst

*einiger Paragrammatum Cabbalisticorum Trigonalium, Auf ihren
Erbarmungs-würdigen Zustand gerichtet worden Durch die mitleidige Feder
Johann Friedrich Riederers.* Nürnberg, **1732**. D-brd: Nst – Will II, 1268.
Paragramma Trigonale auf Herrn Banckier Wagner. Undated manuscript.
Listed as nos. 338 and 339 in *Catalogus derer 700*, and as nos. 470 and 471 in
Catalogus derer 1050. D-brd: Nst – Will 1, 1349.

25 undated paragrams in manuscript, numbered 198 to 223, together with an
incomplete catalogue of paragrams in manuscript, numbered 95 to 250.
D-brd: HS – Sup. ep (4°) 11 Blatt 366 – 403.

Unschuldige Nachrichten von Alten und Neuen Theologischen Sachen. Wittenberg, Leipzig, **1717**. GB: Lbm – P.P. 104 (Wittenberg).

Neue Zeitungen von gelehrten Sachen. Edited by J. G. Krause. Vol. XVII:
Leipzig, **1717**; Vol. XXVI: **1719**. D-brd: Tu – Kb 22 8° Leipzig.

Faber, Johann Christoph. *Neu erfundene Composition.* **1729**. D-brd: W – Cod.
Guelf. 59 musica.

Picander (Henrici, Christian Friedrich). *Ernst-, Schertzhaffte und Satyrische
Gedichte.* Leipzig, **1732**. Reprint edn 1737. GB: Lbm – 1347.d.4–7.

Schmidt, Johann Jacob. *Biblischer Mathematicus Oder Erläuterung der Heil.
Schrift aus den Mathematischen Wissenschaften Der Arithmetic, Geometrie,
Static, Architectur, Astronomie, Horographie und Optic.* Züllichau, **1736**.
GB: Lbm – 3125.c.41.

Mittag, Johann Gottfried. *Leben und Thaten Friedrich August III Des Allerdurchlauchtigsten Großmächtigsten Königs der Pohlen und Churfürsten zu
Sachsen Biß auf gegenwärtige Zeit zusammen getragen und ausgefertigt von
Johann Gottfried Mittag.* Leipzig, **1737**. D-brd: Tu – Fo.XIV.6.

Colonius, Johann Philipp. *SYSTEMA ARITHMETICUM SPECIOSUM Das
ist: Ein auf die neueste Art wohleingerichtetes Vollkommenes Rechen-Buch.*
Frankfurt am Main, **1748**. D–brd: Gs – 8 Math. II 1959.

SELECTED BIBLIOGRAPHY
(excluding sources containing a number alphabet 1525–1748)

Adler, Jeremy and Ernst, Ulrich. *Text als Figur: Visuelle Poesie von der Antike
bis zur Moderne.* Weinheim, 1987.

Aiton, Eric. *Leibniz. A Biography.* Bristol, Boston, Mass., 1985.

Bell, Eric Temple. *The Magic of Numbers.* New York, London, 1946.

Bischoff, Theodor and Schmidt, August. *Festschrift zur 250 jährigen Jubelfeier
des Pegnesischen Blumenordens gegründet in Nürnberg am 16. Oktober
1644.* Nürnberg, 1894.

Bloom, Harold. *Kabbalah and Criticism.* New York, 1975.

Bohse, August. *Letzte Liebes- und Heldengedichte.* Leipzig, 1706.

Brewer, Elizabeth. 'Addenda to the Bibliography of Works of August Bohse',
Wolfenbütteler Barock-Nachrichten, 8 (1981), 274–86.

Breymayer, Reinhard and Häusserman, Friedrich. *Friedrich Christoph Oetinger:
Die Lehrtafel der Prinzessin Antonia.* 2 vols. Berlin, New York, 1977.

Buelow, George J. 'The Loci Topici and Affect in Late Baroque Music:
Heinichen's Practical Demonstration', *The Music Review* 27 (1966), 161–76.

Thorough-Bass Accompaniment according to Johann David Heinichen. Berkeley, Los Angeles, 1966.

'Music, Rhetoric, and the Concept of the Affections: A Selective Bibliography', *Notes* 30 (1973–4), 250–9.

'Symbol and Structure in the Kyrie of Bach's B minor Mass', *Essays on Bach and Other Matters: A Tribute to Gerhard Herz.* Louisville, Ky, 1981.

Bulling, Klaus, 'Bibliographie zur Fruchtbringenden Gesellschaft', *Marginalien* 20 (1965), 3–110.

Butler, Christopher. *Number Symbolism.* London, 1970.

Couturat, Louis. *La Logique de Leibniz d'après des documents inédits.* Paris, 1901.

Dantzig, Tobias. *Number, The Language of Science.* New York, 1959.

David, Hans T. and Mendel, Arthur. *The Bach Reader: A Life of Johann Sebastian Bach in Letters and Documents*, revised edn with a Supplement. New York, London, 1966.

Davis, John J. *Biblical Numerology: A Basic Study of the Use of Numbers in the Bible.* Grand Rapids, Mich., 1968.

Dehnhard, Walther. 'Kritik der Zahlensymbolischen Deutung im Werk Johann Sebastian Bachs', *Kongreßbericht Stuttgart 1985.* Kassel, Basel, 1985.

Das deutsche Bachfest in Berlin 21. bis 23. März 1901: Festschrift. Leipzig, 1901.

Dieben, Henk. 'Bachs Kunst der Fuge', *Caecilia en de Muziek* (1939), 168–71 and (1940), 8–11.

'Getallenmystiek bij Bach', *Musica Sacra* 5 (1954–5), 21–3 and 47–9.

Dornseiff, Franz. *Das Alphabet in Mystik und Magie.* Studien zur Geschichte des Antiken Weltbildes und der Griechischen Wissenschaft, vol. VII. Edited by Franz Boll. Leipzig, Berlin, 1922. Reprint edn Leipzig, 1980.

Dreyhaupt, Johann Christian. *Pagus Neletici et Nudzici, oder ausführliche diplomatisch historische Beschreibung des zum Herzogthum Magdeburg gehörigen Saal-Creyses.* 2 vols. Halle, 1749, 1751.

Drittes deutsche Bach-fest zur Einweihung von Johann Sebastian Bachs Geburtshaus als Bach-Museum: Fest- und Programmbuch. Leipzig, 1907.

Durning-Lawrence, Edwin. *Bacon is Shakespeare.* London, 1910.

Eisler, Robert. *Weltenmantel und Himmelszelt: Religionsgeschichte Untersuchungen zur Urgeschichte des Antiken Weltbildes.* München, 1910.

Elvers, Rudolf. 'Bibliographie Friedrich Smend', *Festschrift für Friedrich Smend zum 70. Geburtstag.* Berlin, 1963.

Emrich, Wilhelm. *Deutsche Literatur der Barockzeit.* Königstein, 1981.

Feldmann, Fritz. 'Numerorum mysteria', *Archiv für Musikwissenschaft* 14 (1957), 102–29.

Fowler, Alastair. *Spenser and the Numbers of Time.* London, 1964.

Friesenhahn, Peter. *Hellenistische Wortzahlenmystik im neuen Testament.* Leipzig, Berlin, 1935.

'Sprechende Zahlen – ein verschollenes Geheimwissen', *Velhagen und Klasings Monatshefte* 52 (1938), 417–22.

Galland, Joseph S. *An Historical and Analytical Bibliography of the Literature of Cryptology.* Northwestern University Studies in the Humanities, vol. X. Evanston, Ill., 1945.

Geiger, Ludwig. *Johann Reuchlin. Sein Leben und seine Werke.* Leipzig, 1871.

Haase, Rudolf. *Leibniz und die Musik. Ein Beitrag zur Geschichte der harmonikalen Symbolik*. Hommerich, 1963.

Handbuch der historischen Stätten Deutschlands. Vol. XI: *Provinz Sachsen-Anhalt*. Stuttgart, 1975.

Hanke, Martin. *Vratislavienses eruditionis propagatores*. Leipzig, 1701.

Harriss, Ernst C. *Johann Mattheson's 'Der volkommene Capellmeister': A Revised Translation with Critical Commentary*. Ann Arbor, Mich., 1981.

Heinichen, Johann David. *Der General-bass in der Composition*. Dresden, 1728.

Herdegen, Johann. *Historische Nachricht von deß löblichen Hirten- und Blumen-Ordens an der Pegnitz: Anfang und Fortgang biß auf das durch Göttl. Güte erreichte Hunderste Jahr*. Nürnberg, 1744.

Hirsch, Samuel Abraham. *A Book of Essays*. London, 1905.

Hofmann, Joseph E. 'Michael Stifel (1487?–1567): Leben, Wirken und Bedeutung für die Mathematik seiner Zeit', *Sudhoffs Archiv* 9 (1968), 1–39.

Hopper, Vincent Foster. *Mediæval Number Symbolism: Its Sources, Meaning and Influence on Thought and Expression*. Columbia University Studies in English and Comparative Literature. New York, 1938.

Houten, Kees van and Kasbergen, Marinus. *Bach en het getal*. Zutphen, 1985.

Humphreys, David. *The Esoteric Structure of Clavierübung III*. Cardiff, 1983.

Hunold, Christian Friedrich. *Geheime Nachrichten und Briefe von Herrn Menantes Leben und Schrifften*. Köln, 1731. Reprint edn Leipzig, 1977.

Jansen, Martin. 'Bachs Zahlensymbolik, an seinen Passionen untersucht', *Bach-Jahrbuch* 34 (1937), 98–117.

'Bach und das Jahr', *Allgemeine Musikzeitung* 70 (1943), 1.

Kahn, David. *The Codebreakers: The Full Treatment of the History of Codes and Ciphers*. London, 1966.

Kellner, Herbert A. 'Welches Zahlenalphabet benützte der Thomaskantor Kuhnau?', *Die Musikforschung* 33 (1980), 124–5.

'Zum Zahlenalphabet bei Guillaume de Machaut', *Musik und Kirche* 51 (1981), 29.

Kircher, Athanasius. *Musurgia Universalis. Mit einem Vorwort, Personen-, Orts- und Sachregister von Ulf Schorlau*. 2 vols. Rome 1650. Reprint edn in 1 vol. Hildesheim, New York, 1970.

Klueber, Johann Ludwig. *Kryptographik. Lehrbuch der Geheimschreibkunst in Staats- und Privatgeschäften*. Tübingen, 1809.

Kommerell, Viktor. 'Michael Stifel: Mathematiker und Theologe 1487–1567', *Schwäbische Lebensbilder* 3 (1942), 509–25.

Krause, Gottlieb. *Der Fruchtbringende Gesellschaft ältester Ertzschrein. Briefe, Devisen und anderweitige Schriftstücke*. Leipzig, 1855. Reprint edn New York, 1973.

Leaver, Robin A. *Bachs theologische Bibliothek: Eine kritische Bibliographie*. Neuhausen-Stuttgart, 1983.

Lewis, C. S. *English Literature in the 16th Century excluding Drama*. Oxford, London, 1954.

Lewis, H. Spencer. *Rosicrucian Questions and Answers with a Complete History of the Rosicrucian Order*. 15th edn. San José, Calif., 1981.

Liede, Alfred. *Dichtung als Spiel: Studien zur Unsinnspoesie an den Grenzen der Sprache*. 2 vols. Berlin, 1963.

D. *Martin Luthers Werke. Kritische Gesamtausgabe*. Weimar, 1883– . Vol. X.I.1, 'Kirchenpostille, 1522' and vol. LIII, 'Vom Schemhamphoras und vom Geschlecht Christi, 1543'.

Mattheson, Johann. *Der vollkommene Capellmeister*. Hamburg, 1739. *Grundlage einer Ehren-Pforte*. Hamburg, 1740.

Menke, Werner. *Thematisches Verzeichnis der Vokalwerke von Georg Philipp Telemann*. Vol. I, 2nd edn Frankfurt, 1988.

Meretz, Wolfgang. 'Standortnachweise der Drucke und Autographen von Heinrich Schreyber (= Grammateus, vor 1496 bis 1525), Christoff Rudolff (1500? bis 1545?), und Michael Stifel (1487? bis 1567)', *Archiv für Geschichte des Buchwesens* (1976), 319–38.

Meyer, Ulrich. 'Johann Jacob Schmidts *Biblischer Mathematicus* von 1736 und seine Bedeutung für das Verständnis der Zahlensymbolik im Werk J. S. Bachs', *Die Musikforschung* 32 (1979), 150–3.

'Zum Problem der Zahlen in Johann Sebastian Bachs Werk', *Musik und Kirche* 49 (1979), 58–71.

'Zahlenalphabet bei J. S. Bach? – Zur anti-kabbalistischen Tradition im Luthertum', *Musik und Kirche* 51 (1981), 15–19.

Mizler, Lorenz Christoph. *Lusus Ingenii de præsenti Bello Augustissimi atque Invictissimi Imperatoris Carolii VI cum Foederatis Hostibus Ope Tonorum Musicorum Illustrato*. Wittenberg, 1735.

Neu eröffnete Musicalische Bibliothek. Leipzig, 1735–54.

Müller, Johann. *Judaïsmus oder Judenthum, das ist ausführlicher Bericht, von des Jüdischen Volkes Unglauben, Blindheit und Verstockung*. Hamburg, 1707.

Neue Zeitungen von gelehrten Sachen. Edited by J. G. Krause. Leipzig, 1715–75.

Neumann, Werner. 'Eine Leipziger Bach-Gedenkstätte. Über die Beziehungen der Familien Bach und Bose', *Bach-Jahrbuch* 56 (1970), 19–31.

Neumeister, Erdmann. *De Poëtis Germanicis. 1695*. Facsimile reprint edn Bern, München, 1978.

Oetinger, Friedrich Christoph. *Öffentliches Denckmahl der Lehrtafel der Prinzessin Antonia*. 2 vols. Tübingen, 1763. Reprint edn Berlin, New York, 1977.

Otto, Gotlieb Friedrich. *Lexicon Oberlausizischen Schriftsteller und Künstler* III, Görlitz, 1803.

Pelargus, Christoph. *Lusum Poeticum Anagrammatum*. Frankfurt, 1595.

Printz, Wolfgang Caspar. *Exercitationum Musicarum Theoretico-Practicarum Curiosarum*. 8 vols. Frankfurt, Leipzig, 1687–9.

Reuchlin, Johann. *De Verbo Mirifico 1494. De Arte Cabalistica 1517*. Facsimile reprint edn Stuttgart, Bad Cannstatt, 1964.

Schering, Arnold. *Das Symbol in der Musik*. Leipzig, 1941.

Schmidt, Johann Michael. *Musico-Theologia Oder Erbauliche Anwendung Musicalischer Wahrheiten*. Bayreuth und Hof, 1754.

Scholem, Gershom Gerhard. *Bibliographica Kabbalistica*. Leipzig, 1927.

Schubert, Ernst. *August Bohse, genannt Talander*. Breslau, 1911.

Schudt, Johann Jacob. *Jüdische Merckwürdigkeiten*. Frankfurt, Leipzig, 1714.

Schultz, Wolfgang. 'Altjonische Mystik', *Studien zur antiken Kultur*, vol. II. Wien, Leipzig, 1907.

Rätsel des hellenischen Kulturkreises, Mythologische Bibliothek, vol. III. 2 vols. Leipzig, 1909–10 and 1912.

Seebaß, Adolf. *Deutsche Literatur der Barockzeit*. Revised edn Basel, 1975.

Selenus, Gustavus (August II of Braunschweig-Lüneburg). *Das Schach- oder König-Spiel. von Gustavo Seleno, in vier unterschiedene Bücher mit besondern fleiß grund und ordentlich abgefasset. Auch mit dienlichen Kupfer-Stichen gezieret: Desgleichen vorhin nicht außgangen. Diesem ist zu ende angefüget ein sehr altes Spiel genandt Rythmo-machia*. Leipzig, 1616. Facsimile reprint edn Zürich, 1978, edited by Klaus Lindörfer.

Shorr, Philip. *Science and Superstition in the Eighteenth Century*. New York, 1932.

Siegele, Ulrich. 'Johann Sebastian Bach – "Deutschlands größter Kirchenkomponist". Zur Entstehung und Kritik einer Identifikationsfigur', in *Gattungen der Musik*. Edited by Hermann Danuser. Laaber, 1988.

Smend, Friedrich. *Johann Sebastian Bach: Kirchen-Kantaten: erläutert*. 6 vols. (Berlin 1947–9). Reprint edns. in 1 vol. Berlin, 1950 and 1966.

Bach in Köthen. Berlin, 1951.

Bach-Studien. Gesammelte Reden und Aufsätze. Edited by Christoph Wolff. Kassel, Basel, 1969.

Söderblom, Nathan. 'Gustav-Adolf-Rede in der Domkirche von Uppsala vom 6. November 1920', *Die Eiche: Vierteljahrsschrift für soziale und internationale Arbeitsgemanschaft* 9 (1921), 15–20.

Spahr, Blake Lee. *The Archives of the Pegnesischer Blumenorden. A Survey and Reference Guide*. University of California Publications of Modern Philology, vol. LVII. Berkeley, Los Angeles, 1960.

Spitta, Philipp. *Johann Sebastian Bach: His Work and Influence on the Music of Germany 1685–1750*. 3 vols. Translated by Clara Bell and J. A. Fuller-Maitland. London, 1883–5. Reprint edn in 2 vols. New York, 1951.

Tatlow, Ruth. 'J. S. Bach and the Baroque Paragram: A Reappraisal of Friedrich Smend's Number Alphabet Theory', *Music and Letters* 70 (1989), 191–205; reprinted with amendments in *Bach: Journal of the Riemenschneider Bach Institute* 20 (1989), 15–33.

Taylor, Archer. *A Bibliography of Riddles*. Helsinki, 1939.

The Literary Riddle before 1600. Berkeley, Los Angeles, 1948.

and Mosher, Frederic J. *The Bibliographical History of Anonyma and Pseudonyma*. Chicago, 1951.

Thorndike, Lynn. *The Place of Magic in the Intellectual History of Europe*. New York, 1905.

Tittmann, Julius. *Die Nürnberger Dichterschule*. Göttingen, 1847.

Tolstoy, Leo. *War and Peace*. Moscow, 1865–9. Translated by Rosemary Edmonds. Harmondsworth, 1957. Reprint edn 1978.

Tworek, Paul. *Leben und Werke des Johann Christoph Männling: Ein Beitrag zur Literaturgeschichte des schlesischen Hochbarock*. Breslau, 1938.

Walther, Johann Gottfried. *Præcepta der Musicalischen Composition*. 1708. Edited by Peter Benary. Wiesbaden, 1955.

Musicalisches Lexicon. Leipzig, 1732.

Weise, Christian. *Curieuse Fragen über die Logica*. Leipzig, 1696.

Werckmeister, Andreas. *Musicalische Paradoxal-Discourse*. Quedlinburg, 1707.

Widmann, Joachim. 'Zur Frage der Zahlensymbolik bei Johann Sebastian Bach', *Musik und Kirche* 52 (1982), 281–92.

Wolf, Johannes. *Handbuch der Notationskunde*. 2 vols. Leipzig, 1919. Reprint edn Wiesbaden, 1963.

Ziebler, Karl. *Das Symbol in der Kirchenmusik Joh. Seb. Bachs*. Kassel, 1930.

Zirnbauer, Heinz. 'Bibliographie der Werke Georg Philipp Harsdörffers', *Philobiblon: Eine Vierteljahrgangschrift für Buch- und Graphik-Sammler*, 5 (1961), 12–49.

Index